2D/3D MultiAgent GeoSimulation

Walid Ali

2D/3D MultiAgent GeoSimulation

The Case of Shopping Behavior in Square One Mall (Toronto)

VDM Verlag Dr. Müller

Imprint

Bibliographic information by the German National Library: The German National Library lists this publication at the German National Bibliography; detailed bibliographic information is available on the Internet at http://dnb.d-nb.de.

Any brand names and product names mentioned in this book are subject to trademark, brand or patent protection and are trademarks or registered trademarks of their respective holders. The use of brand names, product names, common names, trade names, product descriptions etc. even without a particular marking in this works is in no way to be construed to mean that such names may be regarded as unrestricted in respect of trademark and brand protection legislation and could thus be used by anyone.

Cover image: www.purestockx.com

Publisher:
VDM Verlag Dr. Müller Aktiengesellschaft & Co. KG , Dudweiler Landstr. 125 a, 66123 Saarbrücken, Germany,
Phone +49 681 9100-698, Fax +49 681 9100-988,
Email: info@vdm-verlag.de

Zugl.: Quebec City, Laval University, Diss., 2006

Produced in USA and UK by:
Lightning Source Inc., La Vergne, Tennessee, USA
Lightning Source UK Ltd., Milton Keynes, UK
BookSurge LLC, 5341 Dorchester Road, Suite 16, North Charleston, SC 29418, USA

ISBN: 978-3-8364-7229-6

Abstract

In this thesis, we propose a generic method to develop 2D and 3D multiagent geosimulation of complex behaviors (human behaviors) in geographic environments. Our work aims at solving some problems in the field of computer simulation in general and the field of multiagent simulation. These problems are are:

- The absence of methods to develop 2D-3D multiagent simulation of phenomena in geographic environments.

- The absence of gathering and analysis techniques that can be used to collect and analyze spatial and non-spatial data to feed the geosimulation models (input data) and to analyze data generated by geosimulations (output data).

- The absence of a 'realistic' and 'useful' geosimulation prototype of customer's shopping behavior in a mall.

The main idea of our work is to create a generic method to develop 2D and 3D multiagent geosimulations of phenomena in geographic environments. This method contains ten steps, which are summarized as follows:

The first three steps of the method aim to (1) define the geosimulation users' needs, (2) identify the characteristics of the phenomenon to be simulated, as well as its environment, and (3) create the geosimulation models using the multiagent paradigm. The fourth step aims to select the simulation tool/environment/language that is used to develop the geosimulation. In step five, we collect the data which feeds the geosimulation models. In this step, we analyze the collected information in order to define some patterns of the behaviors of the phenomenon to be simulated. In the sixth step, we develop the geosimulation prototype, on the selected simulation platform, using the collected data. In step seven, we collect information about the course of the simulation, once again using the multiagent paradigm. In this step, we deal with the non-spatial and spatial data, generated by the simulation using several analysis techniques: Classical or traditional analysis techniques, our own analysis technique/tool, and the OLAP (On Line Analytical Processing) and SOLAP (Spatial On Line Analytical Processing) technique. In order to ensure the correctness of the simulation models, as well as to enhance the confidence of the simulation users, we need to verify and validate the simulation models. The verification and validation are the purpose of the eighth step of our method. In the ninth step, we test and document the simulation, while in the last step users can use the multiagent geosimulator in order to make efficient spatial decisions about the phenomenon to be simulated or about the configuration of the simulated environment.

The main contributions of this thesis are:

- A new method to develop 2D-3D multiagent geosimulations of complex behaviors (human behaviors) in geographic environments.

- Some models dealing with the shopping behavior in a mall: an initial version of the shopping behavior model based upon a large literature review, an initial version of the multiagent model which is independent of the tool used to execute the simulation, and an agent-based model created according to the selected platform used to develop the geosimulation. All these models are related to the individual shoppers and to the simulated environment representing the mall.

- An illustration of the method using the shopping behavior in a mall as a case study and the Square One mall in Toronto as a case test. This gave birth to a 'realistic' and 'useful' geosimulation prototype called Mall_MAGS.

- A new survey-based technique to gather spatial and non-spatial data to feed the geosimulation models.

- A tool to digitalize the spatial and non-spatial gathered data.

- A new agent-based technique to collect output data from the geosimulation prototype.

- A new analysis technique and tool to analyze spatial and non-spatial data generated by the geosimulation.

- A coupling of the *OLAP* (On Line Analytical Processing) and *SOLAP* (Spatial On Line Analytical Processing) analysis techniques with the shopping behavior geosimulation prototype in order to explore and analyze the geosimulation outputs.

Resumé

Dans cette thèse, nous proposons une méthode générique de développement d'applications de géosimulation, en 2D et 3D, de divers phénomènes ou comportements complexes (exp. comportements humains) dans des environnements géographiques. Notre travail vise à résoudre quelques problèmes dans le domaine de la simulation informatique et, plus particulièrement, dans le domaine de la simulation multiagent. Les principaux problèmes que nous visons à résoudre dans cette thèse sont:

- Absence de méthodes génériques de développement de simulations multiagent de phénomènes ou comportements dans des environnements géographiques.

- Manque de techniques de collecte et d'analyse des données spatiales et non-spatiales : (1) données en entrée de la géosimulation multiagent (qui sont utilisées pour alimenter la simulation) ou (2) données en sortie de la géosimulation (qui sont générées par cette simulation).

- Absence d'un prototype de géosimulation qui peut être, à la fois, 'réaliste' et 'utile' pour simuler le comportement du magasinage des êtres humains dans un environnement georéférencé représentant un centre commercial.

L'idée principale de notre thèse consiste en: (1) la création d'une méthode générique de développement de géosimulations multiagents, en 2D et 3D, des phénomènes complexes (impliquant par exemple des êtres humains) dans des environnements géographiques et (2) l'application de cette méthode en utilisant le comportement de magasinage dans un centre commercial comme cas d'illustration. Cette méthode contient dix étapes qui sont résumées comme suit :

Les trois premières étapes ont pour objectifs de (1) définir les besoins des utilisateurs finaux de la géosimulation, (2) d'identifier les caractéristiques du phénomène à simuler ainsi que celles de son environnement, et (3) de créer un modèle à base d'agents représentent le phénomène à simuler ainsi que son environnement. La quatrième étape vise à sélectionner l'outil de simulation qui va être utilisé pour exécuter les modèles de simulation. Dans la cinquième étape, nous collectons les données spatiales et non-spatiales qui doivent servir à alimenter les modèles de géosimulation. Dans cette étape nous effectuons quelques analyses des données collectées afin de déterminer quelques patrons de comportement du phénomène à simuler. Dans la sixième étape, nous développons le prototype de géosimulation en exécutant les modèles de géosimulation dans la plateforme sélectionnée tout en utilisant les données qui ont été collectées et analysées. Dans la septième étape, nous utilisons une autre fois la technologie multiagent afin de collecter des données spatiales et non-spatiales en sortie de la géosimulation. Ces données contiennent des informations pertinentes concernant le déroulement de la géosimulation. Dans cette étape nous utilisons diverses techniques d'analyse de données spatiales et non-spatiales afin d'analyser ces données. Dans l'illustration de notre méthode nous avons proposé l'utilisation de techniques d'analyse suivantes: techniques/outils statistiques et mathématiques traditionnelles (ou classiques), notre propre technique/outil et d'analyse des données spatiales et non-spatiales, les techniques d'analyse OLAP (On Line Analytical Processing) et SOLAP (Spatial On Line Analytical Processing). Afin d'assurer la fiabilité des modèles de simulation, nous proposons dans notre méthode une huitième étape qui vise à vérifier et valider les modèles de géosimulation. Dans la neuvième étape, nous testons et nous documentons le prototype de géosimulation. Finalement, dans la dixième étape, les utilisateurs finaux peuvent utiliser la géosimulation multiagent comme outil d'aide à la décision. Ces décisions peuvent concerner le phénomène à simuler ou la configuration spatiale de son environnement.

Les principales contributions de cette thèse sont :

- Une nouvelle méthode de développement d'applications de géosimulation multiagent, en 2D et 3D, des phénomènes complexes (tels que ceux qui impliquent des comportements humains) dans des environnements géographiques.

- Quelques modèles représentant le comportement du magasinage dans un centre commercial qui se basent sur une recherche bibliographique solide dans divers domaines de recherche: Une version intégrée du modèle du comportement du magasinage dans un centre commercial, Deux versions du modèle multiagent du comportement du magasinage (la première est indépendante de la plate-forme qui va être utilisée pour exécuter la simulation et la deuxième est dépendante).

- Une application de la méthode proposée en utilisant le comportement du magasinage dans un centre commercial comme cas d'illustration. Le cas de test qui a servi pour développer le prototype de simulation est le centre commercial Square One (Toronto). Ce prototype 'réaliste' et 'utile' est intitulé Mall_MAGS.

- Une technique à base de questionnaire pour collecter des données spatiales et non-spatiales qui servent à alimenter des géosimulations.

- Un outil qui permet de saisir, simultanément, des données spatiales et non-spatiales qui vont alimenter des géosimulations.

- Une technique à base d'agents qui sert à collecter des donnees spatiales et non-spatiales en provenance de la géosimulation en utilisant le paradigme d'agents, ainsi qu'un outil d'analyse de ces données.

- Un couplage des techniques d'analyse et d'exploration de données *OLAP* (On Line Analytical Processing)/*SOLAP* (Spatial On Line Analytical Processing) et de notre prototype de géosimulation du comportement du magasinage des êtres humains dans un centre commercial. Ce couplage sert à analyser et à explorer les données générées par ce prototype.

Acknowledgments

First, I would like to warmly thank my thesis supervisor, Dr. Bernard Moulin, for his invaluable support, patience and confidence, for his precious and never lacking enthusiasm for research and for his continuous assistance in preparing and writing this thesis. I also want to thank him for having so strongly believed in me and provided me with insights which helped me solve many of the problems I encountered in my research. I also acknowledge him for assisting me financially during my Ph.D and for his generosity which gave me opportunities to attend several international and national conferences.

I would like to express my gratitude to my co-supervisor, Dr. Francois Des Rosiers, whose expertise and understanding added considerably to my graduate experience.

I also want to thank Dr. Jean-Pierre Müller from CIRAD (Centre de coopération Internationale en Recherche Agronomique pour le Développement, France), Dr. Christophe Claramunt (École Navale, France), and Dr. Alexis Drogoul from IRD (Institut De Recherche et de développement IRD, France), for having accepted to evaluate this thesis.

I also want to warmly thank Dr. Yvan Bedard and his research team for their collaboration. I have very much enjoyed working with his team's members Mme Sonia Rivest, Mme Marie Josee Proulx and Mr Nadeau.

I want to thank the GEOIDE, the Canadian Network of Centers of Excellence in Geomatics, and the Defence (RDDC Valcartier) which financed part of this research. Many thanks to the managers of Square One who allowed our team to carry out the survey and use their data.

Very special thanks to Mr. Jean Francois and Mr. Pierre-Emmanuel Michon for their help in the preparation and administration of the survey; Mr. Mondher BouDen for devoting time to input the data of the questionnaire in the DataBase; and Dr. Ken Jones's team in Toronto who is in charge of the survey in Toronto. I also would like to thank Mr. Jimmy Hogan and Mr. Jimmy Perron for their help in developping the simulation prototype using the MAGS platform. I most enjoyed working with them and wish them a very good success in their business.

My years as a Ph.D student would not have been as much fun without my friends, particularly my colleagues: Nafaa Jabeur, Nabil Sahli, Jamal Bentahar, Hedi Haddad, Mondher Bouden,

Boubaker Boulekrouche, Mohamed Mbarki, Walid Chaker and Tarek Sboui with whom I shared the laboratory and unforgettable moments.

Finally, I would like to thank my father, my mother and my family in Tunisia for the support they provided me through my entire life, without whose love, encouragement and editing assistance, I would not have finished this thesis.

To my father, my mother, brothers and sister,

to my family and friends

with love and gratitude

Contents

List of Figures

List of Tables

CHAPTER 1: General Introduction

This chapter introduces the context of our research which is related to the multiagent based simulation field, and more precisely multiagent geosimulation. It identifies the motivations, the problems, and the research questions that we address in this dissertation. It also presents our hypothesis, objectives, and the research methodology of our work. Finally, it presents the organization of the rest of this thesis.

1.1. Context of the Research

This thesis is about *multiagent geosimulation (MAGS)*, which is a sub-field of *multiagent-based simulation (MABS)*. It is widely recognized that MABS is one of the main topics of the multiagent systems (MAS) domain. MABS differs from other kinds of traditional computer-based simulations such as *discrete event simulation (DES)*, *continuous event simulation (CES)*, and *object oriented simulation (OOS)*, in that (some of) the simulated entities are modeled and implemented in terms of agents (Davidson, 2000). The agents' capabilities (e.g., autonomy, social ability, reactivity, pro-activeness, etc.) make MABS more attractive than traditional simulation approaches. In the literature, several applications have been created using the MABS paradigm in order to simulate various kinds of systems/behaviors in different areas/domains. In this dissertation, we concentrate our research on the use of MABS to build simulations of human behaviors in virtual geographic environments[1]. The simulation of human behaviors in space is a very interesting and powerful research method to advance our understanding of human spatial cognition and the interaction of human beings with the environment (Frank et al., 2001). Several researchers used the MABS paradigm to simulate human behaviors in geographic environments. For example, (Raubal, 2001) and (Frank et al., 2001) presented an application which simulates human wayfinding behavior in an airport. (Dijkstra et al., 2001) and (Timmermans et al., 2001) presented an application which simulates pedestrian movements in a mall. (Koch, 2001) simulated people's movements in a large-scale environment representing a town. (Moulin et al., 2003) simulated, in a geographic environment representing a part of Quebec City, crowd movements using thousands of virtual agents. Although these applications emphasize the spatial features of the simulation environment (SE), they are distinct in the ways they represent them. Some applications use

---

[1] In this thesis, the term *spatial* can be used instead of the term *geographic*.

cellular automata (CA) to represent the environment, while other approaches use geographic information systems (GIS). The large number of simulation applications that emphasize the spatial features of the environment gave birth to other simulation sub-fields such as *spatial simulation* and *urban simulation* (Benenson and Torrens, 2004). Recently, a new form of simulation, called *geosimulation*, became popular in geography and the social sciences. Geosimulation is a useful tool for integrating the spatial dimension in models of interactions of different types: economic, political, social, etc. (Mandl, 2000). This form is supported by advances, both in the geographical sciences and in fields outside geography (Benenson and Torrens, 2003). (Mandl, 2001) and (Moulin et al., 2003) present multiagent geosimulation (MAGS) as a coupling of two technologies: the MABS technology and that of GIS. Based on the MABS technology, the simulated entities are represented by software agents that autonomously carry out their activities. What's more, they can interact and communicate with other agents, and they may be active, reactive, mobile, social or cognitive (Koch, 2001). Using the GIS technology, spatial features of geographic data can be introduced into the simulation. The GIS plays an important role in the development of geosimulation models. New methodologies to manipulate and interpret spatial data developed by geographic information science and implemented in GIS. They have created added-value for these data (Benenson and Torrens, 2003). Progress in the multiagent and GIS fields makes multiagent geosimulation a promising paradigm which can be used to simulate complex systems and behaviors in geographic environments.

In summary, our research context consists in the *simulation of human behaviors in geographic environments using the multiagent geosimulation paradigm.*

1.2. Motivations

The motivation for this thesis is threefold:

- Multiagent Geosimulation aims to simulate, using agent technology, spatial phenomena or behaviors in geographic environments. Since this field is a recent, we did not find any paper dealing with approaches[2] to develop multiagent geosimulation applications. Thus, our first motivation is *to propose a generic method which can be*

---

[2] The term *method* in this thesis can be used instead of the terms *approach* or *methodology*.

followed to develop multiagent geosimulation applications that simulate human behaviors in geographic environments.

- Our second motivation is *to illustrate our method by developing multiagent geosimulation models and applications which simulate human shopping behavior in a geographic environment representing a mall.*

- It is known within the computer simulation community that simulation output analysis is an important step in a simulation study. This step is necessary to test different ideas and learn about the simulation model and the corresponding simulation system (Anu, 1997), (Alexopoulos, 2002), (Seila, 1992), (Sanchez, 2001), and (Kelton, 1997). Multiagent geosimulation deals with non-geographic and geographic data related to the system/behavior to be simulated and its environment. The spatial characteristic of geographic data used and generated by multiagent geosimulations, make classical analysis techniques, (such as statistical and mathematical techniques) inefficient in providing a better (i.e., easy and rapid) exploitation of simulation outputs. Thus, our third motivation is *to develop a new analysis technique, which is more efficient than the existing ones, in order to easily and rapidly analyze multiagent geosimulation outputs. Of course, this technique must take into account both non geographic and geographic simulation outputs.*

1.3. Problems and research questions

The first problem addressed by this thesis is the *lack of a generic method, which can be followed to develop multiagent geosimulation applications.* Our literature review revealed that there are few papers dealing with methodological issues in the multiagent based simulation field. Furthermore, we did not find any paper that deals with approaches or methodologies which can be followed to develop multiagent geosimulation applications. Thus, the first research question that we address is: *Using the actual progress in the multiagent and GIS fields, is it possible to develop a generic method that can be followed to systematically develop 2D and 3D multiagent geosimulations of systems/behaviors in geographic virtual environments? If yes, what are the important features and steps of such a method?*

The second problem that we explore in this thesis involves *the simulation analysis techniques which are used to analyze outputs generated by the simulation applications.* Based on our literature review, we identified two sub-problems: The first concerns the simulation output generation, and the second is related to the exploitation and manipulation of the simulation output.

- *The simulation output generation*: The literature reveals that, even with the existence of simulation tools that allow output generation such as the SWARM system, the majority of multiagent simulation applications do not profit from this function to generate output data (Minar et al., 1996). Most frequently, the only feedback that exists consists of a mere visualization of the simulation course on a screen (Alexopoulos, 2002). This type of feedback does not aid simulation users to make decisions about the system/behavior to be simulated or the simulation environment. To make efficient decisions, users need output data which can be efficiently stored, analyzed, and well-presented.

- *The exploitation and manipulation of the simulation output*: Some simulation applications generate output data and analysis results for their users. Although this data may or may not be spatial, these applications use classical analysis techniques, such as statistical and mathematical techniques, to analyze and exploit the generated data. Classical analysis techniques are too limited for spatial analysis (no spatial analysis, no spatial visualization, no map-based exploration for spatial data, etc.) (Yougworth, 1995). For a domain such as multiagent geosimulation, geographic data becomes an important issue for decision-makers. Thus, we need more sophisticated analysis techniques that can be used to analyze complex simulation models involving geographic data. These analysis techniques must generate analysis results which can be easily exploited by users. They must also take into account, both the spatial and non-spatial aspects of the output data to be analyzed.

This second problem brings out our third research question which is: *Among the existing analysis techniques, is there an appropriate one which could (i) be used to exploit multiagent geosimulation outputs (non-spatial and spatial), and (ii) present analysis results to users in an efficient (easily and rapidly) manner? If yes, how can we couple this technique with a multiagent geosimulation paradigm?*

1.4. Objectives

The main objectives of this thesis are:

1- *To propose a generic method that can be followed to develop 2D-3D multiagent geosimulation of systems/behaviors in geographic environments. This method will be illustrated by developing a prototype that simulates the human shopping behavior in a mall.*

2- *To design the simulation models: the models for the environment (shopping mall) and those for the shoppers (individual shoppers, group of shoppers, and crowd of shoppers).*

3- *To develop, using empirical data, a multiagent geosimulation prototype that simulates human shopping behavior in a mall.*

4- *To propose an analysis technique to efficiently exploit (in terms of easiness and rapidity) the data generated by the multiagent geosimulation prototype.*

1.6. Methodology

Since we deal with the computer simulation field, at the beginning of this thesis, we studied several research works done in this field, and especially in the field of multiagent simulation. Our literature review revealed that only a small number of works exist, which simulate human behavior in geographic environments. Specifically speaking, there is a noteworthy lack of works that deal with methodological issues for the simulation of systems/behaviors in geographic environments. For this reason, we had the idea to propose a new and generic method which can be followed to develop 2D-3D multiagent geosimulations in geographic environments. In order to illustrate our method, we used the case study of shopping behavior in a mall.

In addition, we noticed that the human behavior simulation applications did not focus on the simulation output generation. The latter is important to end-users who want to use the simulation as a decision-making tool. For this reason, and in order to avoid falling into the same trap, we made some researches in the field of data analysis techniques in order to find efficient techniques which can be used to generate and analyze geosimulation output data. After an in-depth comparison of several analysis techniques, we found that the one most appropriate for multiagent geosimulation is OLAP (On Line Analytical Process) for non-spatial data, and SOLAP (Spatial On Line Analytical Process) for spatial data (Bédard et al., 2001). Thus, we coupled the multiagent geosimulation paradigm and OLAP/SOLAP analysis technique for efficient simulation output analysis and, therefore, for a well-supported decision-making process.

1.7. Organization of the thesis

In the next chapter, we present a literature review with regards to computer simulation. We start by examining some computer simulation sub-fields. Next, we present some simulation applications simulating several systems and behaviors in various domains/areas. Afterwards, we present a number of simulation tools/platforms/languages that can be used to develop simulation applications. Finally, we discuss various methods and approaches that can be followed to develop such tools and applications. It is also relevant to note that our work implicates additional research fields and domains. The literature reviews related to these fields or domains are presented gradually throughout the following chapters of the thesis.

Chapter 3 briefly presents the principal steps of our method that can be followed to develop 2D-3D multiagent geosimulation of systems/behaviors in geographic environments. It also presents the simulation case study that will be used to illustrate the proposed method. This simulation case study consists of developing a multiagent geosimulation application which, in turn, simulates human shopping behavior in a mall.

In chapters 4 to 10, we present the details of each step of the proposed method using the case of human shopping behavior in a mall. In some of these chapters we present certain literature reviews that complement the one presented in Chapter 2.

- Chapter 4 presents the illustration of the first two steps of the proposed method. In this chapter, we specify the needs of the primary users of the shopping behavior simulator for decision-making purposes. We also present the specification of the characteristics of the human shopping behavior in a mall. This specification is based on a large review of the literature produced by several domains and fields related to the shopping behavior.

- Chapter 5: In this chapter, we create the agent-based models of the shopping behavior simulation. These models are created, based upon the literature study results obtained in the previous chapter.

- Chapter 6: This chapter illustrates the step which aims to collect and analyze the empirical input data for the shopping behavior simulation.

- Chapter 7: In this chapter, we select the platform which is used to execute the simulation shopping models. We also present our use of the selected platform and the simulation execution results. In this chapter, we give a complementary literature review which aims to briefly present certain simulation tools and criteria that can be used to select the most suited simulation tool for a given application.

- Chapter 8: This chapter aims to present how we use software agents to collect and analyze the outputs of the shopping behavior simulation. In this chapter, we present a complementary literature review which focuzes on the existing data analysis techniques that can be used to analyze simulation outputs.

- Chapter 9: This chapter illustrates two steps of our method. It first presents the illustration of the method's step in which we verify and validate the shopping behavior simulation models. Secondly, it illustrates the step in which we test and document the simulator of the shopping behavior simulator. Again, in this chapter we present a literature review concerning the verification and validation techniques that can be used to verify and validate the simulation systems or behaviors.

- Chapter 10: This chapter illustrates the final step of the proposed method. In this chapter, we present how the end-users of the shopping behavior simulator (who are mainly shopping mall managers) can use this shopping behavior simulator to make efficient decisions about the spatial configuration of their mall with respect to customers' use.

Chapter 11 begins by summarizing the work done in this thesis. Next, it presents the results and main findings/contributions of our research. Finally, it concludes with possible directions for future works.

CHAPTER 2: Literature Review: Computer Simulation, Multiagent Based Simulation and Multiagent Geosimulation

In this chapter, we provide a literature review about the computer simulation field and its main sub-fields. We, primarily, focus on the multiagent based simulation (MABS) and multiagent geosimulation (MAGS) fields. We also present some simulation development tools, applications, and approaches.

2.1. Introduction:

Today simulation is an important domain, which attracts many researchers from several fields and disciplines (Ruth, 2003). In recent years, extensive research has been conducted in the area of simulation to model large complex systems and understand their structures and behaviors. At the same time, a variety of design principles and approaches for computer-based simulation have evolved. As a result, an increasing number of computer simulation sub-fields and approaches have been proposed, as well as a large number of tools and applications having been designed and developed. This chapter aims to present the state of the art of the computer simulation domain and its main sub-fields. We focus primarily on two recent and interesting computer simulation fields which are *multiagent-based simulation (MABS)* and *multiagent geosimulation (MAGS)*.

This chapter is organized as follows: Section 2.2 aims to present the computer simulation domain and its main sub-fields. In Sections 2.3, 2.4 and 2.5, we deal respectively with multiagent-based simulation, spatial/geosimulation and multiagent geosimulation, in which we are interested throughout this thesis. In Section 2.6, we present some simulation applications and development tools available in several scientific domains and fields. Section 2.7 deals with a methodological perspective of computer simulation and presents existing methodologies and approaches that can be followed to develop computer simulations. Finally, the last section summarizes the chapter and offers conclusion.

2.2. Computer simulation field

2.2.1. What is computer simulation?

Defining computer simulation is difficult, given the many perspectives of its users. The benefits of computer simulation are becoming more generally recognized in several domains and areas (Anthony et al., 2004). To avoid confusion, it is important to clearly and unequivocally define the term and its usage. A typical dictionary definition from the Oxford English Dictionary describes computer simulation as *"the technique of imitating, on digital computer, the behavior of some situation or system (economic, mechanical, etc.) by means of analogous models, situation, or apparatus, either to gain information more conveniently or to train personnel."* (http://www.oed.com).

A second definition, given by (Fishwick, 1995), a specialist in computer simulation, is the following: *"A computer simulation or computer model is a computer program which attempts to simulate an abstract model of a particular system. Computer simulations have become a useful part of modeling many natural systems in physics, chemistry, and biology, human systems in economics, and social sciences and in the process of engineering new technology, to gain insight into the operation of those systems"*.

Based on these definitions, we can identify the key features of a computer simulation:

- there is a digital computer model of a real or theoretical system that contains information on how the system behaves, and

- experimentation can take place by changing the input of the simulation in order to observe how this change affects the outputs.

2.2.2. Good reasons to use computer simulation

(Gaines, 1979) stated a number of good reasons for using computer simulation as a problem-solving tool. In the following points, we list the main reasons:

(1) The physical system is not available: Often, computer simulations are used to determine whether or not a projected system should ever be built; so obviously, experimentation is out of the question. This is common practice for engineering systems (e.g., an electrical circuit) with well established and widely applicable meta-knowledge. It is rather risky to rely on such

a decision in the case of systems from soft science (the so-called *ill-defined systems*) since the meta-knowledge available for these types of systems is usually not validated.

(2) The experiment may be dangerous: Often, simulations are performed in order to find out whether the real experiment might 'blow-up', placing the experimenter and/or the equipment under danger of injury/damage or death/destruction (for example, an atomic reactor, or an aircraft flown by an inexperienced person for training purposes).

(3) The cost of experimentation is too high: Often, simulations are used when real experiments are too expensive. The necessary measurement tools may not be available, or are too expensive to buy. It is possible that the system is used all the time, and taking it 'off-line' would involve unacceptable cost.

(4) The time constants of the system are not compatible with those of the experimenter: Often, simulations are performed because the real experiment executes so quickly that it can hardly be observed (for example, an explosion), or because the real experiment executes so slowly that the experimenter is long dead before the experiment is completed. Simulations allow us to speed up or slow down experiments at will.

(5) Control variables, and/or system parameters may be inaccessible: Often, computer simulations are performed because they allow us to access *all* input (variables), whereas, in the real system, some inputs may not be accessible for manipulation.

2.2.3. Computer simulation classification and sub-fields

In recent years, extensive research has been conducted in the computer simulation field in order to simulate various systems and behaviors in different disciplines (Anthony et al., 2004). At the same time, a variety of design principles and approaches for computer simulation have evolved. As a result, an increasing number of computer simulation sub-fields appeared and researchers, such as (Anthony et al., 2004) and (Maier and Grobler, 1998), tried to categorize them according to a set of attributes or criteria. This categorization is used to establish formal definitions, which are concise and unambiguous for the computer simulation sub-fields. In the following points, we briefly present some categorization criteria and the resulting computer simulation sub-fields.

▪ *The objectives or goals of the computer simulation*: Computer simulations can be classified based upon their objectives and goals. For example, computer simulation may be used to analyze theoretical or real systems in order to understand, or improve, the performance of this system (Ruth, 2003). It may also be used for training objectives (training simulation), which can allow the learners to make potentially fatal mistakes without injury (e.g., flight simulators) (Anthony et al., 2004). Computer simulation can be used for education, design, entertainment, etc.

▪ *The application areas*: There are many application areas in which computer simulation is applied. For example, it is applied to simulate industrial processes or manufacturing systems, or to design mechanical systems or biological systems (Baianu and Lin, 1986). Recently, several researchers in urbanism took a noteworthy interest in computer simulation techniques in order to model and simulate urban phenomena, land use, transportation systems, etc. As a result, a simulation sub-field, called *urban simulation*, appeared. Other domains, in which computer simulation proved its efficiency, are the social sciences. Social scientists have begun to convert social theories into computer programs or computer simulations. It is then possible to simulate social processes and carry out 'experiments' that would otherwise be impossible. In addition, computer simulation has been used as a method to clarify sociological theories (Gilbert and Conte, 1995). The large number of computer simulation applications and works in this area gave birth to a new simulation field, which is called *social simulation* (Gilbert and Conte, 1995).

▪ *The simulation properties*: Another criterion that clearly categorized computer simulation is that it is based upon its properties (Anthony et al., 2004). In fact, there exist many properties that can differentiate one simulation from another. We can cite as examples of computer simulation properties the following:

> ❐ *The presence of time*: This property indicates whether or not the simulation of a system encompasses the time factor. We distinguish a *static simulation*, which does not have time as part of the simulation (there is simply no concept of the passage of time in the system being modeled (Kelton, 1983)) from a *dynamic simulation*, which has time as part of the simulation. In this case, the system being modeled evidently changes over time, and users want to study and quantify this evolution.

❏ *Types of value*: This property specifies the values that the simulated entities can contain. According to this property, computer simulation can be discrete or continuous. *Discrete simulation* has entities that process only one of many values within a finite range, and *continuous simulation* has entities that process only one of many values within an infinite range.

❏ *Behavior*: This property defines how the simulation proceeds. We distinguish *deterministic simulation* from *probabilistic* (or *stochastic*) simulation. A *deterministic simulation* model has no random event occurring, nor any uncontrollable element. In such a model, the exogenous inputs are assumed to be exact in the sense that their values are not random or probabilistic. Thus, as simulation execution under a fixed set of structural assumptions and input parameters values will produce an exact, deterministic set of output responses. In this case, the analysis is quite simple, at least conceptually: A single run of the simulation model produces the exact set of desired values. Further runs of the same model will, of course, produce the same results (Kelton, 1983). A *probabilistic simulation*, as opposed to a deterministic simulation, has random events occurring. Hence, repeating the same simulation often returns different simulation results. As least some of the inputs driving a stochastic model are random quantities without exact values. This appears to be far less desirable than the deterministic case, and from the standpoint of the analysis problem, this is true. However, many systems are inherently stochastic and thus, it is necessary to model them stochastically in order to achieve a level of validity which is sufficient to obtain the desired information (Kelton, 1983). Therefore, given the need to use a stochastic simulation model, we generate observations of random variables from appropriate distributions in order to drive the model, and we use a random number generator (or stochastic algorithms) and appropriate transformation techniques in order to obtain the desired distributions.

Every simulation can be classified, based on the three properties mentioned above. An example of a dynamic, discrete, and probabilistic simulation is to generate a path along which a data packet moves from a source computer host to a destination host in a network. However, simulating the path of a missile, given an initial firing velocity and fixed wind resistance, is an example of a dynamic, continuous, and deterministic simulation. A chess game simulation comprises static, discrete, and probabilistic properties (Anthony et al., 2004).

▪ *The simulation engine*: To model and execute a simulation model, we need a simulation engine. We distinguish three characteristics of a simulation engine:

> ❐ *The execution*: According to this characteristic, a computer simulation can be executed in *serial* (or sequential) mode, i.e., using a single processor, or in *parallel* mode, i.e., using multiple processors. There is an increasing interest in using parallel simulation for modeling complex, large-scale systems because this kind of simulation is not restricted by limited memory and processor power and usually requires a shorter execution time.

> ❐ *The simulation engine*: There exist three types of computer simulation: *Continuous*, *discrete event*, and *hybrid* simulations. In a *continuous simulation*, state changes occur continuously over time. In a *discrete event simulation* (DES), state changes only occur at specific time intervals. *Hybrid simulation* comprises both continuous and discrete-event simulations.

▪ *Modeling framework*: It depicts how a user models the target system to be simulated. In the modeling frameworks, we distinguish:

> ❐ *Entity-based*: Which represents processes to be modeled as entities. Each entity performs its own tasks and communicates with other entities via messaging (Anthony et al., 2004).

> ❐ *Event-based*: In an event-based modeling framework, each task in a modeled process is activated via the arrival of specific triggering events (Anthony et al., 2004).

It is possible to have a modeling framework that implements both entity and event since both frameworks reflect real-world happenings of actual objects (Anthony et al., 2004).

▪ *Programming framework*: The programming framework is a very relevant criterion, which gives birth to several computer simulation sub-fields. It determines the programming paradigm that the developer/user uses to create a simulation application using a simulation language or tool. We distinguish the *structured* programming framework, which implements a top-down structured program design with control passing down the modules in a hierarchy (Anthony et al., 2004), and the *object-oriented* framework expresses the program as a set of objects that communicate with one another to perform tasks. The object-oriented framework is easier to create, maintain, and reuse, compared with the structured programming framework (Anthony et al., 2004). This paradigm gave birth to a new field of computer simulation called *object-oriented simulation (OOS)*. Another programming paradigm, which is often used to simulate urban phenomena in space, is the *cellular automata* paradigm. The decentralized structure of automata systems in space (grid), their ability to directly handle individual spatial and non-spatial elements, as well as the simplicity of formulation, are all features that offer many benefits to model designers and simulation developers (Benenson and Torrens, 2004). Finally, we have the *multiagent system (MAS)* which is a very promising paradigm that has proven its success in modeling and simulating complex systems and behaviors. This paradigm gave birth to the *agent-based simulation (ABS)* and the *multiagent-based simulation (MABS)* fields. In our work we are interested in this kind of simulation. For this reason, we discuss it more thoroughly in the next section.

▪ *Simulation scale*: This criterion determines the level of detail that is possible in the simulation model. According to the level of detail, a computer simulation can be *one-scale* or *multiscale* (Sato, 2003). The scale of computer simulation can be micro, meso, macro, or nano. A micro scale simulation (or microsimulation), is based upon models of individual entities. This type of simulation technique resolves down to individual parameters, and involves a much higher degree of verification and validation. This kind of model building is very expensive, both in time and expertise to interpret the results. A vast array of data input and output can be produced, and it can provide a behavioral test range required for a complete understanding of the system to be simulated (Sato, 2003). A macro scale simulation (or macrosimulation), is usually based on fluid-like models of flows, applied to the average characteristics of the elements in the simulation such as density, flow, and velocity. They do not provide information about particular elements. There is a large body of works associated with macroscopic modeling – fluid dynamics (tried, tested, proven, and applied) uses macroscopic models because you do not model the interaction of every particle in a fluid, but rather rely upon the behavior of the fluid as a large scale interactive system. Thus, frictional forces, flow, and pressure/density are the macroscopic terms associated with fluidic motion. A crowd can be successfully modeled using macrosimulation (Sato, 2003). The meso scale simulation (or mesosimulation) is an intermediary level between the micro and macro simulation (Sato, 2003). Finally, the pico scale simulation (or picosimulation) presents a higher level than the macro one (Sato, 2003).

- *Type of manipulated data/knowledge*: The data/knowledge used by a computer simulation may or may not be geographic (spatial). According to this criterion, we can categorize computer simulations into two categories: classical simulation, which manipulates non-spatial/geographic data/knowledge (numerical and textural data/knowledge), and spatial/geographic simulation, which manipulates spatial and geographic data/knowledge. In the second category of computer simulations, we distinguish the most recent computer simulation fields, which are spatial simulation, *geosimulation* and *multiagent geosimulation*.

In our work, since we are interested in multiagent geosimulation, it is relevant to talk about two main fields. The first one is called 'Multiagent Based Simulation or MABS' and deals with multiagent simulations, while the second one focuses more on spatial/geograpghical data manipulated by the simulation and contains some recent sub-fields such as spatial simulation and geosimulation. These two main fields are presented respectively in Section 2.3 and Section 2.4. In section Section 2.3, we present a recent field called 'multiagent geosimulation' which combines the MABS field and geosimulation one.

2.3. Multiagent based simulation (MABS)

Multiagent based simulation (MABS) is a computer simulation which uses the technology of agents as a programming framework. Before presenting multiagent based simulation, it is relevant to talk about agents and multiagent systems.

The concept of '*agent*' was introduced in computer science during the early' 90s, and multiagent systems (MAS) soon attracted the interest of researchers far beyond traditional computer science. (Wooldridge and Jennings, 1995a) defined an agent as follows: "... *a hardware or (more usually) software-based computer system that enjoys the following properties:*

▪ *Autonomy: agents operate without the direct intervention of human or others, and have some kind of control over their actions and internal states;*

▪ *Social ability: agents interact with other agents (and possibly humans) via some kind of agent-communication language (ACL);*

▪ *Reactivity: agents perceive their environment, (which may be the physical world, a user via a graphical user interface, a collection of other agents, the Internet, or perhaps all of these combined), and respond in a timely fashion to changes that occur in it;*

▪ *Pro-activeness: agents do not simply act in response to their environment, they are able to exhibit goal-directed behavior by taking the initiative. "*

"A multiagent system can therefore be defined as a collection of possibly heterogeneous, computational entities, having their own problem solving capabilities and which are able to interact together in order to reach an overall goal" (Ferber, 1999). *Agents usually operate in a dynamic, non-deterministic complex environment, in which a single input action can often produce unexpected results.*

Multiagent Systems share a number of key features (Jennings et al., 1998).

▪ *each agent has incomplete information or capabilities for solving the problem and, thus, has a limited viewpoint;*

▪ *there is no global system control;*

▪ *data are decentralized;*

▪ *computation is asynchronous.*

MAS could be homogeneous, if agents acting in a complex environment belong to one specific class or type; or heterogeneous, if in a particular environment we find different classes or types of agents that may have different tasks and purposes (Perram and Müller, 1996). These features let MAS be flexible and adaptive enough to solve different distributed problems such as scheduling, internet search, resources allocation, virtual environment for training and education, information retrieval, and military applications. Software agents become a way to help people to manage the increasing volume and complexity of information and computing resources.

Multiagent technology is a promising paradigm which has proven its success in several domains and disciplines. The advanced capabilities of agents make the multiagent paradigm an attractive technique for researchers in the computer simulation domain when trying to simulate various complex systems and behaviors. The widespread use of multiagent techniques in computer simulation gave birth to a new computer simulation field called *multiagent-based simulation (MABS)*. MABS is defined by (Weiss, 1999) as, '*an approach used to simulate the interactions of multiple autonomous agents in an environment*'. The capabilities of the agents in MABS make it more attractive than traditional simulation approaches, such as discrete event simulation (DES), continuous event simulation (CES), and object oriented simulation (OOS). MABS is nowadays used in a growing number of areas and domains, as a result of its ability to cope with very different models of 'individuals', ranging from simple entities (usually called 'reactive' agents (Drogoul, 1995)), to more complex ones ('cognitive' agents (Jennings, 2000) (Castelfranchi and Müller, 1993)). The easiness, with which designers can also handle different levels of representation (e.g., 'individual' and 'groups', for instance) within a unified conceptual framework, is also particularly appreciated (Drogoul et al., 2002).

2.4. Spatial simulation or geosimulation

A recent trend in computer simulation consists in developing what is called *situated* simulation applications. The term *situated* means that the simulation takes place in an environment. Particularly, we can notice that the majority of research works in this trend deal with spatial characteristics of the simulation environment. As a result, several main simulation fields have appeared. As examples, we can cite: *spatial simulation* and recently, *geosimulation*. In this section, we focus on geosimulation as a new wave of spatial simulation which has become proeminent in recent years (Benenson and Torrens, 2003).

As mentioned in (Benenson and Torrens, 2004), geosimulation, as a kind of computer simulation, is a "catch-all title" that can be used to represent a very recent wave of research in geography. In a broad sense, the field of geosimulation is concerned with the design and construction of object-based, high-resolution spatial models, using these models to explore ideas and hypotheses about how spatial systems operate, developing simulation software and tools to support object-based simulation, and applying simulation to solve real problems in geographic contexts (Benenson and Torrens, 2004). Geosimulation models operate with human individuals and infrastructure entities, represented at spatially non-modifiable scales, such as households, homes, or vehicles. In geosimulation models, these entities have behaviors. Many of these entities are animated (visually and dynamically), and animation drives the behavior of inanimate entities in a simulation (Benenson and Torrens, 2004). What's more, the data which feeds the geosimulation models is generally stored in geographic information systems (GIS). According to (Mandl, 2000), four alternatives to couple simulation applications and GIS exist:

- *loose coupling*: GIS- and simulation- software are two different products, and the data of one is integrated into the other.

- *tight coupling*: GIS functionality is implemented in simulation software or vice versa.

- *direct co-operative coupling*: GIS- or simulation- software is working as the server, or client. The two softwares are connected via an interface. The client software is used by the users and the server-software operates in the background.

- *indirect co-operative coupling*: A third programming environment couples the GIS- and simulation- software.

The geosimulation characteristics mentioned above make it a useful tool for integrating the spatial dimension in models of interactions of various types (economics, political, social, etc.) (Mandl, 2000). This form is supported by advances, in both geographical sciences and fields outside geography (Benenson and Torrens, 2003).

Research work in geosimulation mostly focusses on techniques to improve spatial simulation technology: the derivation of new algorithms for spatial processes, new methodologies to conceptualize spatial entities and the relationships between them, the application of simulation models to real-world problems, and new software to experimenting with geographical systems (Benenson and Torrens, 2003).

2.5. multiagent geosimulation

In Section 2.3, we showed that multiagent based simulation (MABS) paradigm is well suited to simulate the interactions between entities having behaviors. We also presented, in Section 2.4, that geosimulation is very appropriate when taking into account the geographic characteristics of the simulation environment. According to these observations, (Mandl, 2000), (Kock, 2001), and (Moulin et al., 2003) combined these two paradigms in order to simulate complex system/behavior in geographic environments. As a result, they present a very recent computer simulation field, called *multiagent geosimulation*, as a coupling of two technologies: Multiagent based simulation (MABS) technology and geosimulation.

- Based on the Multiagent based simulation technology, the simulated entities are represented by software agents that autonomously carry out their activities. Furthermore, they can interact and communicate with other agents. And finally, they may be active, reactive, mobile, social, or cognitive (Koch, 2001).

- Using geosimulation and geographic information system (GIS) technologies, spatial features of geographic environments can be introduced into the simulation. The GIS plays an important role in the development of geosimulation models. New methodologies and tools for manipulating and interpreting spatial data, developed by geographic information science and implemented into GIS, have created added-value for these data (Benenson and Torrens, 2003).

In order to show the efficiency of the multiagent geosimulation paradigm, several researchers have developed simulation applications that simulate complex behaviors in geographic environments. For example, (Koch, 2001) simulates human shopping activities in a town, (Mandl, 2000) simulates pedestrian movements in a town, and (Moulin et al., 2003) developed an application that simulates the crowd movement in a city. It is important to note that only (Moulin et al., 2003) presented a generic platform, which can be used to develop multiagent simulation applications of complex behaviors in virtual geographic environments. We can also cite the platform CORMAS (COmmon-pool Resources and Multi-Agent Systems), which was developed by (Bousquet et al., 1998) and can be used to simulate multiagent systems and behaviors in geographic environments.

Our research aims to the use of the multiagent geosimulation paradigm in order to build simulations of human behaviors in virtual geographic environments. As stated by (Frank et al., 2001) '...*the simulation of human behavior in space is an extremely interesting and powerful research method to advance our understanding of human spatial cognition and the interaction of human beings with the environment*'.

2.6. Simulation applications and simulation tools

In the previous sections, we discussed several types and fields of computer simulation. Inside these fields, researchers developed several applications that simulate various behaviors and systems, or generic tools that can be used to develop simulation applications. This section aims to briefly present some examples of computer simulation applications and tools.

It is important to distinguish between *simulation applications* and *simulation tools*. A simulation application is intended to simulate a specific system or behavior, whereas a simulation tool is a generic software which can be used to develop simulation applications. A simulation tool can be a completely user-friendly environment, or a simple simulation language which can be used with an editor.

Many simulation applications exist that aim to simulate various systems or behaviors in numerous areas. As examples, we cite several of the most well-known simulation applications by domain/area:

- ▪ Human and artificial societies:

    ❑ Wayfinding behavior: In an airport (Raubal, 2001),

    ❑ Shopping behavior: (Dijkstra et al., 2001) (Kurose et al., 1998),

    ❑ Pedestrian behavior: PedSim (http://pedsim.silmaril.org/),

    ❑ Recreational behavior,

    RBSim (http://www.srnr.arizona.edu/~gimblett/rbsim.html),

    ❑ Human crowds: MAGS (Moulin et al, 2001), and ViCrowd (Musse et al., 1999),

▪ Traffic and vehicle simulations: TranSim (http://www-transims.tsasa.lanl.gov/),

▪ Ecology: The following link (http://www.red3d.com/cwr/ibm.html) presents a number of simulation applications in the field of ecology.

A multitude of simulation tools (environments and languages) also exist, some are commercialized, while other are not. As examples, we cite several of them in the following points:

▪ Simulation environments:

❐ MAGS: MultiAgent GeoSimulation (Moulin et al., 2003),

❐ CORMAS (COmmon pool Resources and Multi-Agent Systems) (Bousquet, 1998) (http://cormas.cirad.fr/fr/outil/outil.htm),

❐ GEAMAS: A Generic architecture for agent-oriented simulations of complex processes (Marcenac and Giroux, 1998),

❐ StarLogo (http://education.mit.edu/starlogo/),

❐ RePast (http://repast.sourceforge.net/) (Collier, 2002),

❐ Ascape (Parker, 2001),

❐ AgentSheets (http://agentsheets.com/), etc.

▪ Simulation languages:

❐ MAML (MultiAgent Modeling Language)

(http://www.maml.hu/maml/refman/),

❐ SDML (Strictly Declarative Modeling Language) (http://sdml.cfpm.org/), etc.

▪ Simulation environment and language (hybrid):

❐ SWARM (http://www.swarm.org/wiki/Main_Page),

□ JSim (http://chief.cs.uga.edu/~jam/jsim/),

□ JavaSim (http://javasim.ncl.ac.uk/),

□ ELMS: an environment description language for multiagent simulations (Okuyama, 2005),

□ CSim (http://www.atl.external.lmco.com/projects/csim/), etc.

2.7. Simulation methodologies and approaches

In the previous sections, we presented some technical and practical issues with regards to computer simulation. We also discussed several computer simulation sub-fields, simulations applications, and simulation tools. We recall that one of our research objectives is to present a generic method to develop geosimulations of spatialized behaviors of large groups of agents in geographic environments. Hence, it is relevant to present a literature review about methods and approaches which have been proposed in the computer simulation field. In this section, we discuss methodological issues related to computer simulation. Thus, we present different approaches and methodologies that have been designed in order to develop computer simulation tools and applications for different fields. Considering the large number of methodologies and approaches that exist in the literature, they will be presented in two sub-sections. The first sub-section briefly presents those approaches related to classical simulation (non multiagent-based simulation), such as discrete event simulation (DES), continuous event simulation (CES), object oriented simulation (OOS), etc., while the second sub-section concentrates on the approaches that are related to agent-based simulation and multiagent based simulation.

2.7.1. Classical (non multiagent-based) simulation approaches

Some researchers in the computer simulation field presented generic approaches and methods that can be followed to develop simulation applications. See for example, (Fishwick, 1995) who presented an approach that is composed of three stages: the *simulation model design*, the *simulation model execution*, and the *execution analysis*. (Allen et al., 2001) presented an interesting simulation study approach, which can be followed in order to develop discrete event simulation applications. (Anu, 1997) also proposed a relevant simulation approach for discrete event simulation (DES). This approach contains eleven steps that are grouped under three phases: developing a simulation model, designing a simulation experiment, and performing simulation analysis. (Groumpos and Merkuryev, 2002) discussed a general approach for developing discrete event simulations (DES), which is similar to the approach proposed by (Anu, 1997), although it is composed of twenty one steps. Moreover, (Gilbert, 1993) and (Troitzch, 1997) refined the diagram of (Fishwick, 1995) by adding other relevant steps, etc.

The simulation approaches discussed above, although useful when it comes to understanding how to design simulation applications, have some major critical drawbacks for our purposes: (1) they do not specifically address multiagent based simulation, but rather, computer simulation in general; and (2) they are mainly task-oriented rather than model-oriented, and make it difficult to understand the difficulties found in translating conceptual to computational models (Drogoul et al., 2002). *These drawbacks make the aforementioned methods impractical to develop geosimulations of spatialized behaviors of large groups of agents in geographic environments in geographic environments.*

2.7.2. Multiagent-based simulation methods

Now let us consider multiagent based simulation methods. Our literature review revealed that few researchers proposed methodologies and approaches for multiagent based simulation (MABS). The majority of these methods and approaches are not generic and are specific to simulation applications. In this sub-section, we only present the two generic approaches, found in the literature, which can be followed to develop MABS applications.

a. Drogoul, Vanbergue, and Meurisse's simulation design process

(Drogoul et al., 2002) proposed a generic design process in order to develop multiagent-based simulations (MABS). This process is based upon the notion of '*roles*'. The roles in the design process represent the human actors who will interact to produce a running simulation, along with their contributions. (Drogoul et al., 2002) proposed the following roles:

▪ *The Thematician*: He specifies the intention of the simulation process, i.e. the association between the target system and the application of the simulation. He manipulates three kinds of data concerning the target system (Drogoul et al., 2002):

❐ Theories and assumptions (what he knows or estimates), which define a set of percepts associated with the specific domain.

❐ Observations (what he sees or analyses), which data is relative to the phenomena, such as the parameters and initial conditions of the simulation tool; however, they can also describe qualitative aspects of the phenomena.

❐ Questions (what he wants to understand), which can be classified into three categories: predictive (what will happen in xx years?), speculative (what if we change the parameters?), or theoretical (which of these assumptions may explain the phenomenon?).

(Drogoul et al., 2002) points out that all the thematicians interested in multiagent simulations share the same profile. They usually handle two levels of knowledge at the same time, which we shall call their micro- and macro knowledge (micro-K and macro-K). Macro-K is a set of 'global' knowledge about the target system, mostly obtained from the observations. Micro-K is 'local' knowledge about the individuals, without which the target system would not exist; it is composed of both observations (behaviors, etc.) and assumptions.

▪ *The Modeler*: Since the specifications of the thematician do not allow for a direct transcription of an operational solution, and because the two fields have different semantics, the *domain model* has to be translated into something more formal that can be, eventually, implemented by a computer scientist. This is the duty of the modeler. His role is to make the concepts clear and remove the ambiguities by specifying what the authors call a *design model*. The design model is probably the most difficult model to define, since it depends on the information provided by the thematicians, and on some constraints inherent to the chosen implementation (which may, or may not, be known at the design time).

▪ *The Computer scientist*: The aim of the computer scientist is not only to write a computer program (although it is his main duty), but also to propose a model that may allow for a discussion with the modeler. Without this model, his propositions and choices may not receive any feedback from the other two roles. Shaping the *operational model* is an operation that immediately precedes the actual construction of the *computational system.*

The whole process is described in Fig 2.1 (a detailed explanation of the process can be found in (Drogoul et al., 2002)).

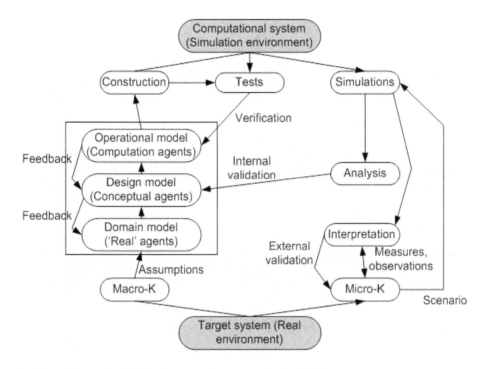

Fig. 2.01. The methodological process of (Drogoul et al., 2002).

b. Ramanath and Gilbert's methodology for developing an Agent-Based Social simulation

(Ramanath and Gilbert, 2003) proposed a simulation research process for developing agent-based social simulations (see Fig 2.2). According to these authors, this process can be considered to be a generic research framework for all simulation studies.

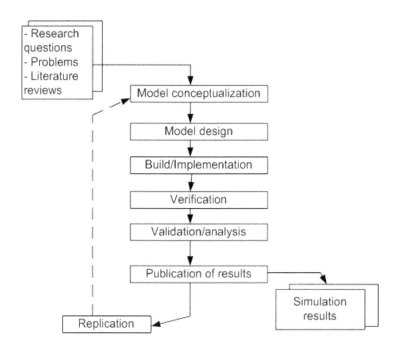

Fig. 2.2. Generic stages in the simulation research process of (Ramanath and Gilbert, 2003).

The stages of the process are the following:

▪ *Model conceptualization:* Once a 'puzzle' (a question or problem whose answer is not known), is identified, conceptualization consists of defining and scoping the target (or problem area) for modeling. This stage may also include some observations of the target, in order to provide parameters and initial conditions required for the model.

▪ *Model design:* Involves making decisions about the type of overarching simulation approach to be followed (e.g., participatory or 'user-centered', conventional or 'researcher-centered', etc.); what to omit and what to include in the simplified version of the target to be modeled (model specification); the assumptions, selection of a software and hardware platform, etc.

▪ *Model construction or build:* This stage refers to the activities involved in writing and testing the computer-based programs necessary to implement the model.

▪ *Verification:* This stage is concerned with the correctness of the transformation from the abstract representation (the conceptual model) to the program code (the simulation model). That is, with ensuring that the program code faithfully reflects the behavior that is implicit in the specifications of the conceptual model.

- *Validation/Analysis:* While verification concerns whether or not the program is working as the researcher expects, validation considers whether or not the simulation is a good model of the target. A model that can be relied upon to reflect the behavior of the target can be considered 'valid'. Validity refers to two aspects: a) 'internal validity', which concerns the correspondence between the theoretical or abstract model to be simulated, and the implementation; and b) 'external validity', or the degree to which the model and simulation correspond to the real world.

- *Publication of results:* The final stage is the sharing, or publication, of results. This signifies, putting the results of the research into a format ready for consumption by the scientific or the practitioner community, or both (e.g., presenting the research at conferences, publishing in a paper, or electronic based journal, on the Internet, etc.).

All of the above stages are carried out for almost all published simulation models. There is, however, another stage of the research process that is infrequent, but which needs to be considered- that is, replication (hence, the dotted line in Fig 2.2 has been used to represent this stage as optional). Replication involves confirming that the claimed results of any given simulation are reliable, in the sense that they can be reproduced by anyone starting from scratch. Ideally, published simulations should be presented in sufficient detail for this to be achieved.

The two approaches proposed by (Drogoul et al., 2002) and (Ramanath and Gilbert, 2003) can be used in order to develop multiagent based simulations, but they do not emphasize the spatial/geographic characteristics of the simulation (the spatialized phenomena to be simulated). According to us, this represents a limitation because in multiagent geosimulations the geographic/spatial characteristics are critical to accurately represent and simulate the spatialized behaviors of the agents which evolve in the geographic environment.

In summary, we can notice that the approaches discussed in this section (for multiagent based simulation or not) underestimate most of the difficulties met when building multiagent geosimulations of spatialized behaviors of the agents which evolve within geographic environments. Let us notice that these approaches do not propose any particular technique to collect the data about the spatial behaviors to be simulated. What's more, they do not provide any technique to analyze the spatial characteristics of the data input of the simulation and to explore the spatial dimensions if the data generated by the geosimulations. This led us to propose our own method to create multiagent geosimulations that can be used:

(1) to gather geographic data relative to the spatialized behaviors to be simulated,

(2) to specify agent models that emphasize spatial behaviors (such as navigation capabilities taking into account the geographic properties of the environment) and plausible interactions with the geographic environment (such as perception and memorization of objects' locations, etc.), and

(3) to carry out practical analyses of the spatial dimensions of the simulation results.

2.7.3. Summary about the simulation methodologies/approaches

The methodologies and approaches which have been presented above are less suitable for developing multiagent geosimulation of phenomena in geographic environments, but they can be used as a base to create a new method that is more suitable for this purpose. The methodologies/approaches presented above contain some interesting steps that can be adapted and integrated into the method we propose for developing 2D and 3D multiagent geosimulations. In the following paragraphs, we present a summary of some steps presented in these methodologies and approaches:

- Develop the simulation models (Annu, 1997): (Fishwick, 1995) called this step "model design". This phase contains the following sub-steps:

  ▪ Identify the problems of an existing system or behavior;

  ▪ Formulate the problems:

    ❏ Select the boundaries of the system/behavior to be simulated;

❑ Define the objectives of the simulation;

❑ Identify the needs of the end-user of the simulation;

▪ Collect and process real system/behavior data (input data);

▪ Formulate and develop the simulation models (Annu, 1997), or model abstraction (Allen et al., 2001), or model conceptualization (Ramanath and Gilbert, 2003).

Develop the simulation models;

❑ Translate the conceptual models into a simulation software acceptable form;

▪ Validate the models;

▪ Test the models (Drogoul et al., 2002);

▪ Document the models for future use;

- Design a simulation experiment (Annu, 1997): (Fishwick, 1995) called this step, "model execution". This phase contains the following steps:

▪ Select the appropriate experimental design;

▪ Establish experimental conditions for runs;

▪ Perform the simulation runs (Annu, 1997) or model implementation (Allen et al., 2001);

- Perform simulation analysis (Annu, 1997): (Fishwick, 1995) called this step, "execution analysis". This phase contains the following steps:

▪ Interpret and present results (Annu, 1997) or output analysis (Allen et al., 2001);

❑ Construct graphical displays of the outputs;

❑ Document results;

▪ Recommend further actions that can be made on the simulation, or on the real system/behavior;

▪ Publication of the results (Ramanath and Gilbert, 2003).

2.8. Conclusion

In this chapter, we presented a literature review about computer simulation, as well as having presented some sub-fields of computer simulation. We were primarily focused on two computer simulation sub-fields, which are multiagent based simulation and geosimulation. Next, we mentioned some applications and tools of computer simulation. Finally, we focused on the methodological aspects of computer simulation, and we presented several approaches that can be followed when developing computer and multiagent simulations. The next chapter aims to briefly present the main steps of our method.

CHAPTER 3: A Generic Method for Developing 2D-3D Multiagent Geosimulations and its Application: The Main Steps and the Case Study

In this chapter, we present the main steps of a generic method that can be followed when developing 2D and 3D multiagent geosimulation applications, simulating various kinds of systems/behaviors in virtual geographic environments. This chapter also presents the case study, which will be used to illustrate the application of this method: The customers' shopping behavior in a mall.

3.1. Introduction

Our literature review revealed that several methods and approaches have been proposed to develop simulation applications using various techniques such as discrete event simulation, continuous event simulation, object-oriented simulation, and multiagent based simulation. However, we did not find any paper or research work dealing with an approach or method that can be followed in order to develop geosimulation or multiagent geosimulation applications, simulating spatial phenomena or behaviors in virtual geographic environments. This lack of methodological works in the multiagent geosimulation field motivated us to propose a generic method to develop multiagent geosimulations in virtual geographic environments. This chapter aims to present an overview of the proposed method. In Section 3.2, we briefly describe the main steps of this method which have been inspired by different methods presented in our literature review (sub-sections 2.6.1 and 2.6.2). Section 3.3 aims to present the case study that will be used to illustrate the proposed method: *the customers' shopping behavior in a mall*. The detailed illustration of the various steps of the method will be presented in the following chapters. Finally, the last section of the chapter states our conclusion.

3.2. A generic method for developing 2D and 3D multiagent geosimulations

This section aims to briefly present the main steps of a method that we propose for developing multiagent geosimulation applications aiming at simulating phenomena in geographic environments. These steps are depicted in Fig 3.1 and will be detailed in the following chapters (chapters 4 to 10) using the shopping behavior case study as an illustration.

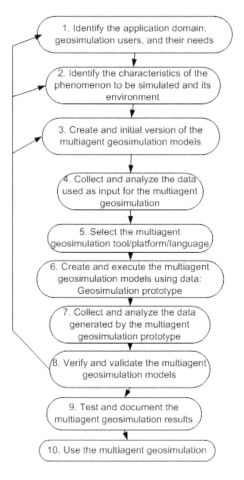

Fig. 3.1.The main steps of our proposed method.

3.2.1. Step1: Identify the multiagent geosimulation users' needs

Simulation applications are generally used to support decision making. In geosimulation applications, decisions are influenced by the spatial characteristics of the simulated phenomenon and the geographic features of its environment. Before developing a multiagent geosimulation application, we must study in detail the needs and goals of its future users. This step is very important because it helps us to identify the future users, the limits of the system and, of course, the spatial limits of the simulation. Identifying the limits of the phenomenon to be simulated and its environment is a very important task because it defines internal and external factors influencing the phenomenon to be simulated as well as the simulation inputs and outputs. This can help to reduce the level of complexity by reducing the size of the phenomenon to be simulated or the complexity of the simulation environment. This step is illustrated in the Chapter 4 of this dissertation using the shopping behavior in a mall as case study.

3.2.2. Step2: Specify the characteristics of the system to be simulated

Based on the users' needs, we must identify the characteristics of the phenomenon to be simulated and those of its environment, including all the relevant spatial and non-spatial features within the limits that were defined in the previous step. This step is important because it prepares the ground for the following steps. This step is detailed in the Chapter 4 of this dissertation using the shopping behavior in a mall case study as an illustration.

3.3.3. Step3: Create the multiagent geosimulation models

In order to be able to simulate the studied system/behavior in a computer, we must model it, as well as its environment, taking into account the spatial and non-spatial aspects. Depending upon the users' needs specified in the first step of the method, we must choose the appropriate level of detail or granularity of the model. Since our method is based upon the multiagent approach to simulate systems, we must use agent-oriented design techniques to create the models and represent the entities of the simulation. The Agent-Based Unified Modeling Language (AUML) (http://www.auml.org/) provides such techniques.

In this step of the proposed method, we can distinguish two categories of entities:

- *Passive Agents (PA)*: This category of agents represents entities that have a structure, without a behavior. Usually, a large part of the elements contained in the simulation environment belongs to this category. Here, we must characterize the spatial and non-spatial structures of the passive agents in both 2D and 3D modes (see Fig 3.2).

- *Active agents (AA)*: This category of agents represents entities, which have structures and behaviors: These entities actively participate in the simulation. For this category, we must specify the data structures of the entities (spatial and non-spatial structures) as well as their behaviors (spatial and non-spatial behaviors) (see Fig 3.3).

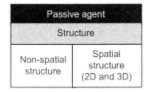

Fig. 3.02.The simulation Passive Agent (PA).

Active agent	
Structure	
Non-spatial structure	Spatial structure (2D and 3D)
Behavior	
Non-spatial behavior	Spatial behavior (2D and 3D)

Fig. 3. 3.The simulation Active Agent (AA).

This step is illustrated in the Chapter 5 of this dissertation using the shopping behavior in a mall as case study.

3.3.4. Step4: Select the multiagent geosimulation tool/platform/language

The conceptual model generated during the last step must be executed on a computer. For this reason, we have two choices:

(1) to implement our simulation models using a standard language, such as C, C++ or Java for example. In this case, we need to select the language to be used for the implementation.

(2) to use an existing simulation tool/platform/language. In this case, we must choose a simulation tool/platform/language that will be used to execute the simulation models. There are several simulation tools/platforms/languages that can be used to create computer simulations. For example, the interested reader can visit the web site

http://www.idsia.ch/~andrea/simtools.html, which presents a good collection of modeling and simulation resources on the Internet. Naturally, a question arises: *How to select the appropriate simulation tool/platform/language for a given application?* Metrics to evaluate simulation tools/platforms/languages include modeling flexibility, ease of use, modeling structure (objects, agents, etc.), code reusability, graphic user interface, animation, hardware and software requirements, output reports, graphical images, customer support, and documentation. It is important to mention that the choice of a suitable simulation tools/platform/language depends upon the characteristics of the system to be simulated and its environment.

This step is detailed in the Chapter 6 of this dissertation using the shopping behavior in a mall case study as an illustration.

3.3.5. Step5: Collect and analyze the data used as input for the multiagent geosimulation

In this step, we collect data and transform it in order to feed the simulation models. If we provide the simulation models with random data, this step can be very simple. However, if we want to use real data we must collect and analyse it before feeding it in the system. Since we deal with geosimulations, we must collect and analyze both non-spatial and spatial data. In our method, we use spatial and non-spatial multidimensional analysis techniques to analyze the multiagent geosimulation input data.

Several techniques exist, which can be used to collect non-spatial and spatial data, as for example:

- *Questionnaires and surveys (pen and paper)*: If the system to be simulated contains people that can be interviewed, we may use surveys and questionnaires to collect non-spatial and spatial data about it. The disadvantage of this technique is that the gathered data is on paper and cannot be used directly by a computer simulation. Hence, the need to digitalize it.

- *Digital questionnaires or Web-based questionnaires*: Some researchers used digital or web-based questionnaires and surveys in order to gather digital data that can be directly used by a simulation.

- *Observations*: We can observe the system/behavior intended to be simulated in order to better understand it. Then, based upon observation results, we can gather data about this system/behavior. The gathered data can be in a digital form or not.

- *Consulting experts*: We can gather data about the system or the behavior to be simulated directly from experts who know the system/behavior.

- *GPS (Global Positioning Systems)*: Taking advantage of the GPS technology, we may collect geographic data about the system/behavior to be simulated. The advantage is that the gathered data can be directly stored in databases or geographic information systems (GIS). Then, after some manipulations (validation, filtering, etc.), this data can be transferred in a computer simulation. However, this technique has a disadvantage because we can gather geographic data about the system/behavior only in areas where GPS signals are available.

After gathering simulation input data, it must be analyzed in order to determine some behavior patterns of the system to be simulated. Since we deal with both non-spatial and spatial data, we propose to analyze these two kinds of data using their respective analysis techniques. In this step, we use a multi-variables analysis approach to analyze the simulation input data. This step is illustrated in the Chapter 7 of this dissertation using the shopping behavior in a mall as case study.

3.3.6. Step6: Execute the multiagent geosimulation models using data

During this step, we perform the simulation models on the selected simulation tool/platform/language, using the data characterizing the system and its environment. During this step, we must respect the constraints and limitations of the selected tool/platform/language, such as the input data structure. This step is illustrated in Chapter 7 of this dissertation using the shopping behavior in a mall as case study.

3.3.7. Step7: Collect and analyze the data generated by the multiagent geosimulation

To be useful, the simulation application must return meaningful results. Based upon the analysis of these results, the users may make informed decisions. In our method, and in order to analyze the simulation output data, we use the multidimensional analysis techniques *OLAP* (*On Line Analytical Processing*) and *SOLAP* (*Spatial On Line Analytical Processing*) (Bédard et al., 2001). It is important to indicate that the simulation output data is generated by specific types of software agents called *Observer agents*. This step is detailed in Chapter 8 of this dissertation using the shopping behavior in a mall as an illustration.

3.3.8. Step8: Verify and validate the multiagent geosimulation models

The verification and validation processes insure that the simulation models accurately represent the real system/behavior to be simulated. These two processes which are theoretically distinct are closely related in practice (Arthur and Nance, 1996) (Balci, 1988). During this step of our method, we can compare the model's performance under known conditions with that of a simulated real system. This step not only insures that the model assumptions are correct, complete, and consistent, but also enhances the users' confidence in the simulation models (Anu, 1997). Based upon the simulation input data and the simulation results, we can verify and validate our simulation models. This step is illustrated in Chapter 9 using shopping behavior in a mall as case study.

3.3.9. Step9: Test and document the multiagent geosimulation results

During this step, we document and test the simulation. In the documentation, we present the results of the system analysis, the simulation models, the selected tool/platform/language, a guide to use the simulation interface, the input/output data analysis results, etc. This step is illustrated in Chapter 9 using the shopping behavior in a mall as case study.

3.3.10. Step10: Use the multiagent geosimulation application

The last step of our method is the use of the multiagent geosimulator. According to (Anu, 1997), multiagent geosimulators can be used to:

- understand the system to be simulated by observing various simulations carried out over long periods of time, using the geosimulation platform.

- test the hypotheses about the system to be simulated. These hypotheses can be fixed by the simulation users.

- compress time in order to observe a system over long periods, or expand time to observe it in detail; to this end, the user can control the simulation time step.

- experiment with the system in new situations or contexts in order to assess the influence of different decisions. As an example, we can mention the assessment of the spatial environment. A user may need to evaluate the influence of important changes of the spatial configuration of the physical environment. Users can use the same simulation scenarios with different spatial configurations and compare the simulation results. The analysis techniques, presented in Section 3.3.7, can be used again for these comparisons.

This step is detailed in Chapter 10 using the shopping behavior in a mall as an illustration.

3.3. An illustration of the method: A Multiagent geosimulation of the customers' shopping behavior in a mall

In order to illustrate our method, we use the case study of customers' shopping behavior in a mall. Since the shopping behavior is carried out by people in geographic environment representing a mall, it is relevant to combine multiagent technology and geographic information systems (GIS) in order to simulate this behavior.

As it will be shown in Chapter 4, the shopping behavior in a mall is very complex given that it is influenced by a large number of factors, some of which are related to the shopper (internal factors), while others come from the mall's environment (situational/contextual factors). The shopping behavior is also composed of several processes which are of different natures: cognitive, spatial, etc. In the following points, we present several aspects of this behavior.

a) *The shopping behavior as a spatial and environmental behavior*: The shopping behavior is performed in a geographic environment (the mall). In a shopping experience, shoppers visit stores, kiosks, and other places. Therefore, their behavior is easily influenced by the geographic characteristics of the environment (mall). The interactions, taking place between the shoppers and the spatial characteristics of the environment, let us consider the shopping behavior as a spatial behavior. In the literature, some researchers such as (Dogu and Erkip,

2001), presented the shopping behavior in a mall as a wayfinding/orientation behavior and mentioned some spatial factors affecting it.

b) *The shopping behavior as an economic behavior*: People go to the mall to visit stores/kiosk in order to purchase items or services. Sometimes, they are confronted with the choice of numerous stores/kiosks to visit, or items to buy. This choice generally depends upon their goals, preferences, and especially, upon the purchasing power of the shopper. Therefore, some researchers consider the shopping activity as an economic behavior, given the fact that it involves financial aspects (spending money).

c) *The shopping behavior as a psychological behavior*: As it will be shown in Chapter 4, the shopping behavior in a mall is influenced by various psychological variables, such as the personality, self-concept, and emotional state of the shopper.

d) *The shopping behavior as a social behavior*: (Fox, 2004) describes well that the mall is not only a place where we spend money. It is also a place to socialize, to meet people, etc.: *"The mall became the new high street, the new town center, the new village green. The mall is usable in all weathers, there is no entrance fee, and there is no harassment. It is all very public and, hence, safe. Malls are colourful and exciting social places. The bustle and the movement, the tremendous variety of things and places, the food people love, and even movies. But most of all, just hanging out, meeting friends, making friends, drinking, gossiping, joking, making dates, etc. And all in a concentrated space – not stretched out over thousands of acres of suburb"*. An important dimension of the shopping behavior in a mall is the social aspect. In addition, the shopping activity can be accomplished individually or in groups (couples, families, with colleagues or friends). The presence of other people in the environment (mall) also shows the social aspect of such behavior.

3.4. Discussion and conclusion

The method's steps discussed in this chapter are based upon the majority of those existing in the literature, and presented in the previous chapter. Our method stands out from these methods and approaches by several characteristics which are presented in Table 3.1.

Characteristics	Classical methods and approaches (see 2.6.1)	Method of (Drogoul et al., 2002) (see 2.6.2.a)	Method of (Ramanath and Gilbert, 2003) (see 2.6.2.b)	Our proposed method
Being generic	x	X	x	x
Usability to simulate complex phenomena such as humans behaviors.	x	X	x	x
Being agent-based simulation		X	x	x
Taking into account the spatial characteristics of the phenomenon to be simulated.				x
Taking into account the geographic features of the simulated environment.				x
Allowing users to integrate and use geographic data in the simulation				x
Integarting spatial analysis of input/outpout data				x
Being used to develop 2D and 3D simulations				x

Table 3.1. Criteria distinguishing our method from those existing in literature review.

As shown in Table 3.1, the majority of methods and approaches can be used to simulate complex phenomena. What distinguishes our method from the other approaches is the fact that it takes into account the spatial characteristics of these phenomena, as well as the geographic features of the simulated environment. Like the methods proposed by (Drogoul et al., 2002) and (Ramanath and Gilbert, 2003), our method is based upon agent technology. It benefits from advanced capabilities of the agents. Unlike the methods proposed by (Drogoul et al., 2002) and (Ramanath and Gilbert, 2003), our method ca be used:

(1) to gather geographic data relative to the spatialized behaviors to be simulated,

(2) to specify agent models that emphasize spatial behaviors (such as navigation capabilities taking into account the geographic properties of the environment) and plausible interactions with the geographic environment (such as perception and memorization of objects' locations, etc.), and

(3) to carry out practical analyses of the spatial dimensions of the simulation results.

Developing such method with such characteristics distinguishing it from others, can be considered as a contribution in computer simulation field, and more specifically, in the multiagent-based simulation field.

As mentioned in Table 3.1, we think that our method is most suitable for developing 2D-3D multiagent geosimulation applications of phenomena in geographic environments.

Besides presenting our method's steps, this chapter also briefly presented the case study, which will be used to illustrate this method: *the customers' shopping behavior in a mall*. The following chapters present details of the illustration of these steps using the shopping behavior case study.

CHAPTER 4: Identification of the Application Domain, the Users' Needs, the Characteristics of the Phenomenon to be Simulated and its Environment

This chapter presents the first two steps of the generic method that we propose in this thesis. The first step aims to identify the geosimulation users' needs, while the second aims to specify the characteristics of the phenomenon to be simulated. This chapter also presents the illustration of these two steps using the customers' shopping behavior in a mall as a case study.

4.1. Introduction and motivations

Geosimulation is a *kind of computer-based simulation which is concerned with the design and construction of high-resolution spatial models of phenomena in order to understand how they behave and operate in geographic environments* (Benenson and Torrens, 2004). The simulated phenomena can be natural or artificial, human or not. Geosimulation is generally used to explore ideas and hypotheses about how phenomena operate and to solve problems in geographic contexts. In the geosimulation field, applications are generally used for decision-making purposes. These decisions are extremely influenced by the spatial characteristics of the phenomenon to be simulated, or by the geographic features of the environment in which the phenomenon occurs. In order to develop useful geosimulation applications, it is relevant to identify the end-users of these applications and to specify their needs. Hence, the importance of our method's first step: '*identification of the application domain, the geosimulation end-users, and their needs*'. In this first step, we attempt to answer the following questions: *what do we want to simulate?*, *where do we want simulate?*, *who are the users of the simulation?*, and *why the users want to use the simulation?*.

In this first step, we define the geosimulation application domain: The phenomenon to be simulated and its environment. If we want to simulate this phenomenon on a computer, we must learn about it in order to know how it operates and behaves in its geographic environment. Learning about the phenomenon to be simulated is the aim of the second step of our proposed method which is called: '*identification of the characteristics of the phenomenon to be simulated and its environment*'.

This chapter presents in detail these two steps and illustrates them using the customers' shopping behavior in a mall as a case study. It is organized as follows: Section 4.1 presents generic descriptions of the two first steps of our proposed method. Section 4.2 aims at illustrating the method's first step by presenting the intended end-users of the shopping behavior multiagent simulator. It also summarizes the main needs of these users. Then, in Section 4.2, we present the illustration of the second step of the method. Hence, we show the results of the shopping behavior study. This in-depth study involved several disciplines related to the shopping behavior in a mall, and to other similar behaviors. Among these disciplines we can cite: discipline dealing with shopping/consumption/buying behaviors, marketing, social behavior, social psychology, etc. Next, Section 4.3 aims at specifying the characteristics and the basic concepts of human shopping behavior in a mall. Section 4.4 then presents shopping in a mall as a social activity. It presents a literature review and specific results related to the shopping activity in groups, and to the structure and behavior of groups in general. Section 4.5 concludes by discussing the issues presented in the chapter.

4.2. Generic presentation of the steps

This section presents generic descriptions of the first two steps of our proposed method and defines some basic concepts.

4.2.1. Definitions of some basic concepts:

This sub-section aims to define some basic concepts presented in this chapter. Here, are some definitions:

- *Simulation*: The act of imitating the behavior of some phenomenon by means of something suitably analogous.

- *Geosimulation*: It is a kind of computer-based simulation that aims to simulate a phenomenon in a geographic environment.

- *Phenomenon to be simulated*: The system to be simulated. This system can be natural (solar system, cell, fire, etc.) or artificial (organization, manufacturing system, traffic system, etc.), human or not (animal, insect), etc.

- *The structure of a phenomenon*: The elements or variables that characterize the phenomenon.

- *The behavior of a phenomenon*: How the phenomenon behaves or acts.

- *Simulated environment*: The geographic area in which the simulated phenomenon exists, operates, and behaves.

- *The geographic limit of the simulated environment*: The geographic boundaries of the environment in which the phenomenon takes place.

4.2.2. Step 1: identification of the application domain, the geosimulation end-users, and their needs:

The first step of our proposed method (see Fig. 4.1) aims at:

(1) *identify the application domain*: We identify the phenomenon to be simulated and the simulated environment. In this sub-step, we attempt to answer the following question: *What do we want simulate and where?*;

(2) *identify the geosimulation's end-users*: We identify the future users of the geosimulation application. In this sub-step, we attempt to answer the following question: *Who are the end-users of the geosimulation application?*;

(3) *identify the main needs of these users*: Once the geosimulation end-users are defined, it is relevant to identify their needs concerning the use of the geosimulation application. In this sub-step, we attempt to answer the following question: *Why the end-users need the geosimulation application?*;

(4) *identify the geographic limits of the simulated environment*: Since we deal with geosimulation, the environment, and especially, its geographic features, influence the behavior of the phenomenon to be simulated. Hence, in order to reduce the complexity of the geosimulation, it is relevant to identify the geographic limits of the simulated environment. In this sub-step, we attempt to answer the following question: *What are the geographic limits of the simulation environment?*

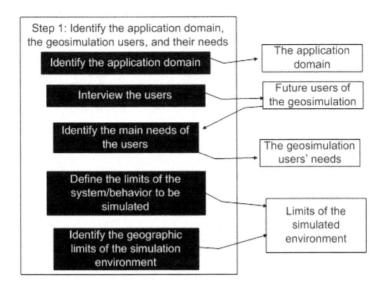

Fig. 4.1.Step 1: identification of the application domain, the geosimulation end-users, and their needs.

As outputs of this step, we have: description of the application domain of the geosimulation, geosimulation future end-users, description of the end-users' needs, and describing the geographic limits of the simulated environment.

4.2.3. Step 2: identification of the characteristics of the phenomenon to be simulated and its environment:

In the previous step, we identified some elements related to the geosimulation application domain (the simulated phenomenon and its environment), the intended users, and their needs. If we want to develop operational computer-based geosimulation of the phenomenon, we must specify its main characteristics and those of its environment, taking into account the elements defined in the previous step. The second step of our method aims at defining these characteristics and contains the following sub-steps (Fig. 4.2):

(1) *Learn about the phenomenon to be simulated and its environment*: Before identifying the characteristics of the phenomenon to be simulated, we must learn about it. Therefore, we can (i) study documents concerning it, (ii) observe it when it behaves (if it is possible), (iii) consult experts or specialists about it, etc. It is important to notice that learning about a phenomenon and its environment can involve several disciplines and science areas.

(2) *Identify the characteristics of the phenomenon to be simulated*: Based upon the study resulting from the previous sub-step, we can identify the characteristics of the phenomenon to be simulated. To characterize a phenomenon, we must identify its structure and behavior. To identify its structure, it is important to identify the *internal elements, factors or variables* that characterize that structure (can come from the system) and that influence its behavior. To identify its behavior, we must characterize the *processes* that compose this behavior. Since we deal with geosimulation, it is important to take into account the spatial aspects of the phenomenon when characterizing its characteristics.

(3) *Identify the characteristics of the simulation environment*: When we deal with geosimulation, the environment, and especially, its geographic features, are important. In this sub-step, we identify the characteristics of the simulation environment within which the phenomenon to be simulated behaves. Hence, we must identify the structures and behaviors of each element belonging to the simulation environment taking into account the geographic limits of such environment.

(4) *Design an initial model of the phenomenon to be simulated and its environment*: This sub-step aims to design an initial version of the model of the phenomenon and its environment. The design of such model is based upon the characteristics of the phenomenon to be simulated and its environment. In this model, we represent the structure of the phenomenon to be simulated, the processes composing its behavior, the structure and behaviors of the elements composing the simulation environment, and the interactions of the phenomenon to be simulated and its environment. This model aims to describe, graphically, the phenomenon and the environment to be simulated in order to better understand them.

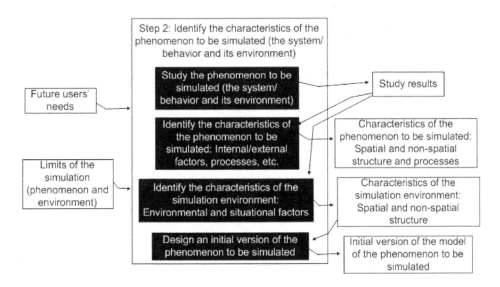

Fig. 4.2. Step 2: identification of the characteristics of the phenomenon to be simulated and its environment.

In sections 4.3 to 4.5, we aim at illustrating, respectively, these steps using customer's shopping behavior in a mall as a case study.

4.3. The users' needs specification: The shopping behavior case study

Like any other software or program, multiagent geosimulations are intended to be used by end-users in order to solve problems and make informed decisions. In multiagent geosimulation applications, decisions are influenced by the spatial features of the phenomenon to be simulated, or by the geographic characteristics of its environment.

In the case of the shopping behavior domain, we can identify:

- *The application domain* - the shopping behavior in a mall (shoppers).

We distinguish two kinds of shoppers: individual shoppers which come to the mall alone, groups of shoppers (which can be couples, groups of friends or colleagues, families, etc.) and a crowd of shoppers that is composed of all the individual shoppers and groups of shoppers within the mall. Hence, the phenomenon to be simulated is composed of individual shoppers and groups of shoppers, while the simulated environment is 'the mall'.

- The users of the geosimulation application - the mall managers:

Mall managers are the primary users of our prototype system for shopping behavior multiagent geosimulation. They will use it to better understand the spatial behaviors of the shoppers visiting the mall and to assess the impact of the spatial layout of the mall on these behaviors.

- The main needs of the users:

The main need of mall's managers is to have access to an efficient simulation prototype that can simulate customers' shopping behaviors in a mall. Mall's managers are particularly interested in understanding which particular categories of shoppers visit specific places (particular stores, kiosks, meeting areas, etc.) and which paths they follow in the mall. They are also interested in better understanding the characteristics of shoppers' flows in the mall. As examples of indicators of interest to mall managers, we can mention: *the number of shoppers entering by a specific door or going through a specific corridor in the mall, the genders and age categories of shoppers going through a corridor, the category of stores visited by particular categories of the shoppers*, etc. When changing the configuration of the virtual mall in the simulation prototype, mall mangers want to observe and assess how the changes may influence the behavior of the virtual shoppers, the evaluation being quantified thanks to the chosen indicators. As examples of modifications that can be carried out in the virtual mall, mall managers can exchange the positions of two places in the mall (stores, kiosks, washrooms, etc.), they can close a corridor or a door, change the position of a door in the mall. It is interesting for mall managers to have an idea of the impacts of these changes, using the geosimulation in the virtual mall, before carrying out these changes in the real mall, changes which may be very costly.

Since the phenomenon to be studied has been defined (individual shoppers and groups of shoppers), the simulated environment is defined (the mall), end-users of the shopping behavior simulator are identified, and their needs are characterized, we can start to study and learn about the shopping behavior in a mall. This study is conducted in several scientific disciplines related to the shopping behavior in a mall, or to other behaviors similar to the aforementioned. The study results are presented in Sections 4.4 (individual shoppers) and 4.5 (groups of shoppers) of the chapter.

4.4. The identification of the characteristics of the shopping behavior in a mall

The first step of our method has been presented in the previous section. This section illustrates the second step whereby the characteristics of the shopping behavior in a mall are identified. Before doing this though, we need to learn more about it. Sub-section 4.4.1 presents the results of an in-depth literature review concerning the shopping behavior in a mall. Based upon this literature review, we then identify the characteristics of the shopping behavior in Sub-section 4.4.2.

4.4.1. A literature survey on the shopping behavior in a mall

The shopping behavior is defined by (Haynes et al., 1994) as follows: '*how individuals or groups choose a store for shopping in a mall*'. Store choice and shopping patterns are based upon customers' perception, images, and attitudes formed from experiences, information, and needs. Furthermore, the shopping behavior involves a decision process related to *where* consumers shop, *how* they shop, and *what* they purchase. This decision process is often initiated by shopping behavior motives, which determine *why* consumers shop and make purchases at certain retail stores (Moschis, 1992) (Stafford and stafford, 1986). As stated by (Haynes et al., 1994), the shopping behavior involves three basic components: The stores' attributes (*where*), the consumers' characteristics (*who*) and the choice context (*how and why*).

The number of studies concerning shopping malls and shopping behavior is very limited (Wakefield and Baker, 1998). Moreover, shopping behavior research frequently concentrates its efforts on individual stores, and not on the mall itself. Furthermore, most research in this area dates back to the 1970s, 1980s, and the early half of the 1990s (Reynolds et al., 2002). What's more, most such studies focused on the shopper (*who*) and its demographic variables (Stone, 1954) (Smith, 1956). These studies gave a detailed taxonomy of customers, but they could not explain *why* people shop (Hassay and Smith, 1996). Some researchers focused on shoppers in a mall according to the '*how*' question of shopping behavior instead of '*who*' they are. For example, (Roberts and Merrilees, 2001) presented a categorization of the shopping activities based upon the mall components. Hence, we can find: *retail-based activities* (buy items and brands), *service-based activities* (buy services), *entertainment activities* (go to the mall for entertainment and play), and *social activities* (go to the mall to socialize and meet people). (Bloch et al., 1994) developed a segmentation model that clusters customers by the shopping activity they perform in a mall, or not (going to a shop, going to a bank, having a snack, etc.). The taxonomy of shopping activities presented by (Bloch et al., 1994) is composed of 13 activities. Their method represents a significant improvement on previous models because it is based upon behavioral variables (action), and not merely descriptive variables such as age and gender. (Bloch et al., 1994) talked about the '*where*' by acknowledging the importance of the environment and atmospheric factors that affect the shopping behavior: '*additional research on the environmental psychology of malls using different measures and methods seems highly worthwhile given the substantial resources being devoted to mall design and rehabilitation*' (Bloch et al., 1994).

In order to better simulate the shopping behavior in a mall we need to understand all the aspects of this behavior. This means we need to better understand:

- *Who* is doing the shopping: shopper characteristics;

- *Why* she/he is doing the shopping: motivations for the shopping;

- *How* she/he is doing the shopping: how the shopper accomplishes the shopping behavior: what are the shopping activities that can be done in the mall, how the shopper makes shopping decisions, etc.;

- *Where* the shopper does his/her shopping: shopping environment characteristics (the mall) and the shopping atmosphere.

The *who, why,* and *how* questions come from the shoppers, while the *where* question comes from the shopping mall.

In addition, we notice a noteworthy lack in terms of empirical research works dealing with the shopping behavior in a mall (Wakefield and Baker, 1998). In our study, we need such empirical research works in order to simulate the shopping behavior in a mall. Fortunately, there are a number of works in the literature that deal with some human behaviors that are very similar to the shopping behavior in a mall. These behaviors are the *consumption behavior* and the *shopping behaviors in stores.*

(Fotheringham, 1998) argued that in shopping behavior in a mall, the choice of the store is classified primarily as a cognitive process. '*Store choice behavior has been found to be similar to items/brand choice by a consumer behavior. The only difference being the importance of the geographic dimension. While the brand choice is devoid of any geography, the choice of a store is very much influenced by its location*'. This dissertation shows the similarity between the shopping behavior in a mall (the shopper decides which store to visit in order to enter and purchase some items or services), and the shopping behavior in a store (the shopper decides to purchase an item or brand inside a store).

In the consumer behavior discipline, (Perner, 2005) defines the consumption behavior as '*the study of individuals, groups, or organisations, and the process they use to select, secure, use, and dispose of products, services, experiences, or ideas to satisfy needs, and the impact that these processes have on the consumer and society*'. Another definition given by (James et al., 1973) is "*acts of individuals directly involved in obtaining and using economic goods and services, including the decision processes that precede and determine these acts*". These definitions show the similarity between the consumption behavior and the shopping behavior in a mall.

Given the high similarity between the shopping behavior in a mall, and both the *consumption behavior (in the consumer behavior discipline)* and the *shopping behavior inside a store*, we can characterize the shopping behavior in a mall based upon the study results and research works of these other fields of research.

4.4.1.1. The shopping behavior in a mall as a consumption behavior

Shopping behavior in a mall is similar to consumption behavior. In order to understand the human shopping behavior in a mall, it is relevant to study the human consumption behavior. This sub-section presents our literature review of consumer behavior, with the goal to understand some aspects of the shopping behavior in a mall.

It is well accepted in the literature concerning consumer behavior that the consumption behavior is influenced by several factors, and is composed by various processes. In the following sub-sections, we present in detail some of these factors and processes.

a. The factors influencing the consumption behavior

(Duhaime et al., 1996) argued that the best way to study human consumption behavior is to find *"Why they act like they do?"*. The majority of the researchers who study this subject are interested to know why humans buy some goods and adopt such consumption behavior, etc. These researchers emphasize that consumption behavior is influenced by two types of factors: *internal factors* (e.g., needs, values, lifestyle, personality, attitudes, gender, lifecycle, etc.), and *environmental and social factors* (e.g., culture, social class, reference groups, family, etc.) (Duhaime et al., 1996). Other factors, which are cited in the literature such as emotion, humour, time, advertisement, etc., are presented as *additional factors or miscellaneous*. They are discussed in the following points.

▪ *Internal factors*:

Internal factors contain the majority of factors that come from the consumer, and that influence his consumption behavior. The main factors are:

❐ *Motivation and needs*: Behavior is initiated through motivations and needs (Bayton, 1958). The author argues that motivation is one of the basic factors in consumer behavior. Motivation arises out of tension-systems which create a state of disequilibrium in the mind of the individual (Helgeson *et al.*, 1984). This triggers a sequence of psychological events directed toward the selection of a goal, which the individual anticipates will bring about relief from such tension, and the selection of patterns of action which he anticipates, will bring about the achievement of the goal. To better understand consumption behavior, we need to know the fundamental needs and motivations, which are the origin of this behavior (Duhaime et al., 1996). Some researchers tried to identify the needs systems of humans. For example, (Maslow, 1954) proposed a theory, with a five-level-hierarchy of human needs (see Fig 4.3). This hierarchy is now central to much thinking in consumption behavior.

Fig. 4.3. The hierarchy of needs proposed by (Maslow, 1954).

(Maslow, 1954) was not the only theorist to focus his efforts on human needs as the motivating force behind human behavior. For example, (Murray, 1938) elaborated a typology of physiological needs even more detailed than that proposed by Maslow.

❏ *Values, beliefs, and attitudes*: Values, beliefs, and attitudes greatly affect human behavior (Duhaime et al., 1996). A value is a standard that guides one's actions, attitudes, comparisons, evaluations, and justifications toward oneself and others (Rokeach, 1960). While motivations and needs of human behavior continually change, values and beliefs are relatively permanent (Rokeach, 1960). Rokeach developed what he called '*Rokeach Value Survey: RVS*', which is an instrument to operationalize the value concept. Researchers closely compare the concepts of attitudes and beliefs when studying values. The idea of studying attitudes and beliefs, when learning about values, is important because the three concepts are closely related to one another. An attitude is a relatively enduring organization of beliefs around an object or situation, predisposing one to respond in some preferential manner (Rokeach, 1960). An attitude is thus, a package of beliefs consisting of interconnected assertions to the effect that certain things about a specific situation are true or false, and other things about it are desirable or undesirable (Morris, 1956). A belief is any simple portion of knowledge, conscious or unconscious, inferred from what a person says or does (Weiner, 1998). According to a study by (Weiner, 1998), all beliefs are a predisposition to action, and an attitude is thus, a set of interrelated predispositions to action, organized around an object.

❐ *Lifestyle*: (Cosmas, 1982) argued that the total assortment of goods and services used by a consumer is hypothesized to be a mirror image of his/her lifestyle. Lifestyle refers to the distinctive ways in which consumers live, how they spend their time and money, and what they consider important- activities, interests, and opinions.

❐ *Perception*: Perception deals with recognizing, selecting, organizing, and interpreting stimuli in order to make sense of the world around us. People receive stimuli from their environment through the five senses, which they then must interpret. People are selective and interpret stimuli that reinforce and enhance their existing beliefs. Consumers tend to interpret what they perceive in such a way so that it does not conflict with their basic attitudes, personalities, motives, or aspirations. They pay attention to stimuli deemed relevant to existing needs, wants, beliefs, and attitudes, and disregard the rest.

❐ *Knowledge and learning*: Consumer knowledge and learning significantly affect consumption behavior (Craik and Watkins, 1973). Information processing describes the series of steps, by which information (or stimulus) is encountered through some exposure to a person's senses, interpreted, understood and accepted, and stored in memory for future use in making of decisions (McGuire, 1976). Elaboration, via mental processing, transforms this information into beliefs, attitudes, and intentions that determine product choice and related aspects of purchase. The degree of integration between the stimulus and existing knowledge that occurs while a stimulus is being processed, will influence the amount of learning that takes place (Craik and Watkins, 1973).

❐ *Self-concept*: (Sirgy, 1982) presented the influence of the self-concept on consumption behavior. Self-concept is an organized set of perceptions of the self, comprised of such elements as the perceptions of one's characteristics and abilities; the perception of oneself in relation to others; and objectives, goals, and ideals that are perceived as either positive or negative (Rogers, 1951).

❐ *Personality*: One of the more engrossing concepts in the study of consumer behavior is that of personality. Personality accounts for consistent patterns of behavior based upon enduring psychological characteristics (Kassarjian, 1971). It is the pattern of traits and behaviors that makes one individual unique and different from all others.

▪ *Environmental and social factors*:

Consumers do not live or make decisions in isolation. The values, beliefs, and opinions of those who surround the consumer affect his/her decisions. Among the environmental and social influences on the consumer are: culture, sub-culture, social class, reference groups, and family.

❐ *Demographic variables*: Demographic variables have a long history in marketing and consumer behavior disciplines (Kalyanam and Putler, 1994). (Kalyanam and Putler, 1994) presented the importance of taking into account the demographic variables in human consumption behavior. The most important variables studied by the researchers of consumer behavior are the following: gender; age group; marital status; occupation and employment sector; habits, and preferences.

❐ *Culture and sub-culture*: Culture consists of a society's beliefs, values, ethics, customs, shared meanings, rules, rituals, norms, and traditions. Culture provides people with a sense of identity and an understanding of acceptable behavior. Culture is deep-seated and enduring, but does change slowly over time (Clark, 1990). Sub-cultures are racial, ethnic, religious, or other groups whose members are distinguishable from the general population and who are held together by common culture and/or genetic ties. To the degree that people in an ethnic group share common customs, values, rituals, and traditions that are different from those of other ethnic groups or the larger society, they constitute a distinct ethnic group (Hirschman, 1982).

❐ *Social classes and stratification*: Social stratification represents the hierarchical division of members of a society into relative levels of prestige, status, and power (Rossides, 1990). Social class refers to divisions, based upon economic and demographic characteristics. Those in the same stratum have roughly similar consumption, lifestyle, and income, and socialize with each other (Gilbert and Kahl, 1982).

❏ *Reference groups*: Reference groups are individuals or collections of people whom the individual uses as a source, or point of comparison for attitudes, beliefs, values, or behaviors. Consumers belong to some of the groups that influence their consumer behavior, and either aspire to join, or work to avoid association with others. Some of these groups are formal groups and others are simply informal groups of friends (Homans, 1961).

❏ *Family*: The most influential reference group is the consumer's family (Qualls, 1982). The family teaches the consumer cultural values that have a substantial impact upon consumption behavior. It continues to be a point of reference, even when the consumer has formed his own household.

▪ *Additional factors (miscellaneous)*:

Consumer behavior is influenced by other additional factors. These factors are presented in the following points:

❏ *Emotion*: A large number of research works presented emotions as an important component of consumer behavior (Richins, 1997) (Lemoine, 2001). In their studies of consumption-related emotions, consumer behavior scholars have based much of their work on frameworks of emotion developed in psychology. The foundation laid by theorists in this field has provided a useful starting point for the investigation of emotions in the consumer behavior field (Richins, 1997). Some scholars have attempted to order the universe of emotions by identifying a set of basic fundamental emotions, although there is no widespread agreement concerning the number or the nature of such basic emotions. The most important scale in the domain of consumer behavior by marketing scholars is the PAD (Pleasure-arousal-dominance) emotion scale developed by (Mehrabian and Russell, 1974). Another interesting emotion scale often used in the sphere of consumer behavior, is the scale proposed by (Richins, 1997). This scale, called *Consumption Emotion Scale (CES)* (see Table 4.1), is specific to consumption behavior.

The Consumption Emotions Set (CES)	
Anger	Frustrated, angry, irritated
Discontent	Unfulfilled, discontented
Worry	Nervous, worried, tense
Sadness	Depressed, sad, miserable
Fear	Scared, afraid, panicky
Shame	Embarrassed, ashamed, humiliated
Envy	Envious, jealous
Loneliness	Lonely, homesick
Romantic love	Sexy, romantic, passionate
Love	Loving, sentimental, warm hearted
Peacefulness	Calm, peaceful
Contentment	Contented, fulfilled
Optimism	Optimistic, encouraged, hopeful
Joy	Happy, pleased, joyful
Excitement	Excited, thrilled, enthusiastic
Surprise	Surprised, amazed, astonished
Other items	Guilty, proud, eager, relieved

Table 4.1. The Consumption Emotions Set (CES) presented by (Richins, 1997).

❒ *The mood*: Mood has been described as a phenomenological property of a person's subjectively perceived affective state. It is viewed as a mild, transient, generalized, and pervasive affective state, not an intense emotion, and not directed at specific target objects (Swinyard, 1993). A positive mood seems to make one kinder, more generous, more resistant to temptation, and more willing to delay self-rewards. Negative moods have produced greater dislike for peers, less volunteering for helping tasks, smaller contributions to charity, less resistance to temptation, and less willingness to delay self-rewards. However, the observed effects of negative moods have been less consistent than those of positive moods. Mood has been shown to have significant effects on consumer behavior (Swinyard, 1993). (Gardner, 1985) observed that the effects of mood may have a special impact on retail or service encounters because of their interpersonal nature, a view also supported by others (Swinyard, 1993). Studies of mood in shopping situations showed its effect on shopping behavior or intentions.

❒ *The role of involvement*: The involvement has a greater effect when the shopping experiences are personally relevant to consumers or are "self-related or in some way instrumental in achieving their personal goals" (Swinyard, 1993). A large number of studies have reported that consumers, involved in a situation or product, are more active processors of related cognitive information. Involved consumers should attend to, and comprehend more information about a shopping situation, and should produce more elaborate meanings and inferences about it.

b. The fundamental processes of consumption behavior

The consumer buying process is a complex matter, since many internal and external factors have an impact on the consumer's buying decisions. When purchasing a product, researchers identified *several processes* through which consumers go (Duhaime et al., 1996) (see Fig 4.4). These processes are discussed in the following points.

Fig. 4.4. The processes of human consumption behavior (Duhaine et al., 1996)

▪ *Needs or problem recognition process*:

Consumer decision making comes about as an attempt to solve consumer problems. A problem refers to '*a discrepancy between a desired state and an ideal state, which is sufficient to arouse and activate a decision making process*' (Duhaime *et al.*, 1996). Consumers often note problems by comparing their current, or actual, situation, explicitly or implicitly, to some desired situation. Problems come in several different types. A problem may be an *active* one (e.g., you have a headache and would like as quick a solution as possible) or *inactive*-- you are not aware that your situation is a problem (e.g., a consumer is not aware that he or she could have more energy taking a new vitamin). Problems may be *acknowledged* (e.g., a consumer is aware that his or her car does not accelerate well enough), or *unacknowledged* (e.g., a consumer will not acknowledge that he or she consumes too much alcohol). Finally, needs can be relatively *generic*, as in the need for enjoyment (which can be satisfied in many different ways), or *specific*, as in the need to eat a chocolate ice-cream (Bettman and Park, 1980).

▪ *Information search process*:

When the consumer recognizes a need (or problem), he/she starts to search for information about the items or services that can be used in order to satisfy that need. There are two principal approaches to searching: internal and external. *Internal searches (via the memorization search process)* are based upon what consumers already know (what is in his/her memory). A problem is that some items or services that can satisfy the need or solve the problem, are not remembered, or have never been heard of, and are therefore, not considered. In this case, the consumer can use *external* searches (*via the perception process*) that get people to either speak to others (getting information by word of mouth) or use other sources (such as advertisements or yellow-page listings) (Bettman, 1979; Punj, 1987). In the search processes, consumers often do not consider all possible alternatives. Some are not known (the *"unawareness"* set), some were once known, but are not readily accessible in the memory (the *"inert"* set), while others are ruled out as unsatisfactory (the *"inept"* set), and those that are considered represent the *"evoked"* set, from which one alternative is likely to be purchased (Beatty and Smith, 1987).

The amount of effort a consumer puts into searching, depends upon a number of factors such as the market (how many competitors there are, and how great are the differences between brands expected to be?), item characteristics (how important is this product? How complex is the product? How obvious are the indications of quality?), consumer characteristics (how interested is a consumer, generally, in analyzing product characteristics and making the best possible deal?), and situational characteristics (Duncan and Olshavsky, 1982).

▪ *Decision-making (purchasing decision) process*:

When evaluating alternatives, consumers choose from a list of acceptable alternatives (evoked set) based upon the criteria they have selected as being important. For a product to be considered by a consumer, he must know that it exists and perceive to be able to satisfy his needs. The criteria a consumer uses to choose between alternative items/services are the item/service attributes the consumer considers to be important. Consumers may make the purchase decision using compensatory or non-compensatory decision rules. Using a *compensatory* decision rule, the consumer identifies the important attributes, rates the alternative products on each attribute, and selects the product with the highest score. With a simple additive rule, the consumer selects the product that is judged to have the largest number of positive attributes. This is a relatively simple rule, used most often when motivation or ability is limited (Alba and Marmorstein, 1987). The weighted additive is a more complex compensatory rule in which the relative importance of each product attribute is also factored into the decision. Therefore, the consumer completes the more complicated task of computing a summated weighted score for each product on the salient attributes, and selects the product with the highest overall score. In contrast, *non-compensatory* decision rules do not balance all attributes and determine whether the positives outweigh the negatives. Rather, if the product does not meet a minimum standard on an important attribute, then it will not be considered. Using a conjunctive decision rule, the consumer sets minimum acceptable standards on all important attributes and eliminates any alternative that does not meet all the minimums. This helps consumers to narrow down the choices for further evaluation. If none of the products meet all the cutoff requirements, either the consumer must change the minimums acceptable, or change his or her decision rule (Grether and Wilde, 1984). With the *lexicographic* rule, the consumer first ranks the attributes in terms of perceived importance. Then, the alternatives are compared on this one most important attribute. If one scores sufficiently high on this most important attribute, then it is selected. If two or more are perceived as equally good, they are then compared on the second most important attribute. This process continues until the tie is broken. Consumers may use a *combination of decision rules* in choosing a product. First, they may use a rule to narrow down the choice set with some simple cutoff, and then they may apply a more complex compensatory rule to make the final choice. Some criteria are more salient than others, and those attributes will have a greater impact, or importance, in determining consumer selections.

▪ *Purchasing process* :

Through the evaluation process discussed above, consumers will reach their final purchasing decision, e.g. they go to the shop to buy the product/service. Purchase of the product/service can either be through the store, the web, or over the phone.

▪ *Post-Purchasing process (Satisfaction, dissatisfaction, cognitive dissonance)* :

❏ *Satisfaction/dissatisfaction*: After the sale, the buyer will likely feel either satisfied or dissatisfied. If the buyer believes that s/he received more in the exchange than what was paid, s/he might feel *satisfied*. If s/he believes that s/he received less in the exchange than what was paid, then s/he might feel *dissatisfied*. Dissatisfied buyers are not likely to return as customers, and are not likely to send friends, relatives, and acquaintances.

❑ *Cognitive dissonance*: Also called buyer's remorse. This post-purchase behavior is more likely to happen when the purchase is a more expensive one. The consumer may experience some regrets, or question himself/herself as to whether or not the purchase was a good one.

c. Consumption behavior models

- The models proposed by (Engel et al., 1968) (Howard and Sheth, 1969) and (Nicosa, 1966):

In order to understand decision-making related to human consumption, many researchers proposed several models for consumer behavior. The three main comprehensive models for this type of consumer decision-making, (Engel et al., 1968) (Howard and Sheth, 1969), and (Nicosa 1966), trace the psychological state and behavior of individual purchasers from the point at which they perceive a need, through the search for information, evaluation of alternatives, purchase, and final evaluation of the consequences. These models are presented in Fig 4.5, Fig 4.6, and Fig 4.7. The assumption in these models is that a purchase act is preceded by a sequence of mental information processing. This involves a cognitive function in forming beliefs, an emotional component in developing positive or negative attitudes, and a reaction, through which one is motivated to select and buy.

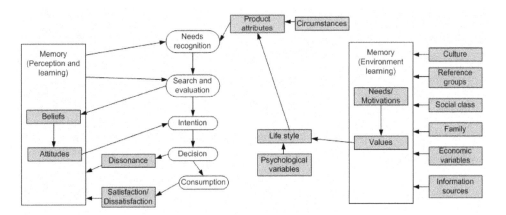

Fig. 4.5. The consumer decision-making model proposed by (Engel eet al., 1968).

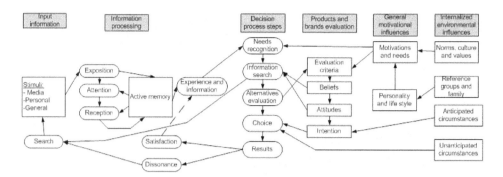

Fig. 4.6. The consumer decision-making model proposed by (Howard ans Sheth, 1969).

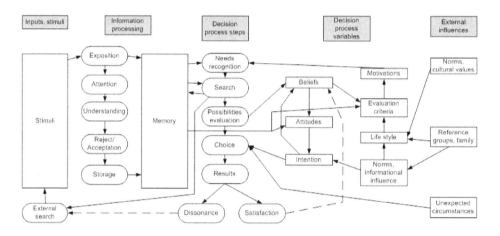

Fig. 4.7. The consumer decision-making model proposed by (Nicosa, 1966).

Although these three models help to understand the consumption behavior, they have specific drawbacks which are:

- They do not consider all the factors that influence consumption behavior. For example, they leave out the majority of external factors that come from the environment, which are presented in the following sub-section;

- They do not present, in detail, how each variable influences another variable, or a process. The relationships between the elements in the model (variables or processes) are presented by descriptive arrows;

- These models are very old and are not updated.

- The CONSUMAT model (Jager, 2000):

Recently, (Jager, 2000) and (Janssen and Jager, 1999) developed what the called *'the CONSUMAT model'*. It is a model of human behavior with the focus on consumer behavior. It combines in an elegant way many of leading psychological theories, such as theories about human needs, motivational processes, social comparison theory, social learning theory, theory of reasoned action, etc. The consumat model represents individual (or *'consumats'*) having needs which may be more or less satisfied, having items (*'opportunities'*) to consume, and various abilities to consume these items. Futhermore, consumats have a certain degree of uncertainty. Depending on the combination of the indicators *'satisfied/not satisfied'* and *'certain/uncertain'*, the consumats are engaged in four different cognitive processes: repetition, deliberation, imitation, and social comparison. When a consumat is both certain and satisfied, it has of course no reason to change its behavior, thus repetition is the strategy chosen. An uncertain but satisfied consumat has a reason to change its behavior. In this case the cognitive process chosen is imitiation of its neighbors. An unsatisfied but certain consumat on the other hand will deliberate. The final strategy is to consult the social network, the strategy chosen by uncertain and unsatisfied consumat (Janssen and Jager, 1999).

The Consumat model proposed by (Janssen and Jager, 1999) is relevant to our work in the sense it presents some variables or 'indicators' which can be integrated in our consumer model such as 'needs', 'satisfaction', 'certainty', etc. But, like the models proposed by (Engel et al., 1968) (Howard and Sheth, 1969), and (Nicosa 1966), the consumat model focuses on the human consumption behavior in general and neither focus on the spatial aspects of the consumption behavior nor on the geographic features of the simulated environment. Since we deal with geosimulation, these apects and features are critical to our work.

- The consumer model proposed by (Ben Said et al., 2001)

(Ben Said et al., 2001) presented a consumer model which was used in a simulation project called CUBES (Customers BEhavior Simulator). The objectives of this model are to develop a software simulating consumers' behavior in a competitive market including several brands and to build a virtual population of consumers including several thousands of individuals, that reproduce real market properties (segmentation, evolution) independently of a given product. The CUBES model provides (1) the simulation of consumers' behavioural attitudes (BA), (the impacts of consumption acts resulting from these attitudes), (3) retroactive effects of these acts on the consumers themselves, and (4) brand reactions to the market evolutions and their retroactive effects on the individual behavioural attitudes. The CUBES model covers the main concepts of previous theoretical works on consumer behavior such as consumer involvement, innovation diffusion and opinion leaders.

The consumer behavioural model presented by (Ben Said et al., 2001) is essentially based on a set of behavioral attitudes (BAs) defined basing on from social processes and personality traits. In this model the authors consider two social processes in order to model the interactions between the individuals of a virtual consumer population: *Imitation_Process* and *Conditioning_Process*. There are three BAs considered by the authors: *Mistrust, Opportunism, Innovation*. These BAs are defined based on consumers' personality traits. In the CUBES model, the behavior of the consumer is based on these BAs.

The CUBES model of consumer presented by (Ben Said et al., 2001) is suited to design and develop an operational simulator of behaviors of thousands consumers in virtual markets. But, like the models proposed by (Engel et al., 1968) (Howard and Sheth, 1969), (Nicosa 1966), and (Jager, 2000) this model focuses on the consumption behavior in general and considers neither the spatial aspects of the consumption behavior nor the geographic features of the simulated environment.

The models discussed above provide a good basis to understand the elements which influence a consumer's decision-making process. We extend them in order to propose an integrated model which includes the main factors influencing both, the consumption and the shopping behaviors, as well as the main processes composing them. This model is presented in Fig 4.8.

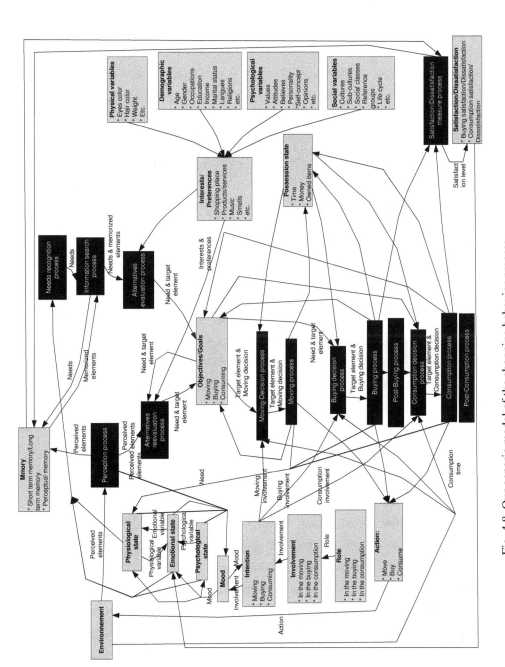

Fig. 4.8. Our generic model of the shopping behavior process.

As shown in Fig 4.8, the initial version of the model contains several factors or variables that influence the shopping behavior (as mentioned in Section 4.3). In order to facilitate the reading of this model, some factors or variables are regrouped together in order to form groups of variables. For example, the shopper's variables *age* and *gender* belong to the *demographic profile*, while the variables *culture* and *social class* belong to the *social profile*. Other variables are grouped together in order to form what we called '*states*'. For example, the variables *time* and *money*, that the shopper has to do shopping, belong to the *possession state*. The model also contains the main processes which are involved in the shopping behavior. For example, we can find the *recognition needs process*, the *perception process*, the *alternatives evaluation process*, the *information search process*, *decision-making process*, etc. (see Section 4.3).

This model will be used as a base: (1) to create the shopping behavior multiagent model (see Chapter 5 for the illustration of the third step of the method) and (2) to gather data concerning the shopping behavior using the survey (see Chapter 6 for the illustration of the fourth step of the method).

Due to the complexity of this model, we cannot take into account all these variables and processes in the shopping behavior geosimulation prototype. For example, in our model, we take into account the following variables: demographic (age, gender, occupation, sector of employments, marital status, etc.), interests, preferences, etc. and the main processes: Need recognition, perception, information search, alternatives evaluation, moving-decision, and moving processes.

4.4.1.2. The shopping behavior in a mall, as a shopping behavior in a store
The shopping behavior in a mall is quite similar to the shopping behavior inside a store, because these two behaviors are performed in geographic environments. In addition, the literature revealed that there exist several studies dealing with the shopping behavior in stores, which can be useful to study the shopping behavior in a mall. This similarity encouraged us to look at these studies in order to better understand the shopping behavior in a mall. In this sub-section we present the results of our study of human shopping behavior in stores. Based upon these studies, we can infer some characteristics of the shopping behavior in a mall. In

addition, we focus only on the factors that come from the environment (the store) and that affect the shopping behavior, because the internal-external factors that influence the shopping behavior are the same factors that influence the consumption behavior and were mentioned in the previous sub-sections.

If we ask a shopper about his/her choice of an item in a store we can expect that he/she answers as follows: "*It depends on when, where, why, etc.*". Consumer behavior depends enormously on the context or the situation. The influence of the situation on consumer preferences for a product or a service has been well documented in prior research on consumer behavior (Belk, 1974) (Srivastava et al., 1981). In line with (Belk, 1974), we define a usage situation as "*those factors particular to a time and place of observation, which do not follow from personal (intra-individual) and stimulus (choice alternative) attributes, and which have a demonstrable and systematic effect on current behavior.*" These factors are called *stimuli* or *situational variables* (Belk, 1974). Previous research such as that done by (Ratneshwar and Allan, 1991), has investigated the impact of different usage contexts on consumer consideration sets, and shown that consumers or shoppers consider different items in different usage situations. These findings are in line with those of (Warlop and Ratneshwar, 1993), who illustrate the importance of the usage context (familiar versus unfamiliar situations) regarding the formation of consideration sets.

(Belk, 1974) presented a situation as a part of a context, which is itself a part of an environment (see Fig 4.9). This distinction is very relevant because the situation is associated with a point in time and space.

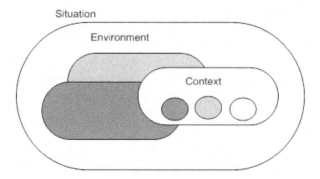

Fig. 4.9. The environment, context, and situation (Belk, 1974).

In our work, we are interested in shopping situations. (Belk, 1974) presented shopping situations, based upon specific aspects, which are presented in the following points.

a. Atmospheric aspect

This aspect contains the following factors:

- *Visual factors*: The visual factors of a physical environment such as a store that influences shopping behavior, are:

  ❏ *Lighting*: Good lighting creates a pleasant atmosphere and encourages the shoppers to stay in the store longer. If customers go into a store that is dull and dingy, they are not encouraged to stay very long (Pellet 1996). However, if the lights are harsh and glaring, retailers are going to find that it takes a toll on employees' performance. Glaring lights are also going to make the customers uncomfortable. If the light does not augment color contrast, it may not be suitable in a fashion wear store (Bandyopadhyay et al., 2001).

  ❏ *Colors and fixtures*: Retailers frequently use colors and fixtures to improve the store environment. (Michon et al., 2005), given that they help provide a classy in-store ambiance. Proper color contrast can enrich the store image and perceived store or merchandise quality.

  ❏ *Layout and displays*: It is an established fact that changes in layout can affect the sales of a store (Bandyopadhyay et al., 2001). These authors' research on the impact of layout and display effects on sales revealed several interesting findings.

- *Non-visual factors*: These factors are

  ❏ *Sound and music*: Sound plays an increasingly critical role in helping retailers to entertain and inform shoppers (Michon et al., 2005). Retailers are now expanding its use beyond the traditional background music application. Sound helps to create a unique environment as merchandisers are confronted more and more with the monotony of merchandise in most stores (Michon et al., 2005). Sound, in the form of music, is commonly used to entertain shoppers. It can also give a significant boost to a store's energy level by creating a sense of excitement. The audio experience, therefore, can be an important component of a store's overall entertainment factor. The main advantage of using sound in the form of music is that it can greatly extend customers' stay time. Music is known to have a classical conditioning effect on consumers (Bandyopadhyay et al., 2001). If the music is likeable, customers not only feel good, but they tend to stay longer likewise. Music also makes the service environment look more positive to customers in waiting lines (Bandyopadhyay et al., 2001).

❏ *Odors and smell*: Studies have shown that ambient aromas both influence a consumer's mood and the time he/she spends in the store. What's more, the sense of smell has the greatest impact on emotions because, anatomically speaking, the nose is directly connected with the olfactory lobe in the limbic system of the brain, which controls emotion (Maclean, 1973).

Much research examined the factors that affect shopping behavior in retail environments. Of existing studies, most have discussed the environmental factors, or physical surroundings, relative to bank, travel agency, hotel, restaurant, hospital, and workplace settings. Table 4.2 shows some of the environmental factors that have been discussed in the literature (Baker et al., 1988), (Bitner, 1992), (Engel et al., 1995) and (Lewison, 1994). (Baker et al., 1988) studied banks, (Bitner, 1992) discussed a typology based upon who performs actions within the environment, as well as having proposed a conceptual framework for three types of service organizations: self-service, interpersonal service, remote service. (Engel et al., 1995) and (Lewison, 1994) provided textbook discussion on the environment factors.

Factors	(Baker et al., 1988)	(Bitner, 1992)	(Engel et al., 1995)	(Lewison, 1994)
Temperature	X	X		
Air quality		X	X	
Lighting	X	X	X	
Noise	X	X		X
Scent/Smell	X	X		X
Music	X	X		X
Layout	X	X	X	X
Flooring	X		X	X
Fixtures/Racks			X	
Aisle placement			X	
Signs	X	X		
Style of decor	X	X		X

Table 4.2. The environmental factors mentioned in the literature.

b. Social aspects

- *Crowding and density*: Retail store crowding influences the confidence of the shopper. According to (Harell and Hutt, 1976), many consumers, after shopping in a crowded store, feel that they somewhat deviated from their original shopping plan. Shoppers tend to shorten their shopping time if they find the store too crowded. They browse less and buy only the basic necessities.

- *Staff or salesperson*: The results of the study made by (Baker et al., 1995) indicated that ambiance and salespeople are more likely to affect customers' perceptions of merchandise and service quality than design factors such as color, displays, store, and merchandise layout. Although there is a wealth of literature on how service quality influences customer satisfaction and purchase intention (see, for example, (Taylor and Baker, 1994), (Gronroos, 1993), (Rust and Oliver 1994)), unfortunately, not much research has been done to explore the impact of the employees on customers' shopping behavior (Michon et al., 2005).

c. Spatial aspects

(Dogu and Erkip, 2000) presented the shopping behavior in a *mall* or a *retail store* as a spatial activity that is completely affected by the geographic characteristics of the environment such as building shape and layout, in addition to geographic configuration. They argued that the shopping behavior inside a mall is a kind of wayfinding/orientation behavior because the shopping activities are also related to the nature of goods to be purchased, and may be affected by the shopper's time and financial constraints.

d. Temporal aspect

The time has played a major function in several research disciplines that are closely related to consumer behavior. This dimension remarkably affects consumption and shopping behavior (Carmon, 1991) and (Dhar and Nowlis, 1999). The importance of time, as a major variable of interest in consumer behavior theory, had already been recognized in the early stages of consumer research. Over the past twenty years, several research streams concerning time have evolved within the consumer behavior literature. These included the effects of time pressure on consumer' decision-making, allocation of their time, and perception of time. Several interdisciplinary reviews also appeared in the marketing literature (Carmon, 1991). The majority of research works addressed the effect of time pressure when consumers are forced to choose. Some researchers such as (Dhar and Nowlis, 1999), examined the decision process and choice outcomes when the no-choice, or deferral option, is available. Studying the no-choice option in consumption or shopping behavior is important for our study because mall's visitors are not always obliged to buy items or to visit stores. (Dhar and Nowlis, 1999) presented a model of the consumer decision-making process (alternative evaluation process) under time pressure. This model is presented in Fig 4.10.

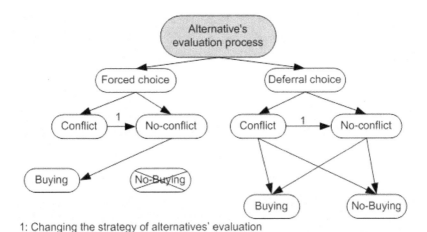

1: Changing the strategy of alternatives' evaluation

Fig. 4.10. The model of the decision-making process under the pressure of time presented by (Dhar and Nowlis, 1999).

These models offer the following options under time pressure:

▪ *Forced choice*: The consumer does not have the choice to buy the item. In the forced choice, we have two issues:

❑ *The consumer can have a conflict*: If there is a conflict (i.e., when the choice is more difficult and the alternatives are similar in terms of importance to the consumer; all the alternatives are attractive), he-she can change the strategy in his-her alternatives' evaluation process. For example, and in order to make a choice, the consumer can change the evaluation of the alternatives' attributes in order to remove the conflict, and he/she buys his-her item because he/she does not have a choice.

❑ *There is no conflict*: The consumer buys his-her item because he-she does not have any choice.

• *Deferral choice*: If they have the choice, consumers are more likely to select the no-choice option when conflict is high (when all the alternatives are attractive) rather than when conflict is low (there is a single superior alternative). An analysis of the decision-making process suggests that consumers who expressed more thoughts, or made more comparisons (and presumably found the choice more difficult), were more likely to choose the deferral option. An implicit assumption that underlies such a pattern of preferences is the notion that selecting the best option, within the choice set, precedes the deferral decision. Thus, the difficulty of making the selection when choice among the alternatives involves conflict, increases the tendency to defer choice.

4.4.2. Specification of the characteristics of shopping behavior in a mall:

Based upon the results of studies presented in the previous sub-sections, dealing with consumption and shopping behaviors in stores, we can list the main characteristics of the individual shopping behavior in a mall.

Shopping behavior in a mall has many dimensions:

• It is a *personal behavior*: It is influenced by personal variables such as demographic variables (gender, age, occupation, marital status, etc), or the position in the family or in a group (who makes the decision.), and other personal characteristics of the individual.

• It is a *psychological behavior*: It is influenced by psychological factors such as motivations, attitudes, values, personality (or self-concept), lifestyle, mood, emotion, involvement, etc.;

• It is a *cognitive behavior*: It is influenced by the perception, memorization, and knowledge of the person about his/her environment;

• It is a *social behavior*: It is influenced by the leading opinion in the family or group, the reference group, the role in the family or group, the social class, the culture, the sub-culture, the religion, etc.; and

• It is an *environmental/situational behavior*: It is influenced by three aspects of the environment:

❏ Spatial aspect: It is spatial behavior because it is influenced by the spatial and geographic characteristics of the environment (mall) such as the layout, the architecture of the environment, the colors and textures, etc.;

❏ Temporal aspect: It is influenced by the temporal factor; and

❏ Atmospheric aspect: It is influenced by the atmosphere of the environment: the music, the odor, the temperature, the humidity, the lighting, etc.

All these factors can be categorized by two classes: Internal or external factors.

The shopping behavior in a mall is composed of the following processes:

▪ The *needs/problems recognition process*: The consumer comes to the mall with the need to visit certain stores in order to purchase specific items or services;

▪ The *information search process* (perception and memorization processes): The shopper perceives the stores, kiosks, etc.;

▪ The *alternatives' evaluation process*: The shopper can have the choice of visiting many stores or kiosks to satisfy his/her needs, so he/she must decide which stores/kiosks to visit;

▪ The *decision-making process*: The customer decides which store to visit;

▪ The *acting process*: The customer acts by moving to his/her selected store; and

▪ The *post-decision process*: The customer leaves the stores, and after his/her shopping trip, he/she leaves the mall.

Based upon the study made in several disciplines, we designed a theoretical model of shopping behavior in a mall. This model contains internal and external factors that affect shopping behavior and processes that compose it. This model is presented in Fig 4.11.

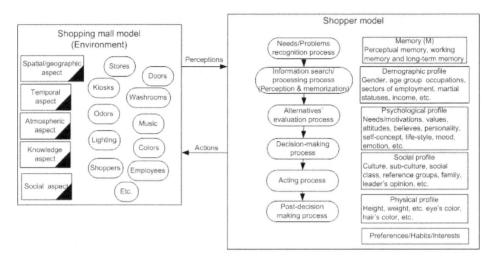

Fig. 4.11. The characteristics of shopping behavior in a mall.

4.5. Shopping in groups

The shopping behavior can be accomplished in groups which can be families, friends, colleagues, etc. The social aspect of shopping behavior brings out the idea of studying the shopping behavior of groups, in addition to the studies done with regards to individual behavior. In order to understand the shopping behavior of groups, we turned towards the discipline of consumer behavior. Unfortunately, the majority of research that involves group consumption behavior deals with one category of group which is *the family*. Moreover, these studies focused on the investigation of family's influence on the decision-making process of one consumer belonging to the family.

Due to the noteworthy absence of studies dealing with the consumption or shopping behavior of groups we turned towards other disciplines that studied groups and their behaviors. Among these disciplines, we can cite: sociology, social psychology, and the discipline that studies group decision-making. In Section 4.4.1, we present respectively, important results of our studies that can help us to better understand the groups, their structure, and their behavior. Then, in Section 4.4.2, we present how we can specify the group within the scope of shopping behavior in a mall.

4.5.1. The study results concerning groups

4.5.1.1. The group definition

In sociology, a group is usually defined as '*a collection consisting of a number of people who share certain aspects, interact with one another, accept rights and obligations as members of the group, and share a common identity*' (Hare, 1976). While an aggregate comprises merely a number of people, a group in sociology exhibits cohesiveness to a larger degree. Aspects that members in the group may share include interests, goals, values, ethnic/linguistic background, and kindship. To define a group, we present the following key points:

- Members have '*self-definition*' as a group member;

- Members are identified by others ('*other-definition*') as a group member. It is especially important that other group members also identify the individual as belonging to the group. Both '*self*' and 'other' definition as a member are necessary. Without self-definition, the individual will lack motivation to act in the group's best interests, and may even think it silly or futile to conform with group norms. Individuals who are compelled to be in a group lacking self-definition may even act to undermine the group. The person may require surveillance to stay in the situation (as for example in a prison). At the very least, someone may enjoy group benefits without contributing (freeloaders) because s/he does not self-define as a group member. Without other-definition, we may perceive the person as a fraud and this could expel him/her from the group. At the very least, we may create distance mechanisms (such as ignoring the person, "rewriting history" to exclude him/her from the group, or literally, "cutting them out of the picture"). Someone who is "in, but not of" the group is not seen as entitled to group privileges or rewards.

- Interdependent and common goals that require membership coordination: This characteristic implies commonality in the group. Interdependence means that people cannot achieve goals individually, but must do so as group members. Interdependent goals require coordination among the members to achieve them. They require the coordinated efforts of at least two people working together. Interdependent goals imply a division of labour so that each member has a unique and specific task i.e., a specialized task.

- A common fate: This characteristic implies commonality in the group.

▪ Direct interaction among members: Ironically, this characteristic typically comes to mind first.

4.5.1.2. Why do groups form?

Two main assumptions for the basis of group formation have been put forward (Hare, 1976):

▪ Functional: such as joint action on a task; face to face interaction or mutually dependent relationships;

▪ Psychological: the perception of a shared identity, attempts to fulfil needs for affiliation, recognition, and self-assertion. In other words, providing individuals with opportunities to fulfil fundamental human needs.

4.5.1.3. The group structure

Groups are more than just averaging individual member's characteristics of feelings, they are more than a collection of individuals. Groups have their own special characteristics and behaviors. The structure of a group reflects the established patterns of behavior that are distinctive within a particular group, and it constitutes a distinctively social aspect of group life. It may act as an objective constraint on a member's activity (Hare, 1976). An important aspect of structure consists of the different categories of membership that the different individuals making up the group occupy:

▪ Early on in the group's history, a group *leader* will often emerge because he or she is perceived by other members as the most competent with regards to the functional requirements of the leadership role.

▪ Group *members* can be defined as individuals who have accepted group goals as relevant and recognize interdependence with other group members as necessary to achieve these goals.

▪ Sometimes, an individual's personal goals conflict with the group's goals; if he or she is not prepared to modify his or her personal goals, dissatisfaction with the group becomes almost inevitable. The individual is then identified as a *deviant*. If deviates resist group pressure, and continue to reject group goals, the group will eventually give up on them and the other group members will leave them alone. They then become *isolates*.

4.5.1.4. Group norms

Norms represent the expectation, within the group, of appropriate behavior by group members. A group's norms do not occur by accident; they represent the interaction of social, historical, and psychological processes, and are thus resistant to change (Hare, 1976).

4.5.1.5. The group types: A taxonomy of types in groups

In the literature, we found several types of groups. For example, theorists often distinguish between *primary groups* and *secondary groups*. The primary group consists of a small group with intimate, kin-based relationships; families, for example. This group is important for the individuals who compose it. In contrast to the primary group, the secondary group is large, whose relationships are formal and institutional. This group is less central for the individuals who compose it (Bishop and Myers, 1974).

The group can be *formal* or *informal*. An informal group is characterized by interaction that is more informal: diffuse, socio-emotional, and particularistic. The informal group dissolves when all the original members leave. While a formal group is characterized by formal interaction. This group survives at least one complete turnover of members. Formal groups often have more resources and advantages than informal groups. For example, a formal group may be more likely to have a group culture containing:

- Codification or some form of recorded information about the group such as minutes or a ledger.

- History, such as a group biography, or an oral tradition of stories or accounts.

- Group symbols, such as a flag, mascots, flowers, or emblems.

- A special group language or set of phrases known only to group members.

- Group rituals, such as a special handshake, or a protocol order for meetings.

A group can include membership or non-membership. We can conceptualize about being a group member or not. One can be a member of a group with very sharp boundaries, such as a classroom. Other group memberships, such as study groups or friendship groups, are more fluid. You come and go at your own convenience, sometimes, defining yourself as a member, and sometimes not.

A group can be *ascribed* or *achieved*. The membership of an ascribed group usually consists of individuals who either are born into the group, marry into the group, or who are otherwise placed there, a priori, by the norms and customs of a culture or subculture. Many important primary groups, such as families or religious affiliations, are ascribed groups. Members in an achieved group must accomplish a task, or demonstrate a skill, in order to enter the group. Recruits to youth gangs, or fraternity and sorority pledges, typically must complete a pledgeship or initiation to show that they deserve membership.

4.5.1.6. Groups and social roles

Social roles emerge from groups. In fact, in nearly all cases, the division of labor or tasks in groups is the major cause of creating social roles. Even the most rudimentary groups tend to create a specialized division of labor and interlocking positions.

As groups survive, they become more complex, taking on many new tasks. Such a proliferation of tasks creates a coordinated and interdependent division of labor. The group can accomplish tasks that no one member could achieve alone. As a group grows in size, it also becomes easier to create a specialized division of labor. The increase in people available to do 'group work' means that we can pick individuals with the appropriate talents, skills, and interests for each job. Thus, from this division of labor frequently comes the development of specialized social roles. A *role* is a social position with an accompanying, attached set of *rights*, *duties*, and *scripts* (Bishop and Myers, 1974). When roles are arranged in some type of hierarchy, or 'chain of command', we have a *stratified social system* (Bishop and Myers, 1974). The most critical aspect of roles is that they transcend individuals because they are social positions: anyone who occupies a specific role is expected to display a minimal level of its scripts and duties. Some role requirements are codified and formal, while others are informal. While latitude often exists in how to play a role, there are also usually minimal defining criteria (Cao and Frada, 1999).

4.5.1.7. Group behavior or processes

Group processes indicate how structures become established and how over time they may change. What characterizes group processes depends upon the length of time a group has been in existence (Cao and Frada, 1999). Generally speaking, groups go through four stages, each with different process issues that members have to deal with:

- *Forming*: Group process at this stage is about exploring and resolving the very fundamental parameters of the group existence.

- *Storming*: Group process at this stage may involve a degree of conflict. Group process may be so destructive at this stage that the group does not survive.

- *Norming*: Members during this period, develop a more positive orientation toward the task, and each other.

- *Performing*: At this stage, process issues are all about achieving group goals. The decision-making process of the group belongs to this process. Groups also utilize a variety of decision-making schemes. Some examples include: voting; compromise averaging (moderating views or plans); 'horse trading' which is a method of compromise, such that various aspects of different members' agendas are adopted; procrastination; delegating decisions (for example, to a committee); implicit consensus (no actual vote is taken); and polarization. The majority of studies dealing with groups focused on the decision-making process. This process is presented, in detail, in the following point.

4.5.1.8. Group decision-making process

Group decision-making has long been a major topic in a wide variety of social sciences: anthropology, sociology, political science, marketing, and psychology (Hare, 1976).The basic thrust of this research has been to determine those factors that affect the process, by which groups make decisions (Swap, 1983). In consumer research, groups that have been studied include families (Davis, 1976) and organizational buying centers (Webster and Wind, 1972). Research has been centered upon identifying the individuals involved in the decision-making process (Davis and Rigaux, 1974), (Silk and Kalwani, 1982), decision role structure (Davis

1976), (McMillan, 1973), and the determinants of relevant influence (Kriewall, 1980), (Thomas, 1982).

In consumer research (or the social sciences in general), limited progress has been made with respect to developing and testing mathematical representations of group processes that can then be used to predict decisional outcomes in consumer behavior. Three exceptions in marketing and consumer research include: (Choffray and Lilien, 1980), (Corfman and Lehmann, 1987), and (Eliashberg and al., 1986).

- (Choffray and Lilien, 1980) proposed a set of four models that mathematically transform a set of individual choice probabilities into a group choice probability. Each model corresponds to a different conceptualization of the interaction process within the group, which, whether or not members vote, uses the inputs of individuals in proportion to their importance, search for consensus, or attempt to be least perturbing to other members. Unfortunately, the authors did not test these models empirically.

- (Corfman and Lehmann, 1987) developed and tested a different set of algebraic models, in which the group members' personal traits (i.e., resources and goals) are used to predict the outcomes of conflict resolutions. The forms of the models are basically linear, or linear with interactions. Models are estimated using data collected on couples' decisions. The dependant variable is the probability of getting one's own way. The independent variables are the resources that an individual brings to the group decision (e.g., expertise, social debt), relative to those of his or her partner(s). While this initial work is a step in the right direction, the particular algebraic forms seem ad hoc and not well-grounded in psychological theory.

- (Eliashberg et al., 1986) tested models from the decision-analysis literature, which follow from sets of axioms, to predict a group's preference judgment as a function of the judgments of its individual members.

(Rao and Steckel, 1991) proposed an interesting model called the 'polarization model'. This model is used to infer the objective of a group from those of the members that compose it.

4.5.1.9. Group cohesiveness

This is defined as the complex of forces, which gives rise to the perceptions by members of a group identity. The cohesiveness of groups has a major impact on their functioning. Its most important effect is the extent to which norms determine behavior within a group. Cohesiveness is central to the study of groups. It is considered vital in group decision-making, goal attainment, identity, and member satisfaction. Typically, cohesion implies a spirit of solidarity, or 'we-feeling'. It is not always clear whether researchers mean the aggregated feelings, beliefs, or actions of individuals towards each other, towards their group, or a total group property. Cohesion has also been conceived as an individual's attraction to the total group, preserving an affective orientation. Envisioning cohesion as attraction to a collectivety can target why people join, or maintain membership in groups that bestow status or other impersonal rewards, even when they do not particularly like other group members (Cao and Frada, 1999).

4.5.1.10. Leadership in a group

The leadership is generally viewed as an attribute of a member in the group. This view of leadership suggests that it resides in personality traits or attributes of the individual. In any situation where leadership is appropriate, the person, with the largest number of desirable traits emerges as the leader. There is a fair amount of consensus about which personality traits, correlate with leadership: effectiveness conscientiousness, extroversion, agreeableness, open to experience, and low on neuroticism. Other traits linked to effectiveness are humility and humour (Hare, 1976).

4.5.2. The specification of groups of shoppers in a mall

Based upon the study results presented in the previous sub-section, we can specify the characteristics of a group of shoppers that come to shop in a mall. Like an individual shopper we propose to characterize a group of shoppers by a structure and a behavior.

4.5.2.1. The structure of a group of shoppers

The literature review dealing with groups presented in the previous sub-section (4.5.1) can be used as a basis to identify the characteristics of a group of shoppers. Based on this literature review, we can characterize a group of shoppers as follows. A group of shoppers is composed of *members* (shoppers) and has a list of objectives to achieve (*shopping list*). The members of the group (individual shoppers) can have roles (e.g., father or mother in a family group) and weight depending upon this role. The objectives belonging to the shopping list of the group aggregate the objectives of each member of the group (individual shoppers). Sometimes, an individual's personal objectives conflict with those of the group. If he/she is not prepared to modify his/her personal objectives, dissatisfaction with the group becomes almost inevitable and the individual may leave the group. This is possible if the group of shoppers is weakly cohesive, otherwise this is impossible. As we can see, the structure of a group of shoppers can be dynamic. The group may also have one or several *leaders*.

4.5.2.2. The behavior of a group of shoppers

In shopping behavior, we are not interested in the processes such as the forming, the storming or the norming of the group. Rather, we are primarily interested in the decision-making (performing) process about the displacements of group's members within the mall in order to achieve the objectives of the group and their individual objectives. In the decision-making process of the group we are more interested in the polarization process which can be used to coordinate the movements of the individuals of the group. Furthermore, besides the decision-making process, we can find other processes, such as the perception process, the navigation process, the association-dissociation process, etc. of the group of shoppers.

4.6. Discussion and conclusion

In this chapter, we presented the two first steps of our proposed method. The first step aims to identify the application domain of the geosimulation, its future end-users, as well as the needs of these users. In the second step we identify the characteristics of the phenomenon to be simulated and those of its environment.

The chapter also presented an illustration of these two steps using the customer's shopping behavior as a case study. In the illustration of the first step, we defined the main users of the shopping behavior geosimulation which are mainly mall managers. These managers need to use the geosimulation as a decision-making tool that helps them to make decision about the configuration of their mall in order to make it more comfortable for the shoppers.

In the literature, we found little research dealing with the shopping behavior in a mall. For example, (Dijkstra et al., 2001) and (Timmermans et al., 2003) simulated the shopping behavior in a mall as a pedestrian behavior. However, they did not study the factors that influence this behavior, the processes that compose this behavior, etc. (Ruiz et al., 2004) examined the shopping behavior and collected relevant data, but they contented themselves with an analysis of this data in order to define the patterns of shopping behavior in a mall. In their study, they omit an important factor, which is the spatial factor that influences the shopping behavior in a mall. Due to this lack of research concerning the shopping behavior within a mall, we turned to other disciplines in order to study such behavior, or similar conduct, such as human consumption behavior. Based upon this study, we were able to specify the shopping behavior in a mall. This specification contains the majority of relevant factors that influence such a conduct, the main processes that compose this behavior, the models that describe it, etc. In our study and specification of the shopping behavior, we are not limited to the individual aspect of this behavior, and we studied the aforementioned with regards to groups. To do that, we turned to the discipline of social sciences in order to investigate a group's decision-making process. Based upon our research, we can assert that there has been no study, nor simulation of a group's shopping behavior in a mall.

Based on all the shopping behavior's studies results which are carried out in several disciplines, we developed an initial version of the shopping behavior model. This model contains the majority of factors influencing the shopping behavior in a mall, as well as the processes that compose it. This model is used as a basis in the next steps of the method. The majority of models proposed in the literature and describing the shopping behavior ((Engel et al., 1968), (Howard and Sheth, 1969), (Nicosa, 1966), etc.), did not take into account the spatial characteristics of the shopping behavior, nor the geographic features of the mall. Since we deal with geosimulation, these characteristics are important to us. For this reason, we integrate them in our proposed shopping behavior model. Presenting such a model can be considered as a contribution in the consumer behavior field and the fields simulating the shopping behavior.

In the next chapter we present the third step of our proposed method in which we design the multiagent geosimulation models. The design of these models is based upon the results of the first two steps.

CHAPTER 5: Creation of an Initial Version of the Multiagent Geosimulation Models

In this chapter we present the third step of our proposed method. In this step, we design an initial version of the multiagent geosimulation models of the phenomenon to be simulated and its environment. We also present the illustration of this step by showing the multiagent-based models of customers' shopping behavior in a mall.

5.1. Introduction and motivations

In the previous chapter, we presented and illustrated the first two steps of our method. In the illustrations we defined: the application domain of the geosimulation, the end-users of the shopping behavior geosimulation application, and their needs. We also specified, in detail, the characteristics of the shopping behavior in a mall based upon in-depth studies in several disciplines related to this behavior. It remains that our goal is to provide end-users (mall managers) with an *operational* geosimulation application that can help them to make decisions. In order to develop a computer-based geosimulation of shopping behavior, we need to model the phenomenon to be simulated (shoppers) and to design the simulation environment (mall). In computer science, it is well-known that the modeling process is very important, because it reduces the complexity of real systems by creating models which can be used in a computer program. Hence, the aim of the third step of our proposed method is to design the geosimulation models which are used to develop the geosimulation prototype.

This chapter is organized as follows: Section 5.2 presents a generic description of the third step of our method. Section 5.3 aims to present the illustration of this step by presenting the shopping behavior geosimulation models, while in Section 5.4, we discuss the issues presented in this chapter and conclude it.

5.2. Generic presentation of the step:

One of the main objectives of this thesis is to benefit from the recent progress made in the *multiagent paradigm* in geosimulation. For this reason, our basic foundation is the agent technology which is used to design the geosimulation models that represent the phenomenon to be simulated and its environment. Hence, we must use agent-oriented design techniques to create the geosimulation models (multiagent-based models) and represent the entities of the geosimulation. The *Agent-Based Unified Modeling Language (AUML)* (http://www.auml.org/) provides such techniques. AUML is a graphical modeling language standardized by the *Foundation for Intelligent Physical Agents (FIPA) Modeling Technical Committee (Modelling TC)* (Odell et al., 2000). AUML was proposed as an extension of the Unified Modeling Language (UML) in order to design agent based systems. AUML contains certain diagrams that can be used to graphically design multiagent based systems. As examples of these diagrams we can mention class diagrams, interaction diagrams, collaboration diagrams, sequence diagrams.

We chose AUML to model our multiagent geosimulation models because it proposes graphical specifications and tools that can be used to design agent-based systems and of course agent-based simulation applications (Peres and Bergmann, 2005). The variety of AUML's diagrams is sufficient to create the various diagrams that we need to specify multiagent geosimulations.

When designing the multiagent model of the geosimulation, we start from the initial model of the phenomenon designed in the previous step. It is relevant to note that the design of the multiagent geosimulation models must be independent from the simulation tool that will be used to execute these models. Naturally, this tool must be intended for multiagent-based simulations. Since we deal with geosimulation, the spatial aspects of the phenomenon to be simulated and the geographic features of its environment must be considered in the multiagent geosimulation models.

In the multiagent geosimulation model, we can distinguish the following categories of agents:

- *Abstract and common agents*: This category contains the agents which do not represent any element in the simulation. They are, mainly, abstract and they are designed in order to contain common and abstract characteristics that may be shared by the other agents of the simulation models (active and passive agents).

- *Passive Agents (PA)*: This category of agents represents entities that have a structure, without a behavior. Usually, a large part of the elements contained in the simulation environment belongs to this category. Here, we must characterize the spatial and non-spatial structures of the passive agents in both 2D and 3D modes.

▪ *Active agents (AA)*: This category of agents represents entities, which have structures and behaviors: These entities actively participate in the simulation. For this category, we must specify the data structures of the entities (spatial and non-spatial structures) as well as their behaviors (spatial and non-spatial behaviors).

Each passive or active agent can have one or more *profiles*. A profile is represented by one or more roles that can be played by the agent in the simulation.

This third step of our proposed method contains the following sub-steps (see Fig 5.1):

(1) *Design the common and abstract agents of the geosimulation*: It aims to design the abstract and common agents (structure and behavior) of the geosimulation models.

(2) *Design the active agents of the geosimulation*: When designing these agents, we start from the initial version of the phenomenon model (part of the system to be simulated) (see step 2 of the method). Hence, the factors or variables belonging to the initial version of the model, are represented by what we call '*attributes*' or '*property*' of the active agents and the processes are represented by what we call '*methods*' of the active agents. Of course, since we deal with geosimulation, we must take into account the non-spatial and spatial aspects of the system in the multiagent geosimulation model.

(3) *Design the passive agents of the simulation*: The design of these agents is based upon the initial version of the phenomenon model (part of the simulation environment) (see step 2 of the method). Hence, each entity belonging to the simulation environment is represented by one or more passive agents. The *factors* or *variables* belonging to the simulation environment are represented by the '*attributes*' or '*properties*' of the passive agents. Of course, since we deal with geosimulation, we must take into account the non-spatial and spatial aspects of the simulation environment.

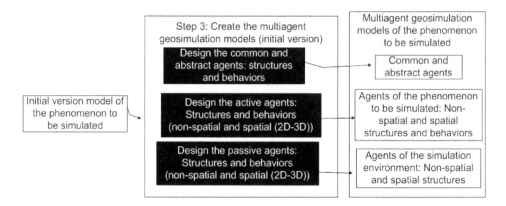

Fig. 5.1. Step 3 of our proposed method.

In the following sections, we present the illustration of this step using the customers' shopping behavior in a mall as a case study.

5.3. Modeling the shopping behavior in a mall using the multiagent paradigm

This section aims to present the details of software agents that build multiagent geosimulation models of shopping behavior in a mall. Such agents can be either passive or active. Passive agents only have structure, having no behavior at all, while active agents have both structure and behavior. Since we deal with geosimulations, agents' structures and behaviors may, or may not, be spatial. Throughout the following sub-sections, we present the agents of the simulation environment, some are passive and other are active (the simulation actors). These actors correspond to the main agents of the simulation: the shopper agents (individuals, groups, and crowd).

5.3.1. Abstract and common agents

This sub-section aims to present abstract and common agents, which will be inherited by all the agents of the simulation model. These agents are the following: The Basic_Agent, the Agent, the Group_Agent, the Active_Agent, the Passive_Agent, the Mobile_Agent, and the Stationary_Agent.

Details of the structure (attributes) and behavior (methods) of these agents is presented in Table 5.1. Since these agents are abstract, they do not have any spatial structure.

Agent name	Agent attributes and methods (with description)
Basic_Agent: This agent is the most abstract in the model. This agent contains all the most common attributes and methods (behaviors).	*Properties*: -**Agent_Id: Integer**: This property represents the identification of the agent in the simulation. -**Agent_Is_Selected: Boolean**: This property indicates if the agent is selected in the simulation by the user. *Methods*: The methods of this agent are trivial and most generic behaviors: +**Basic_Agent_Get_Id** (): This method extracts the identification of the agent. +**Basic_Agent_Is_Selected** (): This method checks if the agent is selected by the user of the simulation. +**Basic_Agent_Execute_Behavior** (): This method executes the behavior of the agent. The agent needs to have a behavior. +**Basic_Agent_Update** (): This method updates the structure and the behavior of the agent.
Agent: This abstract agent represents all the agents of the shopping behavior simulation model.	*Properties*: -**Agent_Id: Integer**: This property represents the identification of the agent in the simulation. -**Agent_Is_Selected: Boolean**: This property indicates if the agent is selected in the simulation by the user. -**Agent_Profile (0-4): Integer**: This property represents the profile of the agent. For example, in the case of the shopping behavior simulation, we can find the following profiles: shopper, store, door, etc. The agent can have, at most, 5 profiles. *Methods*: +**Agent_Add_Profile[3]** (): This method adds a profile to the structure of the agent. +**Agent_Delete_Profile** (): This method removes a profile from the structure of the agent. +**Agent_Get_Basic_Profile** (): This method extracts the basic profile of the agent. +**Agent_Set_Basic_Profile** (): This method sets the basic profile of the agent. +**Agent_Get_Current_Porfile** (): This method extracts the current profile of the agent. +**Agent_Set_Current_Profile** (): This method sets the current profile of the agent.
Group_Agent: This agent represents a group of agents in the simulation. A group of shoppers in the simulation is represented using this agent.	*Properties*: -**Agent_Id: Integer**: This property represents the identification of the agent in the simulation. -**Agent_Is_Selected: Boolean**: This property indicates if the agent is selected in the simulation by the user. **Group_Agent_Members (0-19): Basic_Agent**: This property contains the identification of the agents belonging to the group of agents. The structure of this agent allows for 20 members. *Methods*: +**Associate** (): This method allows the agent to be associated to another agent to form group. +**Dissociate** (): This method allows the agent to be dissociated to form new sub-groups.
Active_Agent: this agent represents the active agents (actors) in the simulation. The active agents have both structure (attributes) and behavior (methods) in the simulation.	*Properties*: -**Agent_Id: Integer**: This property represents the identification of the agent in the simulation. -**Agent_Is_Selected: Boolean**: This property indicates if the agent is selected in the simulation by the user. -**Agent_Profile (0-4): Integer**: This property represents the profile of the agent. For example, in the case of the shopping behavior simulation, we can find the following profiles: shopper, store, door, etc. The agent can have, at most, 5 profiles. -**Position_X: Integer**: This property contains the position (coordinate) X of the agent in the simulation environment. -**Position_Y: Integer**: This property contains the position (coordinate) Y of the agent in the simulation environment. -**Position_Z: Integer**: This property contains the position (coordinate) Z of the agent in the simulation environment. *Methods*: +**Perceive** (): Using this method the agent can perceive the simulation environment. +**Search** (): With this method the agent can access to its memory in order to search data and information. +**Memorize** (): Using this method the agent can memorize elements in its memory. +**Send_Message** (): Using this method the agent can send message to the environment's elements or to other agents.
Passive_Agent: This agent represents the passive agents of the simulation. The passive agents have structure, but do not have behavior.	*Properties*: -**Agent_Id: Integer**: This property represents the identification of the agent in the simulation. -**Agent_Is_Selected: Boolean**: This property indicates if the agent is selected in the simulation by the user. -**Agent_Profile (0-4): Integer**: This property represents the profile of the agent. For example, in the case of the shopping behavior simulation, we can find the following profiles: shopper, store, door, etc. The agent can have, at most, 5 profiles.
Mobile_Agent: This agent represents the mobile, or the moving agent, in the simulation. The moving	*Properties*: -**Agent_Id: Integer**: This property represents the identification of the agent in the simulation. -**Agent_Is_Selected: Boolean**: This property indicates if the agent is selected in the simulation by the user.

---

[3] A profile is a role that can be played by the agent.

agents have a navigational behavior in the simulation.	-**Agent_Profile (0-4): Integer**: This property represents the profile of the agent. For example, in the case of the shopping behavior simulation, we can find the following profiles: shopper, store, door, etc. The agent can have, at most, 5 profiles. -**Position_X: Integer**: This property contains the position (coordinate) X of the agent in the simulation environment. -**Position_Y: Integer**: This property contains the position (coordinate) Y of the agent in the simulation environment. -**Position_Z: Integer**: This property contains the position (coordinate) Z of the agent in the simulation environment. -**Current_Position_X: Integer**: This property contains the current position (coordinate) X in the simulation environment. -**Current_Position_Y: Integer**: This property contains the current position (coordinate) Y in the simulation environment. -**Current_Position_Z: Integer**: This property contains the current position (coordinate) Z in the simulation environment. -**Speed: Float**: This property contains the speed of the movement of the agent in the simulation environment. *Methods*: +**Perceive ()**: Using this method the agent can perceive the simulation environment. +**Search ()**: With this method the agent can access to its memory in order to search data and information. +**Memorize ()**: Using this method the agent can memorize elements in its memory. +**Send_Message ()**: Using this method the agent can send message to the environment's elements or to other agents. +**Move ()**: This is the method used by the agent to move in the simulation environment. +**Stop ()**: This method allows the agent to stop. +**Accelerate ()**: This method allows the agent to increase its speed when it moves in the simulation environment. +**Disselerate ()**: This method allows the agent to decrease its speed when it moves in the simulation environment.
Stationary_Agent: This agent represents the stationary agents of the simulation. Stationary agents do not have a navigation behavior.	*Properties*: -**Agent_Id: Integer**: This property represents the identification of the agent in the simulation. -**Agent_Is_Selected: Boolean**: This property indicates if the agent is selected in the simulation by the user. -**Agent_Profile (0-4): Integer**: This property represents the profile of the agent. For example, in the case of the shopping behavior simulation, we can find the following profiles: shopper, store, door, etc. The agent can have, at most, 5 profiles *Methods*: +**Perceive ()**: Using this method the agent can perceive the simulation environment. +**Search ()**: With this method the agent can access to its memory in order to search data and information. +**Memorize ()**: Using this method the agent can memorize elements in its memory. +**Send_Message ()**: Using this method the agent can send message to the environment's elements or to other agents.

Table 5.1.The structure and behavior of abstract and common agents of the shopping behavior simulation.

5.3.2. Agents of the simulation environment: the virtual mall

In our work, we represent the spatial entities belonging to the geographic simulation environment (mall) by agents. This choice is motivated by the fact that it would be too complex to model and simulate in detail the behaviors of a crowd of shoppers in all the corridors of the mall as well as in all the stores and specific areas that they can visit: we have to set limits to the simulation. Assigning agents to some of the entities of the environment is the way that we have chosen to set these limits. For example, if we concentrate on the study of shoppers' displacements in the mall corridors, we will not be able at the same time to model what happens in each store of the mall. For this reason, we propose to assign agents to specific spatial entities such as stores or restrooms. These agents set the limits of the geosimulation in the sense that the simulation of what happens in these geographic areas (i.e.

stores, restrooms, etc.) can be done using external models such as statistical models. For example, statistical models implemented in the behaviors of the stores can compute the duration of the visit of specific categories of shoppers within the store and the choice of items that a shopper will purchase. Hence, when a shopper agent enters a particular store, the agent associated to the store computes the duration of the visit of the shopper agent and whether it buys some items. After the visit duration computed by the store agent, the shopper agent exists the store and resumes its navigation in the mall's corridors.

Hence, a designer must carefully choose which elements of the virtual environment are parts of the limits of the geosimulation, which behaviors should be assigned to the agents associated to these elements, taking into account available statistical models used to simulate the relevant activities that take place in these elements.

We saw, in the previous chapter (sub-section 4.2.3), that the mall is characterized by many dimensions. Among these dimensions, we have the physical dimension, which represents the spatial/geographic characteristics of the environment, as well as the atmospheric dimension. In this sub-section, we present those agents related to these two dimensions of the mall.

a. The agents of the physical environment (the mall)

The agents of the physical environment represent the physical entities that belong to the simulation environment (the mall). The majority of these entities belong to the spatial aspect of the mall's model, which is presented in the previous chapter (sub-section 4.2.3).

These agents are very important to the simulation because the shopper agents interact with these entities when they accomplish their shopping behavior in the mall. These agents are: Door_Agent, Electronic_Door_Agent, Retail_Agent, Store_Agent, Kiosk_Agent, Room_Agent, Wash_Room_Agent, Cloak_Room_Agent, Desk_Agent, Window_Agent, Product_Agent, Stairs_Agent, Seat_Agent, Notice_Agent, Electronic_Notice_Agent, Escalator_Agent, Elevator_Agent, Area_Agent, Phone_Agent, Fountain_Agent, Slot_Machine_Agent, etc. and the list is not exhaustive. It was shown, in the literature review (Chapter 4), that these physical entities influence the shopping behavior of people in a mall. Details of the structure and behavior of these agents are presented in the Annex B of this thesis.

Since we deal with geosimulation, the spatial features of the agent of the physical environment are important. Hence, it is relevant to design these aspects in the agent's models. The 2D spatial structure of these agents is designed in a geographic information system (GIS) representing the mall (see Fig 5.2). The 3D spatial structure is designed as a 3D model, generated from the GIS of the mall, using 3D studio max software (http://www.the3dstudio.com/) (see Fig 5.3).

Fig. 5.2. The 2D spatial structure of the agents belonging to the physical environment (the mall).

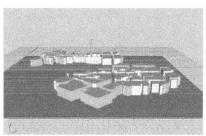

Fig. 5.3. The 3D spatial structure of the agents belonging to the physical environment (the mall).

b. Agents of the atmospheric environment (the mall)

In the previous chapter, we showed the importance of the atmospheric aspect of the mall. The elements of this aspect such as music, odor, lighting, temperature, etc. influence the shopping behavior of people in a mall. For this reason, it is relevant to design these elements in the simulation environment model. As examples of agents we can cite: the zone_Agent, the Odor_Zone_Agent, the lighting_Zone_Agent, the Sound_Zone_Agent, the Music_Sound_Zone_Agent, the Message_Sound_Zone_Agent, etc., and the list is not exhaustive. The detail of these agents is presented in the Annex B of this thesis.

5.3.3. Simulation's actors agents:

In the two previous sub-sections, we presented the passive agents that belong to the simulation environment. We remind that the main objective of our work is to simulate the shopping behavior of persons in a mall. Hence, these persons are represented by shopper agents which belong to the category of *active agents* or *actors*. As shown in the previous chapter (Chapter 4), the shopping activity is social and can be performed individually or in groups. For this reason, in the design of the shopper agents' models we take into account three levels: individuals, groups, and a crowd of shoppers. The *shopper agent* represents an individual shopper, the agent *group of shoppers* represents a group of shoppers who come together to the mall, and the agent *crowd of shoppers* which represent all the shoppers visiting the mall.

In the following points, we present details of the attributes (structure) and methods (behavior) of these actor agents.

a. Shopper agent:

The shopper agent is the most important actor in the simulation, given that our main objective is to develop a simulation prototype of the shopping behavior in a mall in order to understand the interaction of the shoppers with the environment (the mall). The attributes and methods of the shopper agent are presented in the Annex B of this thesis.

b. The Shoppers Group Agent

Some shoppers come to the mall in groups (families, friends, colleagues) to accomplish a shopping behavior. In our simulation, a group of shopper is represented by a Shoppers Group Agent. Unfortunately, in the literature review, we did not find any model of the structure or behavior of a mall's group of shoppers. Therefore, we turned to other disciplines that study groups. Based on the study results related to groups (see Section 4.4), we propose a simple structure for the group of shoppers which is used to record the members of the group. In the following points we discuss the structure and behavior of a group of shoppers.

> • *The structure of the group of shoppers*: A group of shopper contains some members. Each member of the group has his/her goals when coming in the mall. The whole

group has its own list of goals which is based upon the goals of its members. The members of the group are interconnected by weighted relationships. The relationship can be based on family ties (kinship), affection, or friendship. In each group, each member projects a certain weight inside the group. This weight can give a role to the member, and can influence the decision-making process of the group. This weight represents the degree of influence of each member of the group. The member with the highest weight is called the leader of the group; the other members are called the *followers*. What's more, it is possible to find more than one leader in a group.

• *The behavior of the group of shoppers*: The members of a group of shoppers are not independent and, in some situations, they make some collective decisions. Depending upon the objectives (goals) of all the members, we must decide upon the goals of the group as a whole. According to the literature review made in the discipline of group and social psychology, the decision-making process of a group can be based upon several schemes: vote, delegation, polarization, etc. (Rao and Steckel, 1991). In this dissertation, we do not study the decision-making process inside a group. Therefore, we consider the group of shoppers as a whole entity which has its own list of shopping goals to reach.

In our work, the group of shoppers is represented by the Group_Shoppers_Agent. This agent has a special structure that can contain a list of agents. The attributes and methods of the agent Group_Shoppers_Agent are presented in the Annex B of this thesis. The group of shopper agents represents the meso-scale of the simulation model that simulates the shopping behavior in a mall.

c. The crowd of shopper agents:

Until now, we presented the micro-model (structure and behavior) of individual shoppers inside a mall. We also presented the meso-scale of this model, which represents a group of shoppers that come together in order to accomplish a shopping behavior. Inside a mall, we can find numerous individual shoppers, as well as groups of shoppers. These individual and groups form what we call, '*a crowd of shoppers*'. This sub-section aims to present the model of a crowd of shoppers, which represents a macro-scale of the shopping behavior simulated model.

- *The structure of the crowd of shoppers*: The structure of the crowd of shopper agents contains the identifications of the the shopper agents (individuals and groups) existing in the simulation.

- *The behavior of the crowd of shoppers*: The behavior of the shoppers' crowd can be observed basing on the execution of the behavior of the shopper agents (individuals and groups) in the simulation.

The crowd of shopper agent is designed for the purpose to store all the groups of the géosimulation. The model (structure and methods) of the crowd of shoppers is presented in the annex B of this thesis.

5.4. Discussion and conclusion

In this chapter, we presented the third step of our proposed method. This step aims to design the agent-based models of the geosimulation (the phenomenon to be simulated and its environment). We also presented the illustration of this step using the customers' shopping behavior as a case study. Hence, we presented the multiagent-based models of the shopping behavior simulation.

There are several works that use the multiagent paradigm to simulate several behaviors. However, among these works, there are very few that simulate the shopping behavior in a geographic space. For example, we can cite the work of (Ben Said et al., 2001), which simulates general consumption behavior. In their work, the authors simulated the consumption behavior of items without considering the spatial aspect of this behavior. Furthermore, this aspect is very relevant for us given that shopping behavior in a mall is often influenced by the mall's spatial characteristics. (Koch, 2001), (Dijkstra et al., 2001), and (Timmermans et al., 2003) simulated shopping behavior in a spatial context, which can be a city, or a shopping mall. Unfortunately, these scholars did not present the shopping behavior as a pedestrian behavior inside a geographic environment, nor the details of these models as we do in this chapter. Our work presented agent-based shopping behavior models, in detail, based upon a solid literature review, specialized in this subject. We integrated into the multiagent models the majority of factors that influence shopping behavior in a mall (attributes or properties of the agents), as well as the majority of processes that make-up this behavior (methods of the agents).

Moreover, based upon our literature review, we can affirm that there are no research papers involving the simulation of shopping behavior of group in a mall. The majority of works that implicate groups and collective decision-making are restricted to social psychology. In our work, we propose a simple model to represent a group of shoppers. We also propose a simple model representing a crowd of shoppers in the mall. What is important is that we take into account the spatial characteristics of the phenomenon to be simulated and the geographic features of the simulated environment in each scale of the simulation.

Proposing a multi-scale multiagent geosimulation model of shopping behavior in a mall can be considered as a contribution in the computer simulation and multiagent geosimulation fields.

The next chapter aims at presenting our methods for gathering the data which will be used to feed these models.

CHAPTER 6: Collect and Analyze Data Used as Input for the Multiagent Geosimulation

In this chapter, we present the step in which we collect and analyze the simulation input data. This data is used to feed the agent-based simulation models, which were presented in the previous chapter. It also illustrates this step using the customers' shopping behavior in a mall as a case study.

6.1. Introduction and motivations

In the previous chapter, we presented the step in which we design the multiagent geosimulation models of the phenomenon to be simulated and its environment. We also illustrated this step by designing the shopping behavior multiagent geosimulations models. These models are based upon the agent technology and take into account the spatial features of the agents composing them. In order to execute the simulation models on a computer, we need data. Since we deal with geosimuation, a significant part of this data needs to be geographic or spatial.

This chapter aims to present the fourth step of our method, which aims to gather and analyze input data used to feed the multiagent geosimulation models. It also illustrates this step using the shopping behavior as a case study. The remaining part of the chapter is organized as follows: In Section 6.1 we present a generic description of the step. Section 6.2 briefly presents our case study, which is the Square One shopping mall in Toronto, Canada. In Section 6.3, we present how we gathered and digitalized our simulation input data concerning shopping behavior in a mall. Next, Section 6.4 aims at presenting the analysis results of the gathered data. Then, in Section 6.5, we discuss the material presented in this chapter, which is followed by Section 6.6, the chapter's conclusion.

6.2. Generic presentation of the step:

This section aims to present generic descriptions of the fourth step of our proposed method. This step aims to gather the data which is used to feed the multiagent geosimulation model designed in the previous step. It also aims at analyzing this data.

This step has as inputs the initial version of the model of the phenomenon to be simulated (designed in the second step) and the multiagent geosimulation model designed in the previous step (third step). It contains two main sub-steps which are presented in the following points (see Fig 6.2):

(1) *Collect the data*: In this sub-step, we collect data and transform it in order to feed the simulation models. If we provide the simulation models with random data, this sub-step can be very simple. However, if we want to use real data, we must collect it before feeding it in the system. Several techniques can be used to collect non-spatial and spatial data. Here are some techniques: questionnaires/surveys on paper, digital questionnaires, Web-based questionnaires, observations, consulting experts, GPS (Global Positioning Systems) for spatial data, etc. In this sub-step we must:

- choose the simulation case test: Before collecting data, we must choose the case test which is used in the simulation;

- collect data about the phenomenon to be simulated: Here, we must collect non-spatial and spatial data concerning the phenomenon to be simulated. This data is used to feed the non-spatial and spatial structure of the active agents representing the system to be simulated (see the multiagent simulation models developed in the previous steps).

- collect data about the simulation environment: Here, we must collect geographic and non-geographic data concerning the simulation environment. This data is used to feed the non-spatial and spatial structure of the passive agents representing the elements of the simulation environment (see the multiagent simulation models developed in the previous steps). Generally, data about the geography of environments is stored in geographic information systems (GIS).

If we decide to use surveys to collect data, we propose the following directives to be followed (see Fig 6.1):

▪ Preparing the survey's structure and content: The preparation of the survey's structure is based upon the initial version of the model of the phenomenon to be simulated and the multiagent model of the geosimulation. Each factor or variable belonging to these models is formulated by one or more questions in the survey. For each question, we must decide about its formulation and the answers' alternatives. We also need to think about the structure of these answers (one answer, multiple answers, etc.). Once the survey is built, it must be pre-tested before administrating it to the target audience. Hence, we can choose a certain number of persons (colleagues, friends, etc.) and ask them to answer the questions of the survey. After the pre-test, we can modify the survey by adjusting its structure or content. After several adjustments, the survey is ready to be conducted with the target audience.

▪ Conducting the survey: Surveys will be conducted by qualified persons. These persons must be hired and trained to conduct the survey. We also must choose the time and place where the survey will take place. Sometimes, if the survey is intended to collect data about human beings, we need to respect some ethic clauses or constraints before conducting the survey.

▪ Digitalizing the survey data: In order to develop operational computer geosimulations, we need digital data. If the collected data is already digital, we do not need the digitalization process; otherwise (if we use a paper survey) we must digitalize it. To digitalize the data, we must design the structure of files or database intended to contain the data and enter the data in these files or database using an appropriate specific software.

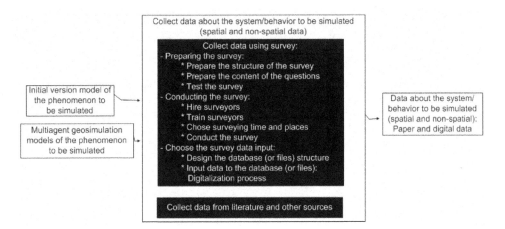

Fig. 6.1. Collect data using a survey.

(2) *Analyze the data*: Once the data are gathered and digitalized, it is relevant to analyze it in order to determine some behavior patterns or categories of the phenomenon to be simulated.

Since we deal with both non-spatial and spatial data, we propose to analyze these two kinds of data.

- Non-spatial analysis: In this category, we analyze the gathered data related to non-spatial variables. These variables exist in the initial version of the model as non-spatial factors. They exist in the multiagent geosimulation model as attributes of the agents (passive or active). The non-spatial analysis results inform us about the distribution of the data based upon the non-spatial variables. Based upon these results, we can define some non-spatial behavior patterns or categories of the phenomenon to be simulated. If the analysis involves one variable, it is called *uni-variable non-spatial analysis;* otherwise, it is called *multi-variables non-spatial analysis.*

- Spatial analysis: In this category, we analyze the gathered data related to spatial variables. These variables represent the spatial characteristics of the simulation environment in both the initial version of the model and the multiagent geosimulation one. The spatial analysis gives us ideas about the frequence of use of the spatial elements belonging to the environment. If the analysis involves one variable, it is called *uni-variable spatial analysis,* otherwise it is called *multi-variables spatial analysis.*

- Spatial and non-spatial analysis: In this category we analyze the combination of non-spatial and spatial variables. This analysis gives us ideas about the use of spatial elements belonging to the environment by other non-spatial elements existing in the simulation. Based upon the results of such analyses, we can define some spatial behavior patterns or categories of the phenomenon to be simulated.

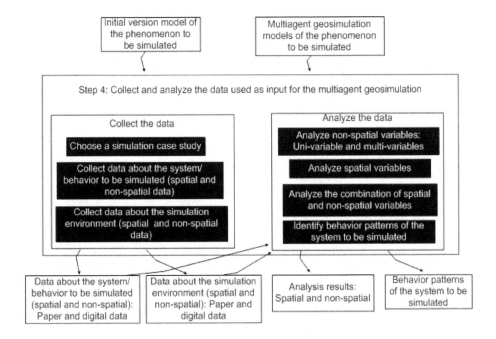

Fig. 6.2. Collect and analyze the data used as input for the multiagent geosimulation.

In the remaining part of the chapter we present the illustration of this step using the customers' shopping behavior as a case study.

6.3. Choosing the geosimulation test case: A brief introduction of the Square One mall

This section aims to present our geosimulation test case, which is the Square One mall. Owned by OMERS Realty Corporation and operated by OMER Realty Management Corporation (http://www.omers.com/scripts/index.asp), the Square One shopping mall (http://www.shopsquareone.com/) is located in Mississauga, Ontario. It is Canada's second largest mall in terms of the number of stores and services offered. With approximately 350 stores and services, it is visited by twenty millions pedestrians each year, averaging 350,000 per week. Square One is the largest shopping mall within the greater Toronto area (GTA), which is the fifth largest metropolis in North America. Mall tenants include Canada's top chains, America's best retailers, and unique speciality shops (OMERS, 2001). Moreover, four major department stores: The Bay, Sears, Wal-Mart, and Zellers anchor the mall, with the latter two being the largest of their kind in Canada. The mall consists of two levels. The upper level boasts a variety of mid to high-end stores with an emphasis on the latest fashions and accessories. The lower level continues the fashion emphasis, but to a more youthful market, and includes speciality tenants. The mall has ample parking and access via local transit, which brings approximately 4.5 million customers annually, accounting for 23% of total visits (shoppers visiting the mall). The mall is well positioned in terms of its trade area, with one of Canada's highest household income values at $67,000 per year. The city of Mississauga grew by 81,000 people between 1991 and 1996 - the largest population increase in any Canadian city. Sales productivity levels for the mall are some of the highest in Canada, at $585 per square foot (OMERS, 2001).

6.4. Simulation input data gathering

Our shopping behavior simulation prototype will be used by shopping mall managers in order to make decisions. For this reason, the simulation prototype needs to be close to reality, or 'realistic'. In order to have a 'realistic' shopping behavior simulation, we need empirical, or 'real', data about both the environment (mall) and the shoppers. In the literature review, we found only one paper that gathered empirical data about the shopper in a mall (Ruiz et al., 2001). The authors focuzed on the non-spatial data regarding shoppers and did not consider spatial aspects, neither about the shoppers, nor about the environment (the mall). In order to geosimulate the shopping behavior in a mall, we need spatial data about both the shoppers and the mall. For this reason, we decided to gather our own data in order to feed the simulation models. With regards to the simulation environment model (the mall), we use data stored in a geographic information system (GIS), and other data sources related to the mall. It has been proven that GIS is very efficient at storing non-spatial and spatial data about geographic environments (Benenson and Torrens, 2001). Regarding the model of the simulation's main actor (the shopper), we use data gathered from real shoppers in the mall using the questionnaire technique. This technique seems to be very efficient at gathering detailed information about the shopper, but it is also very expensive in terms of time and effort. We gathered data at two malls: *Square One* in the Toronto area (October 2003) and *Place De La Cité* in Quebec City (July 2003). For this dissertation, we use the Square One mall as our simulation's test case.

This section aims to present how we gathered the data which feeds the shopping behavior simulation models discussed in the previous chapter. In the previous chapter we presented two kinds of agents that compose the simulation model: passive agents that compose the simulation environment (mall) and active agents that represent the main actors of the simulation (shoppers). In order to feed the simulation models, we need to gather two types of data: the data related to the simulation environment (the mall), and the data related to the shoppers. These two kinds of data are presented, respectively, in the following two sub-sections.

6.4.1. The simulation environment data: The mall

The simulation environment model (the mall) contains geographic and non-geographic data. The geographic data represents the spatial representation of the mall elements (e.g., the geographic structure of a store, kiosk, door, etc.) and the non-geographic data represents the description of these elements (e.g., name, phone number, type of a store, etc.). This data about the simulation environment is gathered from several resources:

- For the geographic data, we used the GIS data of Square One mall (see Fig 6.3).

- For the non-geographic data, we got it from other sources, such as the plans, and brochures and pamphlets of Square One mall. These resources contain non-geographic data, such as the stores' names, door numbers, etc.

In order to simulate in 3D mode, we generated a 3D model of the simulation environment (Square One mall) from the GIS data, using 3D Studio Max software (http://www.the3dstudio.com/). The 3D model is presented in Fig 6.4. In order to develop a more realistic simulation, the graphical aspect of the 3D model is enhanced using some pictures of real stores that are used as facades for the virtual ones.

Fig. 6.3. The GIS (2D), corresponding to the first floor of Square One.

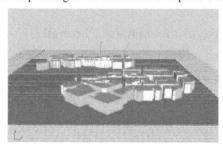

Fig. 6.4. The 3D model of the first floor of Square One (in a 3D viewer).

6.4.2. Data about the shopper: the main actor

In the literature about shopping behavior, we noticed that there are few research works that deal with empirical data about shoppers and shopping behavior in a mall. Furthermore, the majority of existing documents focus on the non-geographic data with regards to shoppers (gender, age, etc.). There is no research involving spatial data neither about shoppers, nor about shopping behaviors in malls (movements, itineraries, etc.). However, since we deal with geosimulation, such data is extremely important to us, and due to this lack of works dealing with empirical geographic data, we decided to gather our own data about shoppers and shopping behavior from spatial Square One mall. This information is both spatial and non-spatial. In order to gather data about shoppers through a questionnaire, we went through a number of sub-steps, which are presented in the following points.

- *Preparing the questionnaire structure*: In this step we prepared the structure of the questionnaire that was used to gather information about shoppers. The questionnaire aimed to feed the shopper model that was presented in the previous chapter. Hence, in the questionnaire preparation, we are based upon the simulation models' structure presented in the previous chapter. What's more, as mentioned in the previous chapter, the shopper model contains a variety of variables that are necessary for the simulation. However, we cannot gather data about all the variables belonging to this model because (1) if we wanted to gather information about all variables, the questionnaire would be much too long and boring. It is difficult to convince a shopper to interrupt his/her shopping trip in order to fill out a long questionnaire, therefore, *the questionnaire must be tight and efficient*, and (2) some of the variables belonging to the shopper model are psychological or social in nature, about which we are unable to gather empirical data, hence, *we needed to exclude such variables from the questionnaire.*

Details of the questionnaire, used to gather data about Square One shoppers are presented in Annex A of this thesis. In the following paragraphs, we briefly present the main sections which compose the questionnaire structure:

The questionnaire is divided into two main parts. The first part aims to gather data about individual shoppers (the individual questionnaire), while the second part focuzes on the groups of shoppers (group questionnaire).

The individual questionnaire is composed of six main sections, which are:

- Section 0: This section aims to identify the questionnaire, describe the project to the respondent, explain the confidentiality instructions, present the recompense and award instructions, and present the general instructions of the questionnaire. This section is read by the questionnaire interviewer.

- Section 1: It contains questions regarding the respondent's demographic profile: gender, age group, occupations, sectors of employment, marital status, life modality, cohabitation, and postal code. The questions asked in this section are useful to better know the respondent. To complete this section we asked the respondent about his/her frequency of visits, from where he/she came (origin), the mode of transportation used to come to the mall, and the household income. This section is filled out by the respondent. The answers of the questions asked in this section will be used to feed the demographic variables (age, gender, occupations, etc.) shopper's model presented in Chapterc 4.

• Section 2: It contains an oral interview concerning the patron's general and specific mall-visit objectives. This section requires pre- and post-shopping interviews during which the surveyor establishes the initial goals of the subject, and whether or not those goals were accomplished.

• Section 3: Also in an interview mode, the surveyor examines the individual's spatial usage of the two levels of Square One mall. In this section, we record the patron's parking location, point of entrance, usual shopping itineraries, and shopping area preferences.

• Section 4: The fourth segment of the individual questionnaire investigates the habits, preferences and interests of the respondent. These questions can be related to mall usage and mall environment (atmosphere).

• Section 5: Also in an interview mode, the surveyor asks the respondent about his/her reactions and emotional states when he/she is found in some specific shopping situations.

The group questionnaire is composed of three sections, which are:

• Section 0: This section aims to identify the group questionnaire, and present its general instructions. This section is read by the questionnaire interviewer.

• Section 1: It contains some questions about the group identification, the persons who compose it, etc.

• Section 3: The last section contains an oral interview concerning the group's usual shopping itineraries in Square One mall.

- *Conducting the survey*: In order to conduct the survey, the surveyors selected three entrances based upon customer flow meters and suggestions from mall management as to which entrances showed the highest activity. The survey was carried out in two parts, one upon the individual's arrival into the mall, and the other upon his/her exit. This enabled the surveyors to collect information regarding the individuals'/groups' planned activities, as well as unexpected activities which were done during the mall visit.

The goal of the overall survey process was to gather data about a typical week at the Square One shopping mall center. As a result, the questionnaire was administrated over the course of four days, two of which were during the week and the other two were on the week-end. The survey was carried out during the full duration of the mall's operating hours in order to capture the whole variety of mall users throughout the course of a normal day.

After four days, we gathered 390 completed individual questionnaires. However, the surveyors did not collect any data about groups of shoppers. During the survey carried out at Place De La Cité mall in Quebec City, we got few completed group questionnaires. This was not enough to carry out meaningful statistical analyses.

- *Digitalizing survey data*: Until this sub-step, the gathered data existed in paper format. To be used by a computer simulation prototype, this data needed to be digitalized. The digitalization process involves the following steps:

- *The design of the database structure, which contained the gathered information about the shoppers*: The shopper's database structure is based upon the structure and content of the questionnaire. Since we have two kinds of questionnaires (for individuals and groups), we have two parts in the shopper's database structure: one for the individual shoppers and the other for the groups. The structure of this database was designed using Microsoft Access software. A brief description of this structure (the tables' names) is presented in Fig 6.5 and Fig 6.6 for the individual questionnaire, and Fig 6.7 for the group questionnaire.

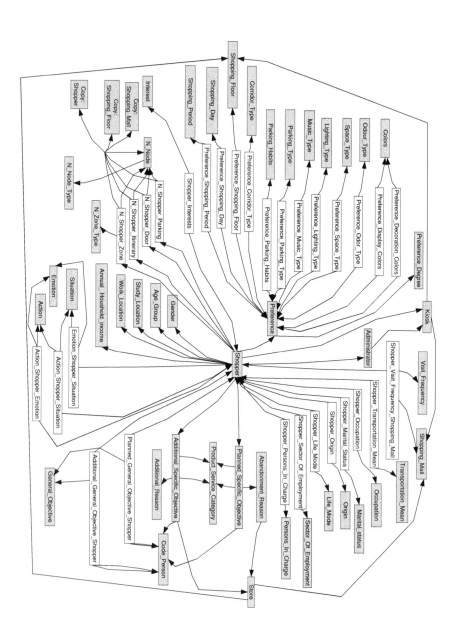

Fig. 6.5. The structure of the individual questionnaire.

125

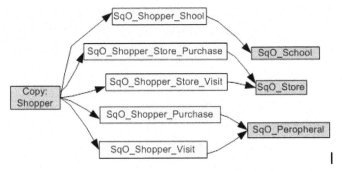

Fig. 6.6. The structure of the individual questionnaire (Specific for Square One mall).

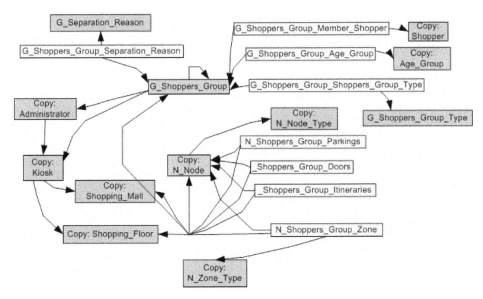

Fig. 6.7. The structure of the group questionnaire.

- *The data input into the database*: In order to input the gathered geographic and non-geographic data into the database, we used a specific user-friendly software that we developed using Microsoft Visual Basic 6.0. Fig 6.8 presents one of the screenshots[4], which is used to input non-geographic data about a shopper (demographic data), and Fig 6.9 presents an example of screen used to input geographic data (itineraries of the shopper).

---

[4] The software contains about fifteen windows which are used to record the collected data into the shopper's database.

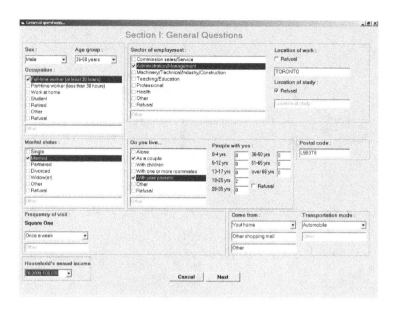

Fig. 6.8. A screenshot to input non-geographic data (demographic data).

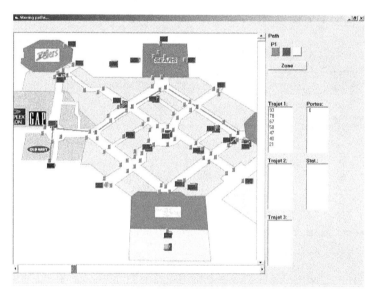

Fig. 6.9. A screenshot to input geographic data (the shoppers' itineraries).

The gathered data aims to feed the shopping behavior multiagent model presented in Chapter 5. To gather data about the shoppers we used a survey. The structure and the content of this survey were defined based upon the initial version of the shopping behavior presented in Chapter 4. In this survey, we were not able to collect data about all the variables presented in the initial version of the model for the following reasons:

- Some variables are psychological, such as personality and values, and we did not find an easy and efficient way to gather data related to these variables;

- The survey is conducted during the respondent's shopping trip, and must take little time5.

6.5. Simulation input data analysis

The spatial and non-spatial data gathered during the survey must now be analyzed for different reasons:

- they can be used to understand how the shoppers use the environment (mall) and interact with its spatial elements when they perform their shopping behavior;

- they can be used to define the patterns of shopping behavior in a mall. These patterns will be used by the simulation engine of the simulation platform which will be used to execute the shopping behavior simulation models;

- they can give us an idea about the frequency of usage of the mall's elements (doors, stores, corridors, etc.) by the shoppers;

This section aims at presenting specific analysis results, which are performed on the input data using an analysis tool that we developed for this purpose. Since we deal with geosimulation, spatial data has the same importance as non-spatial data. Referring to the two types of gathered data (spatial and non-spatial), we present two kinds of analysis: spatial and non-spatial.

---

[5] Actually, the survey tooks about 30 minutes to interview a shopper. This is a long survey duration, and we are surprised by the cooperation of the shoppers who answered the questions.

6.5.1. Non-spatial analysis

The non-spatial analysis is related to the non-spatial gathered data. This kind of analysis is important, because it shows the distribution of the gathered data based upon the non-spatial variables of to the multiagent geosimulation model.

This sub-section briefly outlines some non-spatial analysis results of particular variables belonging to the model of the shopper agent. These results can inform us about the nature of shoppers that frequent the Square One mall. This will help us to define the categories of shoppers frequenting the mall (e.g., younger, older, students, etc.) and their typical behavior (e.g., browsing, making exercice, visitic specific stores, etc.). In the following points we present specific analysis results based on some non-spatial variables coming from the shopper model. The analysis results for all the variables belonging to the shopper's model are not presented in this manuscript.

- *The variable 'Gender of the shoppers'*: As Table 6.1 and Fig 6.10 illustrate, there is a relatively even split of respondents between genders with 55% female, and 44% male.

Gender	Clients Number
Female	214
Male	173
Refusal	3

Table 6.1. Gender of the questionnaire respondents.

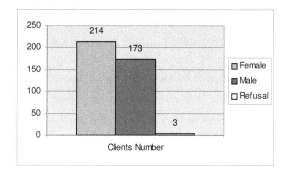

Fig. 6.10. Gender of the questionnaire respondents.

- *The variable 'Age group of the shoppers'*: As shown in Table 6.2 and Fig 6.11, the largest age group by percentage was that of 18-25 years, representing 28% of the questionnaire respondents. People younger than 17 years of age made up about 17% of the survey, and those aged between 26 and 35 years represented 24%. Respondents between 36 and 50 years old represented 21% of the interviewees. What's more, it is interesting to notice that there were only 4% over the age of 66 years, and 6% who are between 51 and 65 years.

Age group	Clients Number
0-4 years	0
13-17 years	65
18-25 years	113
26-35 years	94
36-50 years	78
51-65 years	22
Over than 66 years	16
Refusal	2

Table 6.2. Age group of the questionnaire respondents.

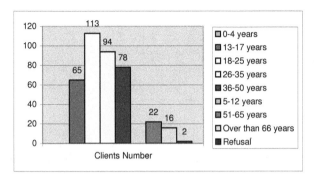

Fig. 6.11. Age group of the questionnaire respondents.

We also analyzed the following variables belonging to the demographic profile of the shopper: household income, occupation, sector of employment, mean of transportation, origin (from where the shoppers come), the life modality, and marital status, etc. The analysis results of these variables are not presented in this dissertation.

- *The variable 'General objectives (planned objectives)'*: Table 6.3 and Fig 6.12 show that the majority of respondents come to the mall in order to do some window shopping (51%), or to accompany a person (62%).

Planned general objectives	Clients Number
Do some window shopping	202
Accompany a person	244
Join a person	2
Meet a person	24
People watch	55
Walk in the mall for exercise	49
Be for a spectacle or an or more event-s	5
Other	240

Table 6.3. The general objectives of shoppers (planned).

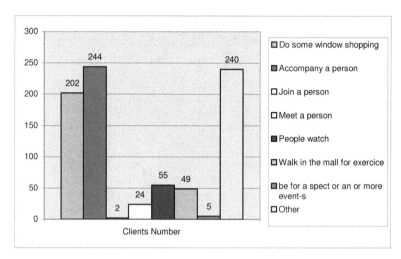

Fig. 6.12. The general objectives of shoppers (planned).

- The variable of 'Shopping period in the day': Table 6.4 and Fig 6.13 demonstrate that the most preferred periods in the day for shopping are in the afternoon and evening.

Shopping period	Number of clients
Morning	71
Before noon	39
Noon	55
Afternoon	141
Evening	123
It varies	113
I don't know	9
Refusal	6

Table 6.4. The shopping period in the day.

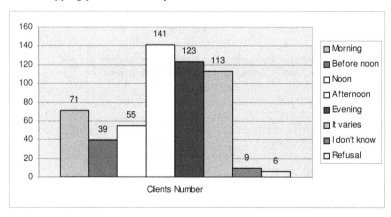

Fig. 6.13. The shopping period in the day.

We also analyzed the following variables related to the shopper's preferences: shopping day, type of corridors in the mall, parking type, used parking, lighting type, display and decoration colors, mall visit frequency, and musical choices.

- *The interest variable*: Table 6.5 shows the analysis results of the interest variable of the respondents. As demonstrated in this table, the majority of respondents are always interested in travels/tourism, cultural activities, music, cinema/television, etc. On the other hand, they are not always interested in society games or land vehicles.

Table 6.5. The analysis results of the interest variables.

Interests/ Degree	Always	Often	Sometimes	Rarely	Refusal	Indefinied
Cultural activities	155	121	67	8	0	133
Theatre shows	110	107	94	41	0	132
Music	179	135	49	6	0	115
Cinema-Television	165	150	54	9	0	106
Reading	130	96	105	32	0	121
Other cultural activities	2	1	0	0	0	481
Motorsports	50	61	95	125	0	153
Automobiles	85	91	89	65	0	154
Motorcycles	34	45	59	151	0	195
Marin vehicles	24	39	62	154	0	205
Land vehicles	25	32	62	158	0	207
Other motorsports	0	0	0	0	0	484
Tourism-Travels	183	118	71	29	0	83
Games	47	52	91	139	0	155
Video games	47	37	64	153	0	183
Society games	32	60	133	93	0	166
Other games	1	2	0	0	0	481
New technologies	108	84	93	60	0	139
Computer-Internet	110	80	91	0	0	203
TeleCommunication	72	79	89	72	0	172
Other new technologies	0	0	0	0	0	484
Home decor	72	106	87	73	0	146
Interior design	88	113	76	62	0	145
Crafts	48	79	98	96	0	163
Gardening	40	64	93	120	0	167
Other home decor	0	2	0	0	0	482
Sports	129	106	81	33	0	135
Outdoor sport	137	117	64	39	0	127
Indoor sport	90	83	98	57	0	156
Other sports	1	2	1	0	0	480
Clothing-Fashions-Accessories	131	0	0	148	0	205
Beauty	70	71	91	127	0	125
Beauty products	57	71	89	91	0	176
Beauty services	47	62	82	109	0	184
Other beauty	0	1	0	0	0	483
Jewelry	46	75	153	167	0	43
Cooking	134	160	113	41	0	36
Other interests	4	5	0	0	0	475

Non-spatial analysis results presented in this sub-section are related to some variables related to the individual shopper model. These analyses involve one variable at a time. These results help us to create some categories of shoppers visiting Square One mall. For example, as mentioned above, the analyses results related to the non-spatial variable *'General objectives (planned objectives)'* related to the shopper model inform us about the categories of shoppers visiting Square One mall. Most of these shoppers are browsers which come to the mall to do some window shopping, or individuals that accompagny another person. These results are also used as a base for multi-variables analysis which is discussed in sub-sections 6.4.3 and 6.4.4 which is important to define the shopping behavior patterns. The definition of these patterns is discussed in the next chapter.

6.5.2. Spatial analysis:

Since we deal with geosimulations, spatial and geographic data should be carefully analyzed. The majority of spatial data belongs to the environment model. This analysis aims to examine the frequencies of usage of the environment's spatial entities (parking, doors, corridors, shopping areas, etc.).

In this sub-section, we present some analysis results related to some spatial variables (or entities) belonging to the environment model such as the parkings and the entrance doors. These analysis results inform us about the frequency of usage of these spatial variables by the shopper. These analyses, which involve one spatial variable at a time, provide the basis for multi-variables analyses that are important to define the shopping behavior patterns. The definition of these patterns is discussed in the next chapter.

> - *The 'parking' variable*: This analysis shows the percentage use of parking areas by shoppers. Table 6.6 and Fig 6.14 indicate that the parking areas on first floor of Square One are not excessively frequented by shoppers. On the other hand, the parking areas on second floor are used very frequently (see Table 6.7 and Fig 6.15). These results

are presented cartographically in Fig 6.16 and Fig 6.17. In these figures, the numbers in the circles identify the parking areas and the colors are proportional to the number of shoppers who use the parking areas. The higher the number, the darker the color.

Parking	Clients number
0	7
1	13

Table 6.6. The parking variable

(first floor of Square One mall).

Parking	Clients number
0	8
1	28
2	53
3	10
4	1
5	27
6	7
7	2
8	4
9	49

Table 6.7. The parking variable

(second floor of Square One mall).

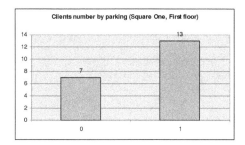

Fig. 6.14. The parking variable

(first floor of Square One mall).

Fig. 6.15. The parking variable

(second floor of Square One mall).

135

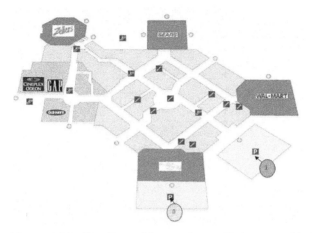

Fig. 6.16. The parking variable (first floor of Square One mall) (cartographically).

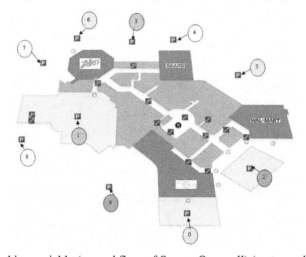

Fig. 6.17. The parking variable (second floor of Square One mall) (cartographically).

- *The entrance door variable*: This analysis shows the percentage of use of the mall's entrance doors by shoppers. The analysis results in Table 6.8 and Fig 6.18 indicate that the most frequented entrance doors on first floor are doors 10 (32%) and 0 (24%). These results are presented cartographically in Fig 6.19. Here, the numbers in the circles identify the doors, and the colors are proportional to the flow of shoppers who reach the mall by this entrance. If the flow increases, the color of the circle becomes darker.

Door	Number of clients
0	97
1	0
2	2
3	3
4	9
5	12
6	1
7	1
8	4
9	4
10	126
11	9
12	2
13	1
14	0
15	3
16	0
17	4
18	1
19	3
20	14
21	3
22	1
23	5
24	12
25	7
26	23

Table 6.8. The entrance door variable (first floor of Square One mall).

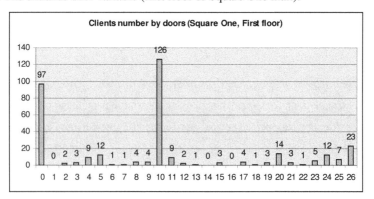

Fig. 6.18. The entrance door variable (first floor of Square One mall).

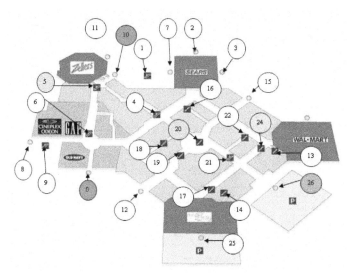

Fig. 6.19. The entrance door variable (first floor of Square One mall) (cartographically).

6.5.3. Multi-variables non-spatial analysis

In the analysis results presented above, we deal with one variable at a time. In order to see the effect of each variable on the others, we analyzed the combination of several variables. This can help us to define more detailed behavior patterns for the system to be simulated. For example, for the shopping behavior in a mall, two-variables analysis results, related to the variables *general objectives* and *gender*, can inform us that the majority of browsers are females. Based upon this information, we can define two detailed shopper categories (browsers females and browser males) and we define a specific pattern for each category of shoppers. Multi-variables analysis is more interesting if we analyze more than two variables. For example, a three-variables analysis (*general objectives, gender,* and *preferred music*) can inform us that the majority of the females browsing the mall like classical music. Hence, we can design a more detailed classification of the shoppers visiting the mall based on these variables.

In this sub-section, we present an example of analysis, in which we combine non-spatial variables related to the shoppers: gender and age group. Table 6.9 and Fig 6.20 show that among the respondents who are between 13 and 17 years of age (teenagers), the majority are female (47/65 or 72%), while males represent only 27% (18/65). On the other hand, we can see that the percentage of females who are between 18 and 35 years of age is almost equal to the percentage of males in this age category.

Gender/ Age_Group	Male	Female	Refusal	Total
13-17 years	18	47	0	65
18-25 years	56	57	0	113
26-35 years	49	45	0	94
36-50 years	32	45	1	78
51-65 years	9	13	0	22
Over than 66 years	9	7	0	16
Refusal	0	0	2	2
Total	173	214	3	390

Table 6.9. Combination of gender and age group variables.

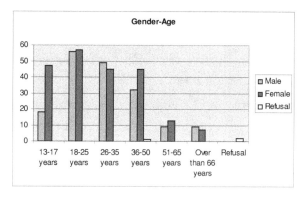

Fig. 6.20. Combination of gender and age group variables.

6.5.4. Multi-variables spatial and non-spatial analysis

In geosimulation, analyzing the combination of the non-spatial variables related to the model of the system to be simulated and the spatial variables related to the simulation environment model is very important because we can determine how spatial variables can influence non-spatial one. For example, in our shopping behavior case, if we combine the non-spatial variable *gender* of the shopper with the spatial variable *entrance door* of the simulation environment (mall), we can identify precisely which kinds of shoppers attend the entrance door. Then, and based upon this information, we can define more detailed *spatial* categorization of the shoppers by entrance door.

The spatial analysis results presented in Table 6.8, Fig 6.18, and Fig 6.19 show us that door number 0, on first floor, is frequented by 97 shoppers, while door number 10 is frequented by 126 shoppers. Nevertheless, this kind of analysis cannot answer the following question: *Who are these shoppers?* In order to answer this type of question, we need to combine the spatial variables of the environment (entrance doors, parking areas, etc.) with the non-spatial variables related to the shoppers (age group, gender, etc.).

In order to know what is the gender of those shoppers frequenting the door number 0, we made a non-spatial/spatial analysis of the combination of two variables: the variable entrance door number 0 (spatial analysis) and the variable gender of the shoppers (non-spatial analysis). The analysis results in Table 6.10 and Fig 6.21 demonstrated that among the 97 shoppers who frequented door 0, 60 were female and 37 were males.

Gender	Number of clients
Female	60
Male	37
Refusal	0

Table 6.10. Combination of gender and entrance door variables (door 0).

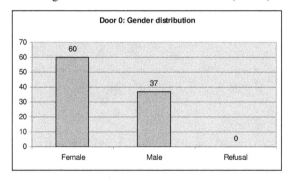

Fig. 6.21. Combination of gender and entrance door variables (door 0).

We can analyze a combination of more than two variables in order to know, in more detail, who are the shoppers that frequent a specific area in the environment. For example, we can combine the variables: gender, age group (non-spatial variables), and entrance door (spatial variable) to know exactly who are the shoppers that frequent door number 0. The results presented in Table 6.11 and Fig 6.22 show that the majority of females who frequent entrance door 0 (60 females) are between 13 and 17 years of age (20/60).

Among these 60 female clients, we can do multidimensional analysis to find the number of females from each age group, giving us the following results:

Age group	Number of clients
13-17 years	20
18-25 years	11
26-35 years	11
36-50 years	15
51-65 years	2
Over than 66 years	1
Refusal	0

Table 6.11. Combination of gender, age group, and entrance door variables (door 0).

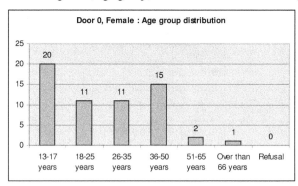

Fig. 6.22. Combination of gender, age group, and entrance door variables (door 0).

The shoppers' database contains numerous spatial and non-spatial variables that can be combined together. These variables are summarized in Table 6.12.

Non-spatial data	General and demographic data	Gender, Age group, Occupations, Sectors of employment, Means of transportation, Origin, Modalities of life, Marital status.
	Objectives	Planned general objectives, Planned specific objectives Additional general objectives, Additional specific objectives.
	Habits and preferences	Shopping periods, Shopping days, Shopping floors, Corridors, Nice odor, Crowded space, Parking types, Display color (Degree 1), Display color (Degree 2), Display color (Degree 3), Decoration color (Degree 1), Decoration color (Degree 2), Decoration color (Degree 3), Shopping mall visit frequency.
		Musical preferences — Classic, Alternative, Country, Dance, Jazz and Blue, Pop R&B and HipHop, Others
	Interests (39 interests)	Cultural activities, Theatre-Shows,Music, Cinema-Television, Reading, Other cultural activities, Motorsports, Automobiles, Motorcycles, Marin vehicles, Land vehicles, Other motorcycles, Tourism-Travels, Games, Video games, Society games, Other games, New technologies, Computer/Internet, TeleCommunication, Other new technologies, Home decor, Interior design, Crafts, Gardening, Other home décor, Sports, Outdoor sport , Indoor sport, Other sports, Clothing-Fashions-Accessories, Beauty, Beauty products, Beauty services, Other beauty, Jewelry, Cooking, Other (Interests)
Spatial data	Entrance doors	Entrance doors (Floor 1) and Entrance doors (Floor 2)
	Used and preferred parking	Used and preferred parking (Floor 1) and Used and preferred parking (Floor 2)
	Shopping itineraries	Itineraries (Floor 1) and Itineraries (Floor 2)
	Shopping zones	Shopping zones (Floor 1) and Shopping zones (Floor 2)

Table 6.12. The analyzed variables.

The analysis results of the simulation input data gathered during this step will be used in the sixth step of our method in order to define some shopping behavior patterns and to initialize the execution of the geosimulation (see Chapter 7 of this dissertation).

6.6. Discussion and conclusion

This chapter presented the step in which we gather and analyze the input data used to feed the simulation models designed in the previous step. We claim that the geographic data is a key element in geosimulation. Hence, spatial or geographic data has the same importance as non-spatial variables. For this reason, we need to gather and analyze spatial and non-spatial data related to the phenomenon to be simulated and to its simulation environment. Since geosimulation is a young field, we did not find in the literature any method's or and approach's step that deal with spatial data analysis of the simulation input. Referring to the shopping behavior simulation models presented in the previous chapter, we collected empirical data about the simulated environment (the mall) and information about the simulation's main actor, which is the shopper. In order to be used by a computer simulation, the gathered data was digitalized and stored in a database. Moreover, in order to find some shopping behavior categories and patterns which can be useful for the simulation, we analyzed the gathered data. The important part of this study is the analysis of the combination of non-spatial data related to the shopper's model and spatial data related to the mall's model. This analysis can give us an idea about the frequency of use of the mall's geographic elements.

In this chapter, we presented an interesting step in which we collect and analyze data before using it to feed the geosimulation models. This step is, generally, neglected by research works dealing with simulation methods and approaches such as (Anu, 1997), (Fishwick, 1995), (Allen et al., 2001), (Groumpos and Merkuryev, 2002), (Drogoul et al., 2002), (Ramanath and Gilbert, 2003), etc. Introducing such a step in our method can be considered as an original work in the field of simulation. What's more, (1) developing a software to digitalize non-spatial and spatial simulation data at once and (2) analyzing these two kind of data can also be considered as original work. It is interesting to note that the preliminary findings derived from the collected data and presented to the managers of *Place De La Cité* mall raised a lot of interest.

In this chapter we presented a survey method to collect spatial and non-spatial real data about a phenomenon for geosimulation. This method which is illustrated using the shopping behavior case study can be considered as a contribution, because we did not find any similar method or technique that can be used to collect spatial empirical data about a specific phenomenon which operates in geographic context.

Another contribution consists in the development of a technique that can be used to analyze uni-variable or multi-variables spatial and non-spatial input data of a geosimulation.

The next chapter aims at presenting the implementation of the shopping behavior simulation models presented in chapter 5, using the gathered data presented in this chapter.

CHAPTER 7: Selection of the Simulation Tool and the Cretaion/Execution of the Multiagent Geosimulation Models Using Data

In this chapter, we describe and illustrate two steps of the proposed method. First, we present how we select the simulation platform that is used to execute the geosimulation model using the gathered data. In the second step we present how we create the agent models in the selected platform and how we can execute the geosimulation in this platform.

7.1. Introduction and motivations

To develop an operational computer geosimulation we need to implement the simulation models on a computer. Hence, we have two choices:

(1) we can program our own geosimulation prototype using a standard programming language or (2) we can use an existing simulation tool which can be a simulation language, environment, or platform. In the two cases, the choice of the language or the simulation tool is not made in an ad-hoc manner, but it depends upon several criteria which need to be defined and discussed. Hence, the importance of the step *'Select the simulation tool'* of our method. Once the language or the simulation tool is selected, the developer can use it in order to develop the geosimulation prototype and to execute the simulation models using the collected data. This chapter aims to present two steps of our proposed method. In the first step, we choose the simulation tool, while in the second step we present how we use this selected tool to create and execute the geosimulation models. The chapter is organized as follows: In Section 7.1, we present the generic descriptions of these steps. In Section 7.2, we illustrate the first step by showing how we selected the simulation tool6 that is used to execute the shopping simulation models. Section 7.3 aims to present, in detail, the selected tool which is used to develop the shopping behavior geosimulation. Section 7.4 demonstrates how this tool

---

[6] The term 'tool' can be used instead of the terms 'platforms', 'language', 'program', or 'software'.

is used to specify the geosimulation models of the shopping behavior in a mall, while Section 7.5 presents the execution of the shopping behavior geosimulation models (the geosimulation shopping behavior prototype), and discusses the execution results. Finally, Section 7.6 discusses the issues presented in the chapter and concludes the chapter.

7.2. Generic presentation of the steps:

In this section we provide a generic presentation of the two steps of our method: *Select the geosimulation tool/platfor/language and create and execute the géosimulation models using the selected platform.*

7.2.1. Select the geosimulation tool/platform/language:

In the previous steps we designed the simulation models and we gathered the gathered data concerning the phenomenon to be simulated. In order to develop an operational geosimulation, we need to create and execute, on computer, the agent-based simulation models using the gathered data. For this reason, we may have two choices:

- to implement our simulation models using a standard language, such as C, C++ or Java for example. In this case, we need to select the language to be used for the implantation.

- to use an existing simulation tool/platform/language. In this case, we must choose a simulation tool/platform/language that will be used to execute the simulation models. There are several simulation tools/platforms/languages that can be used to create computer simulations. For example, the interested reader can visit the web site http://www.idsia.ch/~andrea/simtools.html, which presents a good collection of modeling and simulation resources on the Internet. Naturally, a question arises: *How to select the appropriate simulation tool/platform/language for a given application?* Metrics to evaluate simulation tools/platforms/languages include modeling flexibility, ease of use, modeling structure (objects, agents, etc.), code reusability, graphic user

145

interface, animation, hardware and software requirements, output reports, graphical images, customer support, and documentation. It is important to mention that the choice of a suitable simulation tools/platform/language depends upon *the characteristics of the system to be simulated and its environment*.

This step contains the following two sub-steps (see Fig 7.1):

(1) *study the existing simulation tools/platforms/languages*: In this sub-step, we must study several simulation tools/platform/language in order to choose the one which can be used to develop the geosimulation prototype.

(2) *choose the tool/platform/language*: In this sub-step, we must choose the suited tool/platform/language based upon several selection criteria and the characteristics of the phenomenon to be simulated.

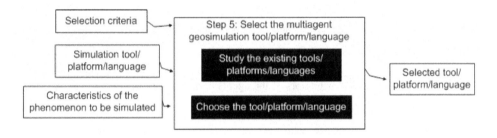

Fig. 7.1. Select the multiagent geosimulation tool/platform/language.

7.2.2. Create and execute the geosimulation models:

Before presenting the details of this step, let us define some basic concepts:

- Scenario: It is defined in the Oxford English Dictionary as follows: *(a) an outline of any possible sequence of future events; or (b) an outline of an intended course of action; (c) a scientific model or description intended to account for observable facts).*' (http://www.oed.com/)

- Simulation scenario: It is defined as the definition of the sketch or the outline of a simulation. This sketch or outline involves the following elements: actors of the simulation, the simulation environment, the simulation time period, circumstances or future events occurring during the simulation execution, etc.

During this step, we perform the simulation models on the selected simulation tool/platform/language, using the gathered data characterizing the system/behavior to be simulated and its environment. This step contains the following sub-steps (see Fig 7.2):

(1) *Create the multiagent geosimulation models in the selected tool/platform/language*: In this sub-step, we translate the multiagent geosimulation model into the selected tool's formalism in order to create the agents' models in the simulation platform. Hence, the structures and behaviors of the agents belonging to the multiagent geosimulation models (abstract, common, active, passive, etc.) are represented by the structures and behaviors of the agents using the selected tool. Sometimes, the selected tool may be based on a specific formalism that we must respect when defining the structures and behaviors of the agents. In this sub-step, we also must create the simulation scenario.

Generally, the structures and behaviors of the agents representing the system to be simulated, the agents representing the simulation environment, and the geosimulation scenarios, are stored in specific files or databases which are managed by the simulation tool.

(2) *Execute the multiagent geosimulation models in the selected tool/platform/language*: In this sub-step, we execute the geosimulation models that were created in the previous sub-step and stored in files or databases, using the input data which is gathered in the fourth step of the method.

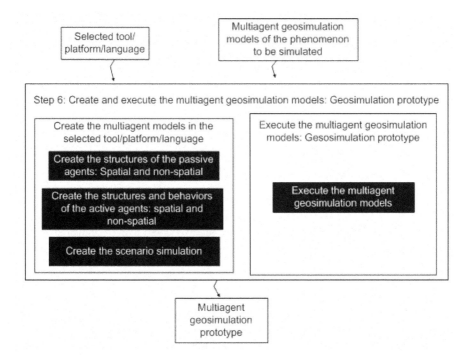

Fig. 7.2. Create and execute the multiagent geosimulation models: Geosimulation prototype.

In the remaining part of the chapter, we illustrate these two steps using the customers' shopping behavior as case study.

7.3. Select the tool suited to execute the geosimulation model

In order to run the simulation models on a computer, we need to use a simulation tool. Due to variety of types of simulations, several simulation tools exist that can be used to execute the simulation models. Naturally, a question arises: How to select the appropriate simulation tool for a given application? Metrics to evaluate simulation tools are numerous. In the following points, we present the most important ones, which can help the designer, to choose the suitable simulation tool for his applications.

• *Ease of using simulation tool*: One of the main criteria considered when selecting a simulation tool is its ease of use. For most developers, the use of simulations to obtain results will be the most interesting part of work. Therefore, the quicker a model can be implemented and experimented with, the better. The main factor influencing how easy it is to use a tool is how much, and what type, of programming experience is required. Some tools require the developer to have an extended knowledge of a particular language, while, other tools allow the user to do most implementation via a relatively user-friendly graphical interface, or by employing selected 'English-like' programming commands.

• *Flexibility*: If we have a system/behavior that we would like to simulate, the question is: 'Is the tool capable of implementing the system/behavior in which we are interested?'. Without looking at each individual case, there is no easy way to answer this question. However, it may be useful to look at models that have already been implemented using the tool to see whether or not there are common points with the models we want to simulate.

• *Background support*: An important point to consider when choosing a simulation tool is the amount of background support (manuals, newsgroups, support groups, etc.) available, as well as the quality and the openness of the source code. If the developer has a problem with the implementation, it is very useful to draw upon outside help and examples.

• *Ability to support agent technology*: Since we deal with agent-based simulation, it is important that the selected simulation tool supports the agent technology (agent- based tool).

• *Characteristics and capabilities of the agents*: An important and critical point is related to the agent's capabilities. If we want to simulate complex behaviors in geographic environments such as human behavior, it is important that the tool provides agents with advanced capabilities. Moreover, since we deal with

149

geosimulation, the agents must have knowledge-based capabilities which enable them to apprehend space (perception of space features, reasoning capabilities, etc.).

- *Ability to support spatial and geographic data/knowledge*: The final point to consider concerns geographic data. If we want to simulate systems or behaviors in spatial contexts or environments, we need a simulation tool that supports and able to integrate geographic data.

Several simulation tools exit, that may or not may be commercial, but they have proven their efficiency in the simulation of complex systems and behaviors. These simulation tools can be in the form of a language simulation program, a simulation development environment, or both. In the following points, we present some well-known multiagent simulation tools existing today.

- *The Swarm system*: It was originally developed by the Santa Fe Institute (http://www.santafe.edu/), specifically for multiagent simulation of complex adaptative systems. The Swarm system provides a set of libraries that the developer uses to build models, as well as to analyze, display, and control experiments performed on these models. The libraries are written in Objective C (http://theory.uwinnipeg.ca/gnu/libobjects/objective-c_toc.html), and until recently, building a simulator meant programming in a combination of Objective C and Swarm. However, it is now possible to use Java (along with Swarm) to call upon the facilities offered by the libraries. In the Swarm system, the fundamental component that organizes the agents of a Swarm model is a 'swarm'. A swarm is a collection of agents whose the behavior is controlled by a schedule of events. The swarm represents an entire model: it contains the agents as well as the representation of time. The Swarm system supports hierarchical modeling whereby an agent can be composed of swarms of other agents, in nested structures. In this case, the higher level agent's behavior is defined by the emergent phenomena of the agents inside its swarm. This multi-level model approach, offered by the Swarm system, is very powerful. Multiple swarms can be used to model agents that themselves build models of their own world. In the Swarm system, agents may themselves own swarms, which are models that an agent builds for itself to understand its own world. The Swarm system is a powerful tool that can be used to develop agent-based simulation, but it is limited for geosimulation because it does not support and integrate geographic data in the simulation.

▪ *AgentSheets*: It is an agent-based simulation tool, founded upon a spreadsheet approach. Instead of the spreadsheet grid's cells being occupied by numbers, they are instead occupied by agents. The simulations then take place on the grid where the agents live. AgentSheets is very simple to use because it employs the visual programming paradigm, meaning that all development is completed via a graphical interface (dragging and dropping elements from toolboxes, etc.). Agents are created in a window called a 'gallery' and have an associated behavior, specified by sets of rules (methods) and events. The way that AgentSheets operates is intuitively easy to understand, which makes it remarquably quick to develop simple simulations. This tool has three particular limitations: the first, one agent cannot send information to another agent (this would be problematic if we wanted to model the communication of information between agents in a simulation); the second, one agent cannot change the attribute of another agent (this could be problematic if we wanted to model a situation where one agent influences a second agent); and the third which is critical for us, the tool can not support geographic data and the agents are not equipped with advanced spatial capabilities such as apprehending space for example.

▪ *MAML (Multi-Agent Modeling Language)*: It was developed by the Complex Adaptative Systems Laboratory at the Central European University in Hungary. The language was initially developed to help social science students, with limited programming experience, to create agent-based models quickly. The ultimate goal of the project is to develop a user-friendly environment (complete with a graphical interface). MAML actually sits on top of the Swarm system, and is intended to make the latter easier to use by providing macro-keywords that define the structure of the simulator and access the Swarm libraries. MAML works at a higher level of abstraction than the Swarm system and with clearer constructs. However, in addition to learning MAML, the developer also needs to know Objective C language, as well as the Swarm system. This point currently limits MAML's usefulness to unexperienced programmers. Another point that limits MAML's use in geosimulation is that it does not support geographic data and the agents are not equipped with spatial cognitive capabilities which are important to develop geosimulation applications.

- *The MAGS (MultiAgent GeoSimulation) platform*: This platform has been developed in our lab, in the Computer Science Department at Laval University (Moulin et al., 2003). It aims to develop simulation applications that simulate complex behavior in georeferenced environments. This platform is based upon recent progress in the fields of multiagent systems and geographic information systems, in order to provide more realistic simulations of spatial behaviors in geographic environments (Moulin et al., 2003). The agents in MAGS are equipped with advanced knowledge-based capabilities (perception of space, memorization, etc.) that are useful to simulate complex behaviors in geographic environments such as human behavior. Furthermore, the MAGS platform supports geographic data which can be easily integrated and used in it (see Section 7.4).

- *The CORMAS platform (COmmon pool Ressources and Multi-Agent Systems)* (http://cormas.cirad.fr/): CORMAS is a multi-agent simulation platform specially designed for renewable resource management. It provides a framework to build models of the interactions between individuals and groups using natural resources. Using CORMAS, the design of the spatial features of the simulation is represented by a hierarchy of 'spatial entities'. A spatial entity represents the smallest homogeneous portion of the geographic environment in the simulation model. For example, these spatial entities can be elementary (cells in a grid) or compound (sets of spatial entities). When these spatial entities yield resources, it falls within their competence of arbitrating, according to some pre-defined protocols, between potential concurrent demands formulated by the agents exploiting these resources. The way the agents are exploiting the resources may depend on their own representation of the environment, which they build from these same spatial entities (Bousquet et al., 1998). As one can see, CORMAS is dedicated to the creation of multi-agent systems, specifically for the domain of natural-resources management which is far from our working domain. It is relevant to notice that the CORMAS system can use geographic data stored in a GIS but it needs some conversions of geographic data into text files that can be used to create the spatial entities in the grid.

▪ *The GEAMAS platform ((GEneric Architecture for Multi-Agent Simulation systems))* (Marcenac et al., 1998): GEAMAS is a multi-agent software platform intended to develop simulation applications. Based upon a layered architecture, GEAMAS allows a better understanding of how the emergence of a global behavior occurs, and why the multi-agent approach works in this context. The version 2.0 of GEAMAS is structured in three modules: the *Kernel*, the *Generation Environment* and the *Simulation Environment*. The *Kernel* implements an object model for agents and provides generic classes (create the structures and the behaviors of agents). The *Generation Environment* allows the graphical design of simulation environment (create the simulation environment). The *Simulation Environment* enables the observation of the simulations evolution via Graphical User Interface tools (the interface of the simulation). The implementation uses the Java language (Marcenac et al., 1998). The GEAMAS can be ffectively used to simulate social behaviors but, it does not take into account the spatial aspects of the simulation which are important in the géosimulation and is not able to take advantage of geographic data stored in a GIS.

Our main objective is to simulate complex behaviors in geographic environments using agent technology. In order to simulate a complex behavior such as human behaviors in geographic environments, we need a tool whose agents are equipped with advanced spatial and 'cognitive' capabilities which enable them to apprehend space. The tool must be able to integrate and use geographic data in order to represent the spatial features of the simulation environment. Given our main objective and taking into account the most important selection criteria of simulation tools, we chose the MAGS platform to develop our shopping behavior simulation prototype. This choice was motivated by several factors, the most important of which are:

- The agents of the MAGS platform are equipped with advanced knowledge-based and spatial and non-spatial capabilities: such as perception, navigation, memorization, communication, etc.

- In the MAGS platform, it is easy to integrate in the simulation platform geographic data, coming from GIS or other data sources. Moreover, this data can be in 2D or in 3D modes.

- The MAGS platform is a user-friendly environment that can be easily used to develop complex geosimulations in georeferenced environments. As will be mentionned in Section 7.4, The MAGS platform has a user-friendly module which can be used to specify simulation scenarios and which is independent from the geosimulation engine.

We present the MAGS platform in more details in the following section.

7.4. The MAGS (MultiAgent GeoSimulation) platform

MAGS is a generic platform that can be used to simulate, in real-time, thousands of knowledge-based agents navigating in a 2D or 3D virtual environment. MAGS agents have several knowledge-based capabilities such as perception, navigation, memorization, communication, and objective-based behavior, which allow them to display an autonomous behavior within a 2D-3D geographic virtual environment (Moulin et al., 2003). The agents in MAGS are able to perceive the elements contained in the environment, to navigate autonomously inside it, and to react to changes occurring in the environment. These agents have several knowledge-based capabilities (Moulin et al., 2003).

- *The agent perception process*: In MAGS, agents can perceive (1) terrain characteristics, such as elevation and slopes; (2) the elements contained in the landscape

154

surrounding the agent, including buildings and static objects; (3) other mobile agents navigating in the agent's range of perception; (4) dynamic areas or volumes whose shape changes during the simulation (ex.: smoky areas or zones having pleasant odors) (Bouden, 2004); (5) spatial events, such as explosions, etc., occurring in the agent's vicinity; (6) messages communicated by other agents (Moulin et al., 2003).

- *The agent navigation process*: In MAGS, agents can use two navigation modes: *Following-a-path-mode*, in which agents follow specific paths that are stored in a bitmap called ARIANE_MAP, or *Obstacle-avoidance-mode*, in which the agents move through open spaces avoiding obstacles. In MAGS, the obstacles to be avoided are recoded in a specific bitmap called OBSTACLE_MAP.

- *The memorization process*: In MAGS, agents have three kinds of memory: *Perception memory* in which the agent stores what it perceives during the last few simulation steps; *Working memory*, in which the agent memorizes what it perceives during a bit of time , and *Long-term memory* in which the agent stores what it perceives during one or several simulations (Perron et al., 2004).

- *The agent's characteristics*: In MAGS, an agent is characterized by a number of variables whose values describe the agent's state at any given time. We distinguish *static states* from *dynamic states*. A static state does not change during the simulation, and is represented by a variable and its current value (ex.: gender, age group, occupation, marital status). A dynamic state is one that can possibly change during the simulation (ex.: hunger, tiredness, stress). A dynamic state is represented by a variable, associated with a function which computes how its values change during the simulation. The variable is characterized by an initial value, a maximum value, an increase rate, a decrease rate, an upper threshold, and a lower threshold, which are all used by the function. Using these parameters, the system can simulate the evolution of the agents' dynamic states, as well as trigger the relevant behaviors (Moulin et al., 2003).

- *The objective-based behavior*: In MAGS, an agent is associated with a set of objectives which it tries to reach. The objectives are organized in hierarchies that are

155

composed of nodes which represent composite objectives, and leaves which represent elementary objectives associated with actions that can be performed by the agent. Each agent owns a set of objectives corresponding to its needs. An objective is associated with rules, containing constraints on the activation and completion of the objective (Moulin et al., 2003).

- *The agent communication process*: MAGS agents can communicate with each other by exchanging messages using mailbox-based communication.

The spatial characteristics of the environment and static objects are generated from data stored in Geographic Information Systems and other related databases. These characteristics are recorded in a raster mode which enables agents to access the information contained in various bitmaps, that encode different types of information about the virtual environment, in addition to the objects contained within it. In MAGS, the simulation environment is not static and may change during a simulation. For example, we can add new obstacles, or gaseous phenomena, such as smoke, dense gases, and odors, which are represented using particle systems, etc. (Moulin et al., 2003).

The MAGS platform offers to its users a user-friendly module that can be used to specify geosimulation scenarios. In the scenario specification, the user specifies the characteristics of the simulation agents, their behaviors, the features of the simulation environment, and some events that may occur during the simulation (Bellafkir, 2003).

7.5. Execute the shopping behavior simulation models using MAGS: The Mall_MAGS platform

This section presents how we use the MAGS platform in order to specify (create) and develop (execute) the shopping behavior simulation models and scenarios.

The MAGS platform has two main modules that are used to specify and execute all simulation models. The first one is used to specify the simulation (the agents' structures and behaviors, as well as the simulation scenario), while the second one is the simulation engine which executes the simulation. These modules are presented in Fig 7.3.

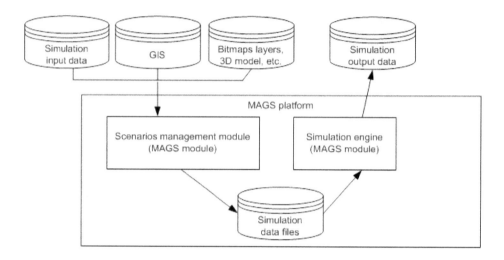

Fig. 7.3. The two modules of the MAGS platform.

To use the MAGS platform' modules in order to develop a geosimulation prototype, we need to follow the following steps:

- Specify the structures of the agents belonging to the simulation: This specification is based upon the structures of the agents' models which were designed in the third step of our method. The agents specified at this step can be active (actors) or passive (agents belonging to the simulation environment).

- Integrate the geographic data in the simulation: At this point, we integrate the geographic characteristics of the simulation environment into the simulation. These characteristics can be in 2D or 3D modes.

157

- Specify the behavior of the active agents that represent the actors of the simulation: This specification is based upon the behaviors of the agents' models which were designed in the third step of our method.

- Specify the simulation scenarios: At this step we specify the events that can occur during the simulation execution. As example of events we can cite: an explosion that occurs in the simulation in a specific place and time.

- Execute the specification mentioned above in the simulation engine of the MAGS platform.

The details of use of these two modules for the specification and execution of shopping behavior simulation models are presented in the following sub-sections.

7.5.1. The specification of a simulation scenario and agents' structures:

Before executing the simulation models in MAGS, they must be specified. In this specification, we need to respect a specific formalism of the MAGS platform. This specification is made using a specific module of the MAGS platform which is called the '*scenarios management module*'. This module is also used to enter the input data into the simulation models. This data, which is related to the agents and the simulation environment, is stored in specific simulation binary files that are then executed by the MAGS engine. This module is presented as a user-friendly interface (see Fig 7.4).

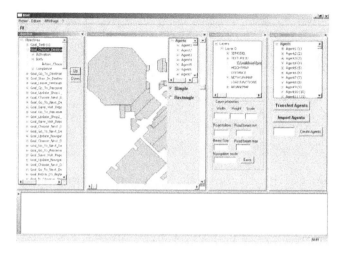

Fig. 7.4. The MAGS interface of simulation specification.

The Scenarios Management Module allows users to enter into the simulation two categories of data:

- non spatial/geographic data: This data feeds the non-spatial structures and behaviors of the simulation agents.

- spatial/geographic data: This data is related to the simulation environment (bitmap layers for the 2D and 3D models). This geographic data is used by the agents when they accomplish their spatial behaviors in the simulation.

Before demonstrating how we use the interface to specify and feed the simulation models, it is relevant to present some information about the formalism used with the MAGS platform. It is important to understand this formalism in order to comprehend the simulation specification.

a. The MAGS platform's formalism
■ *The environment in MAGS: The spatial/geographic data of the environment*

Using specific MAGS utilitary modules, the spatial characteristics of the simulation environment are generated from data stored in a geographic information system (GIS) and other databases. These characteristics are recorded in a raster mode which enables agents to access the information contained in various bitmaps, which encode different types of information about the virtual environment, in addition to the objects contained within. The main bitmaps used by the agents are:

- AgentsMap: It contains information about the locations of agents belonging to the environment;

- ObstacleMap: It contains the locations of obstacles in the environment;

- AriadneMap: It contains the paths that can be followed by mobile agents;

- HeightMap: It represents the elevations of the environment;

- TextureMap: It is used to visualize the simulation in 2D mode;

The information contained in the various bitmaps is used by the agent's fundamental mechanisms: perception, navigation, decision making, etc.

The 3D spatial characteristics of the environment are recorded in a 3D file with .X extension (Microsoft direct X format), which is used by MAGS's visualization module in order to display the simulation in a 3D mode. The 3D model is also generated from data stored in the GIS.

• *The agents' structures in MAGS*

The characteristics of the agents are specified by two *states*: *static states* and *dynamic states* (Fig 7.5). We recall that a *static state* does not change during the simulation and is represented by a variable and its current value, while a *dynamic state* is a state which can possibly change during the simulation (e.g., the agent's tiredness, hunger, etc.). A dynamic state is represented by a variable associated with a function which is used to compute how this variable changes values during the simulation.

160

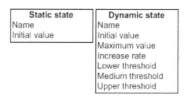

Static state	Dynamic state
Static state	**Dynamic state**
Name	Name
Initial value	Initial value
	Maximum value
	Increase rate
	Lower threshold
	Medium threshold
	Upper threshold

Fig. 7.5. States of the agents in the MAGS platform.

Based upon this formalism, all the elements belonging to the agents' structures designed in Chapter 5 are specified using static or dynamic states. The laters are related to some needs which can change during the simulation. In order to characterize the needs we can use the hierarchy of needs proposed by (Maslow, 1954).

▪ *The agents' behaviors in MAGS*

In MAGS, an agent can have one or more *profiles*. A *Profile* is a role (or several roles) that can be played by the agent during the simulation. According to each profile, the agent can accomplish a specific behavior. An agent's profile is associated with a set of objectives that it tries to reach. An *objective* is a goal that the agent intends to attend during the simulation. The objectives are organized in hierarchies, that are trees composed of nodes representing composite objectives, as well as leaves representing elementary objectives, which are associated with actions that the agent can perform (see Fig 7.6).

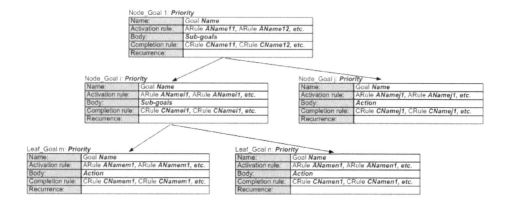

Fig. 7.6. The tree of objectives that composes the behavior of an active agent in MAGS.

An objective is associated with two groups of rules:

- *activation rules* which contain constraints about the activation of the objective.

- *completion rules* which contain constraints about the completion of the objective.

The constraints are dependent on time, on the agent's states and the environment's states. These constraints are specified, using so- called '*Preconditions*', and each precondition is composed of one or several '*FormulaElements*' (see Fig 7.7). A FormulaElement represents a numeric, or logical, operation that relates two operands, representing two states values of an agent.

Rule i:

Name:	Rule *Name*
Precondition	Precondition i1: FormulaElementi11, FormulaElementi12, etc. Precondition i2: FormulaElementi21, FormulaElementi22, etc. Etc.
Action	Action *Name*

Fig. 7.7. The structure of an objective in MAGS's formalism.

An objective can be *recurrent* or not. If the objective is recurrent, it is activated and executed continually during the simulation, otherwise, it is executed once. In MAGS, the objective has a *life-cycle*. This life-cycle can have the following values: *activated* (if the objective is activated), *inactivated* (if it is not activated), *current* (if it is in execution), *interrupted* (if it is interrupted and another objective is being executed), *finished with success* (if its execution is finished with success), and *finished without success* (if it is finished without success).

The selection of the current agent's behavior depends upon the priorities of the objectives (Moulin et al., 2003). The priority of an objective varies depending on the priority of the need related to this objective. Each agent's need is associated with a priority, which varies according to the agent's profile. An objective priority is primarily a function of the corresponding need's priority. It is also subject to modifications brought about by the opportunities that the agent perceives, or by temporal constraints (see Fig 7.6).

b. The specification of the geographic characteristics of the simulation environment: The shopping environment (the mall)

In the MAGS platform, the 2D geographic characteristics of the simulation environment are stored in separate bitmaps. Fig 7.8 presents a screenshot of the spatial configuration of Square One mall's first floor obtained from GIS data (using GeoMedia software). Figs 7.9 to 7.12 present, respectively, the bitmaps that are generated from this GIS.

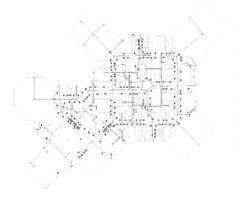

Fig. 7.8. A screenshot of the GIS of Square One mall's first floor.

Fig. 7.9. The TextureMap.   Fig. 7.10. The ObstacleMap.

Fig. 7.11. The AriadneMap.   Fig. 7.12. The AgentsMap.

The 3D characteristics of the simulation environment (the mall) are stored in a 3D file. Fig 7.13 presents the 3D model, designed using 3D Max Studio software, which is generated from the GIS data of Square One mall.

Fig. 7.13. The 3D model of Square One mall's first floor.

The geographic characteristics of the environment are then specified using the scenario management module of the MAGS platform. Fig 7.14 presents the interface windows used to specify these characteristics.

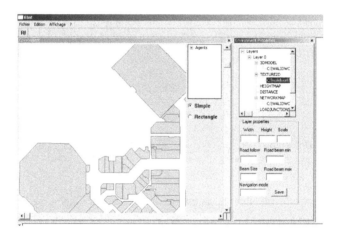

Fig. 7.14. The screen of specification, of geographic data in the simulation environment.

c. The specification of the structures of the simulation agents (passive or active):

The structures of the agents (active or passive) are specified through profiles, as well as static, and dynamic states. Fig 7.15 presents the interface module windows, which is used to define the agents' profiles in MAGS. Figs 7.16 and 7.17 present the windows that are used to indicate, respectively, the static and dynamic states of the agents in MAGS.

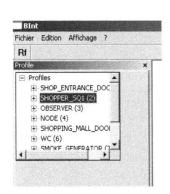

Fig.7.15. The profile
definition of an agent in the
MAGS platform.

Fig. 7.16. The specification of
an agent's static states in the
MAGS platform.

Fig. 7.17. The specification
of an agent's dynamic states
in the MAGS platform.

d. The specification of the simulation scenario

Using MAGS's scenario management module, the user can specify a simulation scenario. For example, one can indicate which agent will be created in a precise location of the simulation environment, at a specific time. The user can also specify some events that can be triggered during the simulation. For example, he can specify the time of the creation of a specific agent, the time of deleting an agent, an explosion, etc. What's more, in the specification of the simulation, the user can initialize the simulation with a population of the agents that compose the simulation. To do that, the user must choose a data source that contains data about the population of agents in the simulation (e.g., the database shopper in the shopping behavior simulation case), and import, in a batch manner, this data into the simulation. We developed a specific module to carry out this kind of population generation from the database containing the results of the analysis of the survey data. Fig 7.18 presents the window of simulation scenario creation.

166

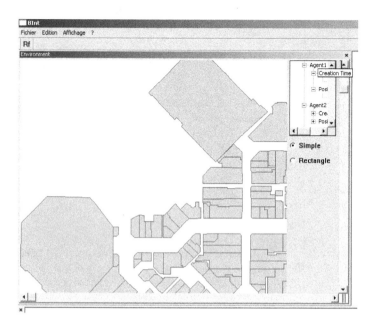

Fig. 7.18. The window of the simulation scenario specification.

7.5.2. The specification of the simulation agents' behaviors (active agents)

Using the MAGS's scenario management module, the user can specify the behavior of the active agents of the simulation. In this sub-section, we introduce how we use this module to specify the behavior of the most important active agent in the shopping behavior simulation, which is the shopper agent. Before specifying the shopping behavior of the shopper agent in MAGS, we present some shopping behavior patterns that we created in order to specify the shopping agents' behaviors.

a. Shopping behavior patterns in a mall:

Supported by our collected data concerning shoppers in Square One mall, we notice that these shoppers come to the mall with various purposes and intentions. Some shoppers intend to buy products or services, others wish to explore the mall, while still others go specifically to meet friends, etc. These activities can be categorized by definite shopping behavior patterns

167

discussed in the literature. Shoppers can be categorized particularly by the activities' taxonomy described by (Ruiz et al., 2004):

- *Recreational mall shoppers*: They go to the mall for the exercise, to talk to other shoppers, to see other clients, to have a snack, etc. The shoppers having this behavior pattern are especially motivated by social interaction and leisure;

- *Full-experience mall shoppers*: They go to the mall to talk with other customers, browse, buy snacks, and to purchase things or services (planned and unplanned). They are the 'best' customers for the mall, they seem to enjoy life at the mall;

- *Traditional mall shoppers*: They are concentrated on purchasing activities: they browse and make purchases; however, they do not make unplanned purchases; and

- *Mission mall shoppers*: They go to the mall to buy something specific. They only purchase selected items that they already planned to buy.

The taxonomy of behavior patterns presented above is relevant, but not useful to us because the descriptions are not precise enough to develop a computer simulation. If we want to simulate shopping behaviors in a mall, we need more detailed and precise shopping behavior patterns. (Bloch et al., 1994) presented an interesting and detailed taxonomy of shopping behavior patterns based upon shoppers' activities in the mall. This taxonomy is presented in Table 7.1.

Mall activity item
1.Walk in the mall for exercise
2.Look at mall exhibits or shows
3.Talk with other shoppers met in the mall
4.Socialize with friends or family in the mall
5.Go to movie playing in the mall
6.Play a video game in a mall arcade
7.Visit a medical/dental/vision care office in the mall
8.Had a haircut or styling in the mall
9.Browse in a mall store without planning to buy
10.Buy a snack in the mall
11.Have a lunch or dinner in the mall
12.Do shopping in a mall store to buy something today
13.Make an unplanned purchase

Table 7.1. The shopping behavior taxonomy presented by (Bloch et al., 1994).

Supported by our literature review, we can affirm that the taxonomy presented by (Bloch et al., 1994) is not complete. (Bloch et al., 1994) did not present certain shopping behavior activities in a mall (go to a restaurant to eat, go to an exit door to leave the mall, etc.). Furthermore, (Bloch et al., 1994) presented the shopping behavior based upon the activities that a shopper can do in a mall. In our work, we look at the shopping behavior as the activities that the mall can offer to its shoppers. These activities essentially depend upon the spatial characteristics of the mall (the areas contained in a mall), because each spatial entity in the mall offers different kinds of activities to the shoppers. Hence, we extended the taxonomy presented by (Bloch et al., 1994) as follows:

- Based upon the activities presented in the (Bloch et al., 1994)'s taxonomy of shoppers, we noticed that shoppers always have one or several destinations (in the mall) in order to accomplish their activities. Also, we noticed some general activities such as browsing. In our taxonomy, these types of activities are detailed in different specific activities related to some places in the mall.

- Shoppers inside the mall may feel hungry or thirsty. Therefore, they may go to a restaurant. They also may feel the need to use the restrooms, which they will visit. They may also visit a store because they heard music playing or because they smelled a pleasant odor coming from a store. Furthermore, if they need to exit the mall, they will go to an exit door in order to leave. Therefore, as one see, a shopper always has a place to go, based upon the internal and external factors that influence it.

The taxonomy of shopping activities that we use to specify mall's shopping behavior of the shopper agents is presented in Table 7.2.

The taxonomy of activities in a mall
o Go to a specific store (to browse or purchase): In this shopping behavior activity, the shopper agent's destination is a store or kiosk. If the shopper agent has several stores to visit, it can decide which one to visit based upon various variables: The known store, the closest store, the most preferred store, the planned store, etc.

o Explore the mall: In this case we distinguish two exploration modes:
    • Exploring for 'exploration': In this situation, the shopper explores the mall without visiting a specific place. Technically, it visits the nodes of the mall network. It is more influenced by its preferences, the environment, ads, the music, etc. If it is in exploration mode, has time, so if perceives something interesting, it can go see it.
    • Exploring for 'search': In this case, the shopper agent explores the mall in order to search for a target

> or place which can be a store, an exit door, an information desk, etc. During this exploration, if it finds its target, it goes to it.
>
> In the exploration mode, the destination of the agent is a node that belongs to the mall network.
>
> o Go to a restroom: In this case, the destination of the agent is a restroom. The shopper always determines which destination is the most preferred, the closest, etc.
> o Go to a restaurant or food court: In this case, the destination of the shopper is a restaurant. The agent decides to go to a restaurant when he feels hungry.
> o Go to a snack place: If the shoppers want to purchase a snack, their destination is a snack place in the mall
> o Go to a socialization place:
> o Go to an entertainment zone or place:
> o Go to a relaxation area:
> o Go to an information desk:
> o Go to the stairs, an elevator, or an exit door: When the shopper decides to leave the mall's floor, he or she can look for this destination. In this case, we can distinguish between two modes of leaving the mall:
>   • Leave the mall normally, when the shopper decides to leave. He decides to leave the mall when he has reached his maximum shopping time, or when he has visited all the desired stores or places in the mall.
>   • Leave the mall in a panic situation: If there is a fire or other emergency.

Table 7.2. The taxonomy we propose for shopping activities' patterns.

The destination choice related to the shopping activity depends upon many factors. It can depend upon the agent's preferences, the distance between the agent and the destination, the environment's elements perceived by the agent, etc. The activities' patterns are identified in the MAGS platform in terms of a hierarchy of objectives whose root is the global objective '*Do shopping*' for the shopper agent (see Fig 7.19).

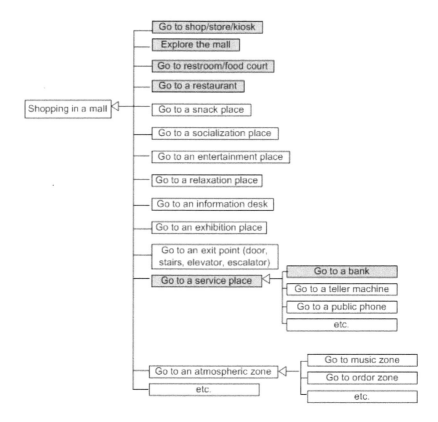

Fig. 7.19. The hierarchy of shopping activity patterns in the MAGS platform.

It is essential to note that all the activity patterns of the proposed taxonomy do not have the same priority. For example, visiting a store, browsing, or going to a restaurant do not have the same priority as going to the restroom or leaving the mall. The differences in priorities fit well with the structure of objectives that takes into account the concept of priority. It is also important to mention that the priority can change from one shopper agent to another.

At every moment of a shopping trip, the shopper agent makes decisions regarding its next destination. Based upon internal variables (objectives, preferences, etc.), external variables (the environment), and priorities of objectives, the agent must choose its destination.

b. Specification of shopping behavior patterns in MAGS:

In the following paragraph, we present details of the MAGS' specification of the objective that initialise the shopping behavior: The *Goal Start_Shopping*. The other objectives representing the main patterns of shopping behavior are presented in the Annex C of this thesis.

The objective Goal Start_Shopping aims to initiate the shopping behavior. It is composed of two sub-goals: in the first goal the agent chooses the next destination in the mall, and in the second it moves to this destination. The specifications of this objective are presented in Fig 7.20.

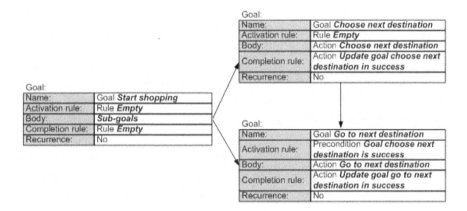

Fig. 7.20. The specification of the objective Start_Shopping.

The sub-goals composing the Goal Start_Shopping are specified in MAGS as the following:

- Sub-Goal *Goal Choose_Next_Destination*: With this sub-goal, the shopper agent makes decisions about its next destination. This destination may be a store, an exit door, restroom, etc.

  ▪ Recurrence: This sub-goal is not recurrent.

172

▪ Activation rule *Empty*: This sub-goal does not have any activation rule. Hence, it is executed only at the beginning of the simulation.

▪ Body Action *Choose_Next_Destination*: Within this sub-goal, a shopper agents chooses its mall's next destination. The choice depends upon several factors: its shopping list items, its preferences, the perceived elements in the environment, the elements in its memory, the distances between it and destinations, etc.

▪ Completion rule *Action_Update_Goal_Choose_Next_Destination_Success*: This rule contains only an action, which updates the sub-goal's life-cycle as finished with success.

the next sub-goal is:

- Sub-Goal *Goal Go_To_Next_Destination*: This sub-goal allows the shopper agent to move to the chosen destination in the previous sub-goal.

▪ Recurrence: This sub-goal is not recurrent.

▪ Activation rule *Precondition Goal_Choose_Next_Destination_Is_Success*: If the previous sub-goal successfully completed, this goal can be activated. This rule links this sub-goal with the previous one.

▪ Body Action *Go to next destination*: Using this action, the shopper agent moves to the next chosen destination.

▪ Completion rule Action *Update goal go to next destination success*: This rule contains an action that updates the sub-goal's life-cycle as finished with success.

7.6. Execute the shopping behavior simulation models using MAGS: The Mall_MAGS platform: the prototype mall_mags

All the specifications mentioned in the previous sections are stored in the simulation binary files related to the shopping behavior prototype. These files are then opened by the second module of MAGS: the simulation engine. In Fig 7.21, we display a 2D screenshot of a simulation that involved some of the 390 software shopper agents, all navigating in the virtual shopping mall. Figs 7.22 and 7.23 show 3D screenshots of this simulation.

Fig. 7.21. The 2D simulation in the MAGS platform (Square One mall).

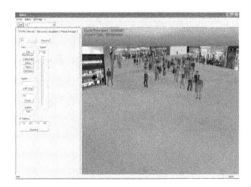 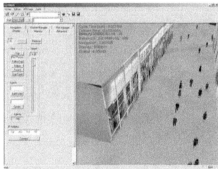

Fig. 07.22. The 3D simulation in the MAGS platform (Square One mall).

Fig. 7.23. The 3D simulation in the MAGS platform (Square One mall).

In the simulation prototype, which we called Mall_MAGS, each shopper agent comes to the mall in order to visit a list of specific stores or kiosks that are chosen before the simulation, on the basis of the agent's characteristics. It enters through a particular door and begins its shopping trip. Based upon its location in the mall, its knowledge (memorization process), and what it perceived in the mall (perception process), it decides which store or kiosk to visit next (decision making process). When it chooses a store or kiosk, it moves in its direction (navigation process). Sometimes, when it is moving toward the chosen store or kiosk, it may perceive another store or kiosk (perception process) that belongs to its shopping list, and that it did not know before. In this case, the shopper agent goes to this place, and memorizes it (memorization process) for its next shopping trips. The shopper agent accomplishes this behavior continually, until it visits all the stores or kiosks, or until it has no time left for the shopping trip. If the agent still has time to shop, and some stores or kiosks that are on its list are located in the mall, but it does not know where they are, the agent starts to explore the shopping mall in search of these stores or kiosks. When the shopper agent reaches the maximum time allowed for its shopping trip, it leaves the mall.

A shopper agent can also come to the mall, without a specific list of stores or kiosks to visit. It goes to the mall to explore it, to see people, or to do exercise, etc. In the exploration mode, the shopper agent follows its preferred paths. In this mode the moving actions of the agent, to the stores, kiosks, music zones, odor zones, lighting zones, are all directed by its habits and preferences. For example, if the shopper agent likes *cars*, and it passes in front of a car exhibition, it can attend it. To extend our simulation prototype we can simulate the shopper's reactions to the mall's atmosphere. We can insert special agents that emit music, lighting, or odor. If the agent is in the exploration mode and likes the music, or the lighting, or the odor broadcasted by these special agents, the shopper agent can move toward them and possibly enter a store.

During its shopping trip, a shopper agent may feel the need to eat or to use the restroom (simulated by a dynamic variable reaching a given threshold). Since these needs have a higher priority than that simply to shop or play, the agent temporarily suspends its shopping trip and goes to the locations where it can eat something or use the restrooms. In our geosimulation prototype, the priorities of the shopping behavior activities are defined, based upon Maslow's hierarchy of needs (Maslow, 1970).

Using the MAGS functionalities the user can manipulate the simulation with flexibility. For example, he/she can control the time of the simulation, he/she can access all the information about the agents in the simulation (states values, behaviors, memory, etc.), and he/she can control the visualization of the simulation in 2D and 3D, as well as navigate in the 3D environment during the simulation.

7.7. Discussion and conclusion

This chapter presented and illustrated the two steps belonging to our proposed method. The first one aims to select the simulation platform, which is used to develop the simulation models, while the second one presents the creation of the agents in the selected platform, as well as the execution of these models using the selected platform. For the shopping behavior case study, we chose the MAGS (MultiAgent GeoSimulation) platform in order to create the shopping behavior simulation prototype. What motivated us to choose this platform is the fact that it allows us to use advanced spatial and knowledge-based capabilities of its agents to develop simulations in georeferenced environments. What's more, the MAGS platform can integrate and use easily geographic data, which is an extremely an important aspect for a geosimulation. The second part of this chapter presented in detail how we used the MAGS platform in order to develop the shopping behavior simulator which is called Mall_MAGS.

When executing the Mall_MAGS prototype, we can see hundreds of shopper agents navigating in a georeferenced environment representing a mall and performing shopping behavior. In the simulation, the shopper agents are equipped with advanced spatial knowledge-based capabilities which increase the realism of the behavior simulation. The simulation is presented in 2D and 3D modes. It is known, that simulating in 3D mode increases the realism of the visualization of the simulation. In the literature, we did not find any geosimulation prototypes exhibiting, simultaneously, these characteristics. Hence, our prototype can be considered as a contribution to the field of computer simulation, and especially, to the field of multiagent geosimulation.

The next chapter presents how we can generate and analyze output data from the simulation for the end-users in order to help them assess the simulation.

CHAPTER 8: Collect and Analyze the Output Data Generated by The Multiagent Geosimulation

In this chapter, we present the method's step in which we collect and analyze the output data generated by the geosimulation prototype. We also illustrate this step using the customers' shopping behavior in a mall as case study.

8.1. Introduction and motivations:

To be useful, geosimulation applications must return meaningful results. Simulation output generation and analysis is an important step in a simulation study (Anu, 1997). This step is necessary in order to test various ideas and to learn about the simulation model, as well as the corresponding simulated phenomenon. A user must better understand the simulation model's output, and consequently, he/she needs appropriate tools/techniques to collect and analyze the output data generated by the simulation. Hence, it is relevant to integrate in our method a step aiming to *collect and analyze the data generated by the geosimulation*. This step is presented and illustrated in this chapter using the shopping behavior as a case study. This chapter is organized as follows: Section 8.1 presents a generic description of the step aiming to generate the geosimultion output data and to analyze it. In Section 8.2, we illustrate the generation of the geosimulation outputs, using the shopping behavior case study. Section 8.3 illustrates the analysis of the output data collected from the geosimulation in the first sub-step. Finally, Section 8.4 discusses the issues presented in this chapter and concludes it.

8.2. Generic presentation of the step:

This step is composed of two sub-steps aiming, respectively, to collect data from the geosimulation and to analyze this data (see Fig 8.1). Details of these sub-steps are presented in the following sub-sections.

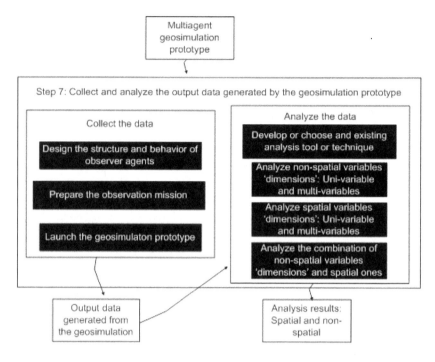

Fig. 8.1. Collect and analyze the output generated by the geosimulation prototype.

8.2.1. Collect outputs data from the geosimulation:

In order to collect meaningful output data from the geosimulation execution, we use specific agents called 'observer agents'. These agents have to perform what we call an '*observation mission*'. During this mission the observer agents: must be located in a place within the virtual environment, observe the geosimulation execution, and record the observed data in databases or files. In order to collect geosimulation data using observer agents we must prepare an '*observation scenario*'. In this scenario we design the structure/behavior of the observer agents and define their *observation mission* (the place and time of the observation in the virtual environment, as well as the targets (elements) to be observed during the simulation execution). The observation scenario is defined using the selected platform which is already used to develop the geosimulation prototype (see the fifth step of the method presented in Chapter 7).

179

Using agents to collect simulation output data is relevant for the following reasons:

- the user can easily define the observer agents' observation mission. He/she can modify the positions of the observer agents in the simulation environment, the observation duration, the observed targets in the geosimulation, the structure of the generated files (or database) that will contain the observation data (outputs), etc.

- the user can specify several observer agents with different observation missions. For example, in the virtual shopping mall, he/she can create observer agents that gather data concerning shopper agents or observer agents that gather data concerning other agents in the geosimulation (e.g., store agents, door agents, etc.). In addition, the user can gather data in specific places or areas in the virtual environment (as for example the west side of the virtual mall, main corridors, entrance doors, etc.).

- since an observer agent is assigned to a specific geographic place in the virtual environment, the generated data is related to this place and can be analyzed taking into account the geographic features of this place.

8.2.2. Analyze output data generated by the geosimulation:

In order to be useful to the geosimulation's users, the collected simulation output data must be analyzed and the results of analysis presented to users. At this point, there are two possibilities: (1) we can develop an analysis tool to analyze the geosimulation output data, or (2) we can choose one of the existing analysis tools or techniques to analyze the geosimulation output data. In the two cases, a question arises: *What are the characteristics of the technique or tool which is appropriate to analyze the geosimulation output data?* We think that the characteristics of such a tool or technique depend on the characteristics of the geosimulation which are:

- Geosimulation focus on spatial and geographic data. Hence, we need an analysis tool or technique that takes into account spatial data.

- The great potential of the geosimulation is to explain the interactions of a large number of actors in complex social phenomena taking into account the geographic aspects of the simulation environment. Hence, we need an analysis tool or technique that can analyze combinations of variables in order to identify the influence of one or more variables on the others.

- In addition, the complexity of the geosimulation models, as well as their visualization capabilities, make them more realistic and, therefore, closer to users' mental models. Hence, we need an analysis tool or technique that can present the analysis results in a manner which is close to user's mental model.

To sum up, in order to analyze the outputs of multiagent geosimulations, we need sophisticated analysis tools or techniques, which:

- take into account the spatial aspects of the output data to be analyzed;

- take into account multi-variables analysis in order to define the influence of some variables on others. This is relevant if we want to understand the interactions between some geosimulation actors and the simulation environment;

- offer better manipulation, exploitation, and visualization of the analysis results which must be realistic and, therefore, closer to users' mental models;

- are able to analyze data generated from several executions (compare several simulation scenarios and analysis results).

This step is illustrated in Sections 8.3 and 8.4 using the customers' shopping behavior in a mall case study.

8.3. Collect the output data, generated by the shopping behavior geosimulation

Concerning the shopping behavior geosimulation output data, we are interested in data related to the software shopper agents, their behavior, and interaction with the virtual mall. Hence, we need to collect data about the shopper agents during the course of the simulation. Depending on the nature of data to be collected from the shopping behavior geosimulation, we consider several categories of observer agents:

- *Traffic observer agents*: These agents have the mission to collect data concerning the traffic flow of the shopper agents inside the virtual mall. Each observer agent, belonging to this category, is established in a corridor and collects information concerning each shopper agent passing through this corridor during its shopping trip. The data collected by this category of agents can be used to compare the corridors' frequentations for several configurations of the simulated environment;

- *Visit observer agents*: These agents have the mission to collect data concerning the shopper agents visiting specific places within the virtual mall (e.g., store). Each observer agent, belonging to this category, is assigned to the choosen area (as for example a store) and collects information concerning each shopper agent visiting this area. The data collected by this category of agents can be used to compare the frequentations of specific area for several configurations of the simulated environment;

- *Shopping observer agents*: These agents have the mission to collect data concerning the shopper agents' shopping trip. The mission of these agents is the following: (1) when simulation starts, they are located in specific places within the virtual mall; (2) when a shopper agent enters the mall, they collect data concerning this agent and its planned shopping trip before it starts its shopping trip; and (3) before the shopper agent leaves the mall, they collect data concerning this agent and its performed shopping trip. As we can see, the observer agents belonging to this category mimic the behavior of the '*surveyors*' who were hired to collect geosimulation input data concerning the real shoppers (see Chapter 6) (see Fig 8.2). The data collected by this category of agents can be compared to the input data collected by the *'surveyors'*. Hence, the analysis of this data can be used to calibrate or validate the geosimulation models.

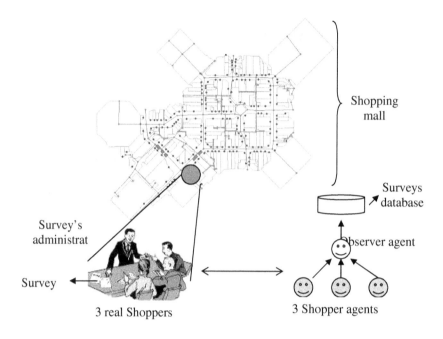

Fig. 8.2. The usage of *shopping observer agents* to collect data about the virtual shoppers.

In our work, we developed the first category of the observer agents (traffic observer agents). These agents must be established in the corridors of the virtual mall and when they perceive a virtual shopper agent passing by this corridor, they must observe it, and record information about it (e.g., its identification) in a data file or database. The structure/behavior of the observer agents, as well as their observation mission are specified in the MAGS platform. In the following sub-sections, we present the structure/behavior and observation mission of the traffic observer agent used to collect data from the shopping behavior geosimulation.

183

a. The structure of the traffic observer agent:

The structure of the observer agent is composed of the following fields:

- *Observer_Id* (Integer): This field presents the identification number of the observer agent in the MAGS platform (Moulin et al., 2003).

- *Observer_Direction* (Integer): This field represents the direction of the observer agent in the geographic simulation environment.

- *Observer_Pos_X* (Integer): This field represents position X of the observer agent in the geographic simulation environment.

- *Observer_Pos_Y* (Integer): This field represents position X of the observer agent in the geographic simulation environment.

All these fields are represented in the MAGS platform by static states (Moulin et al., 2003). We suppose that the observer agents do not have any characteristics that change during the simulation. Therefore, they do not have dynamic states in MAGS (Moulin et al., 2003).

In MAGS, the observer agents have a spatial representation in 2D and 3D (Moulin et al., 2003). In 2D mode, they are represented by a red triangle. In 3D mode, they are represented by a human shape, dressed in red. The red color in 2D, and the red dressing in 3D, distinguish them from the shopper agents in the simulation (see Fig 8.3).

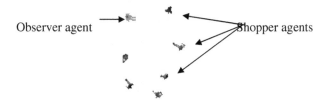

Fig. 8.3. An observer agent and some virtual shopper agents in 3D mode in the MAGS platform.

b.The behavior of the traffic observer agent (the observation mission):

In the MAGS platform, we need to specify, in very detailed manner, the behavior of the observer agent. When the simulation starts, the observer agent must:

- Put on a red dressing: In order to be distinguished from the shopper agents, the observer agent performs this specific behavior by putting on a uniform red dressing (see Fig 8.3);

- Go to the X, Y positions in the virtual mall. These locations are specified in its static states Observer_Pos_X and Observer_Pos_Y: At the beginning of the simulation, the observer agent moves to its assigned observation location within the virtual mall. It is relevant to note that the positions of the observer agents can be defined by the geosimulation user using the scenarios management module of the MAGS platform; and

- Begin to observe the shopper agents and record information about them in data files until the end of the simulation.

All these behaviors must be specified in the scenarios management module of the MAGS platform, using its formalism (objectives, rules, preconditions, actions, etc.) (see previous chapter). Fig 8.4 presents an observer agent that is affected to a corridor, perceiving certain shopper agents passing by this corridor, and recording information about them. The information is stored in a data files related to the observer agent.

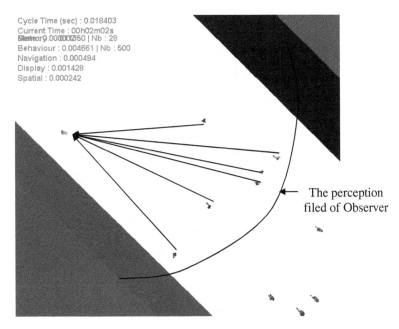

Cycle Time (sec) : 0.018403
Current Time : 00h02m02s
Stustreor9.000000350 | Nb : 28
Behaviour : 0.004661 | Nb : 500
Navigation : 0.000494
Display : 0.001428
Spatial : 0.000242

The perception filed of Observer

Fig. 8.4. A 3D simulation of an observer agent that observe virtual shoppers.

In the case of the prototype of shopping behavior in Square One mall, the positions of the observer agents are presented in Fig 8.5.

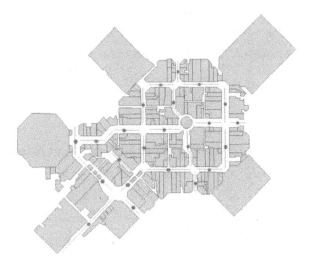

Fig. 8.5. The positions of the observer agents in the virtual mall (Square One mall).

186

The data collected by the traffic observer agents is stored in data files whose the structure is presented in Fig 8.6.

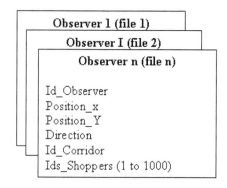

Fig. 8.6. The structure of files storing the geosimulation output data (n observers).

Independently of their category (traffic, visit, or shopping), the observer agents are assigned to a specific geographic place in the virtual shopping mall. Hence, the generated data is related to this place and can be analyzed taking into account the geographic features of this place. In the next section we present the illustration of the second part of the step which aims at analyzing the geosimulation generated data. This illustration is made using the shopping behavior case study.

8.4. Analyze the output data, generated by the geosimulation

Our literature review revealed that there exist some analysis techniques and tools that can be used to analyze the collected data generated by the geosimulation using observer agents. In the following sub-sections, we present some analysis techniques and tools which can be used to analyze output data generated from the shopping behavior geosimulation prototype. In each sub-sections we present the advantages and the limits of such tool or technique.

8.4.1. Classical or traditional analysis techniques:

In order to analyze the geosimulation outputs, we tried to use some existing analysis tools or techniques. Hence, we made an in-depth literature survey about the analysis techniques and tools that can be used to analyze simulation outputs. We found out that there exist some researches dealing with simulation output analysis. As examples, several authors (Sanchez, 2001), (Kelton, 1997), (Alexopoulos et al., 1998), (Alexopoulos, 2002), and (Seila, 1992) propose different analysis techniques for simulation outputs. Unfortunately, these techniques which are called '*traditional or classical techniques*' present some limitations. One limitation is the statistical and mathematical aspects of these techniques which make them usually difficult to use by computer scientists in order to build relevant visualizations and outputs for end-users (decision-makers). To overcome this problem (Grier, 1992) proposed a graphical, statistical analysis technique that can be used to analyze simulation outputs. The visual display of the results quickly conveys information about the simulation models. Users, who rely on simulations to support their decisions, prefer graphical analyzes because they are easy to understand. (Blaisdell et al., 1992) proposed SIMSTAT, which is a tool to analyze simulations, based upon a graphical analysis technique, and which is combined with several simulation tools. Using graphical analysis is efficient for several kinds of simulations that do not deal with spatial or geographic data. However, for multiagent geosimulation, spatial data represent an important issue for end-users (decision-makers). In such a simulation fields, a classical or traditional analysis technique based upon tables and graphs, is too limited for spatial analysis (no spatial analysis, no spatial visualization, no map-based exploration of spatial data, etc.). Consequently, we can conclude that traditional or classical analysis techniques are less suited for the analysis of multiagent geosimulation outputs.

8.4.2. Our proposed analysis technique/tool:

To overcome the limitations of traditional analysis techniques, we decided to develop our own analysis tool. This sub-section aims at presenting this tool and at demonstrating how it can be used to analyze and exploit the data generated from the shopping behavior geosimulation prototype. This tool, which is developed using Microsoft Visual Basic 6.0, is coupled with the geosimulation prototype as follows: it exploits the data generated by the observer agents and stores them in files, analyzes them, and presents results to end-users via a friendly user-interface (see Fig .8.7).

Fig. 8.7. Coupling of the geosimulation prototype and our analysis tool.

The analysis results are stored in some data files (analysis files) whose structures are presented in Fig. 8.8.

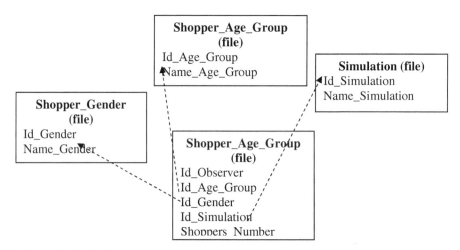

Fig. 8.8. The analysis files' structures.

In the following points, we present some advantages of our tool that make it more suited, than traditional tools and techniques, for analyzing geosimulation outputs.

a. Spatial analysis:

In geosimulation spatial data is extremely important. To be compatible with geosimulation, an analysis tool which is intended to analyze geosimulation outputs, must take into account the spatial aspect of these outputs. Our analysis tool can analyze spatial and non-spatial data generated from the geosimulation and presents the analysis results to its users. For the shopping behavior case study, presenting the distribution or the flow of shopper agents passing through the corridors of the simulated environment (mall) can be considered as spatial analysis results that can be relevant to a user of the shopping behavior geosimulation. Our tool can do that by displaying for each corridor of Square One virtual mall the flow of shopper agents passing through. It can present the analysis results as follows: each corridor' flow is presented using a line that is attached to this corridor. The width of the line is proportional to the flow of the shopper agents that pass through the corridor. As an example, Fig 8.9 presents the results of the simulation, using 390 shopper agents in the virtual mall representing Square One (Toronto). As shown in Fig 8.9, since a large number of shoppers agents go to the department store, Wal-Mart, we can note that the corridors taken to go to this store are the most frequented by the shopper agents.

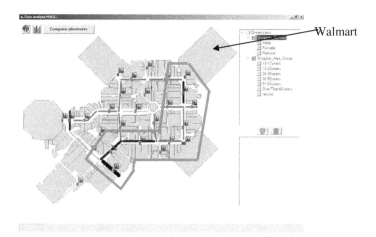

Fig. 8.9. The simulation analysis results for the frequentation of Square One by 390 virtual shoppers.

b. Analyzing of combinations of non-spatial and spatial variables:

It is important to be able to analyze the combinations of non-spatial and spatial variables (multi-variables) in order to understand the interdependency of various factors, and especially to understand how the spatial factors derived from the geographic features of the environment influence the other factors as well as the agents' shopping behavior. When developing our tool, we took into account this characteristic of the analysis. In the following points, we present some multi-variables analyses that can be done using our analysis tool. This is illustrated with the shopping behavior as case study. In these analyses, we combine non-spatial variables belonging to the shopper agents and spatial variables belonging to the simulated environment.

- Using our tool, the user can get the analysis results of the combination of the spatial variable for *corridor frequenting*, with the non-spatial variable for *gender of the shopper agent*. To do that, the user must select, by a simple mouse click, a corridor (or an observer agent related to this corridor) on the map, and select the variable gender from the variables list (at the right in Fig 8.10). Fig 8.11 presents the analysis results of the combination of the spatial variable (corridor X) and the non-spatial variable

191

gender. We can see that corridor X is frequented by 46 shoppers agents. Among these, there are 22 males (47.82%) and 24 females (52.17%) (see Fig 8.12). When the user clicks on the observer agent related to corridor Y, the tool indicates that this corridor is visited by only 45 shopper agents, 26 males (57.77%) and 19 females (42.22%) (see Fig 8.13).

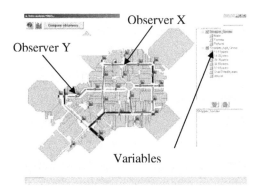

Fig. 8.10. The selection of the observer and the variables to be analyzed.

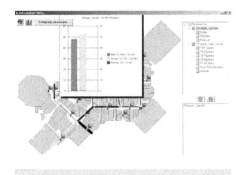

Fig. 80.11. The analysis results for visitation of the corridor related to observer X.

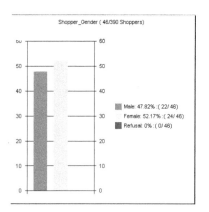

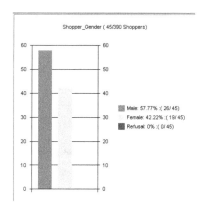

Fig. 8.12. The frequentation analysis results for corridor X.

Fig. 8.13. The frequentation analysis results for corridor Y.

- The user can combine the spatial dimension (i.e. a corridor) that belongs to the environment, with more than one non-spatial variable belonging to the shopper. For example, he/she can combine the non-spatial variables *gender* and *age_goup*, belonging to the shopper, with the spatial variable *corridor* belonging to the geographic environment. To do that, the user needs to select two variables, *gender* and *age_group*, and then he needs to select a corridor (or the observer agent related to this corridor). He can directly see the analysis results on the screen. Figs 8.14 and 8.15 present details of these analysis results. For example, for corridor X, we find that among the 46 shoppers, 19 females are between 26 and 36 years old, and 2 males are between 13 and 17 years old. The user can also compare the analysis results of the combination of several variables related to several corridors (where observer agents are located) in order to explore and compare them.

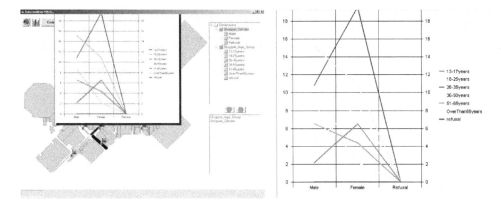

Fig. 8.14. The analysis for the combination of the gender/age_group and the corridor.

Fig. 8.15. Details of the analysis combining gender/age_group and the corridor.

c. Comparing several simulation execution output results:

Using our tool, the user can compare the output data generated by different geosimulation executions. The comparison of results is useful to compare different geosimulation scenarios. This tool's functionality is presented in details in Chapter 10 of this dissertation.

To sum up, our analysis tool has several advantages because users can use it to perform spatial analysis, to analyze multi-variables, to analyze the combination of non-spatial variables with spatial ones, and to compare outputs of many simulation runs. Yet, this tool has some limitations:

- it is limited in terms of the number of variables to be combined and analyzed. Therefore, using the current version of the analysis tool, we cannot analyze more than four variables, whether they are spatial or not. However, this could be extended. We must also emphasize that beyond four combined variables the results would be difficult to interpret.

■ our tool is limited with regards to the exploitation of the analysis results. It uses only the following visualization modes to explore the analysis results: pie charts, diagrams, and tables.

8.4.3. The OLAP and SOLAP technique:

In the previous sub-section, we presented our own analysis tool that is coupled to the geosimulation engine in order to analyze its outputs. This tool offers some interesting functionalities concerning the analysis of geosimulation outputs, but, it presents some limitations concerning the visualization and exploitation of the results. For this reason, we turned to the literature in order to find other tools or techniques that can overcome the limitation of our tool. We selected the technique called *OLAP* (*On Line Analytical Processing*) which allows users to make uni-variable and multi-variables analysis where each variable is called 'dimension'. Recently, the OLAP technique has been extended in order to analyze spatial variables or 'dimensions'. This extension is called *SOLAP* (*Spatial On Line Analytical Processing*) (Bédard et al., 2001).

This sub-section aims to present the fundamental concepts, on which OLAP and SOLAP are based. It also presents how we used OLAP/SOLAP technique to analyze the outputs of the shopping behavior geosimulation prototype.

a. OLAP analysis technique

OLAP (On Line Analytical Processing) has been defined as "*...the name given to the dynamic enterprise analysis required to create, manipulate, animate and synthesize information from exegetical, contemplative and formulaic data analysis models. This includes the ability to discern new or unanticipated relationships between variables, the ability to identify the parameters necessary to handle large amounts of data, to create an unlimited number of dimensions, and to specify cross-dimensional conditions and expressions*" (Codd et al., 1993). Other OLAP definitions have since been proposed, including "*A software category intended* *for the rapid exploration and analysis of data based on multidimensional approach with several aggregation levels"* (Caron, 1998).

The multidimensional approach is based on two notions: *dimensions* and *measures*. *Dimensions* represent analysis axes which represent a variable to be analyzed, while *measures* are the numerical attributes being analyzed against the different dimensions. A dimension contains members that are organized hierarchically into levels, each level having a different granularity going from coarse at the most aggregated level, to fine at the most detailed level. The members of one level can be aggregated to form the members of the next higher level. The measures at the finest level of granularity can be aggregated or summarized, following this hierarchy, and provide information at the higher levels according to the aggregation rules or algorithms.

A set of measures, aggregated according to a set of dimensions, forms what is often called a *data cube* or *hypercube* (Thomsen et al., 1999). Inside a data cube, possible aggregations of measures on all the possible combinations of dimension members can be pre-computed. This greatly increases query performances, in comparison to the conventional transaction-oriented data structures found in relational and object-relational database management systems (DBMS).

The common OLAP *architecture* can be divided into three parts: the multidimensionally structured database, the OLAP server that manages the database and carries out the different calculations, and finally, the OLAP client that accesses the database via the OLAP server. This access allows the end-user to explore and analyze the data, using different visualization methods and adapted operators (Bédard et al., 1997), such as *drill-down* (show-details), *roll-up* (show a more global picture, also called *drill-up*), *drill-across* (show another theme with the same level of details) and *swap* (change a dimension for another one).

Finally, it is commonly found in the literature that the multidimensional approach of analysis is more in agreement with the end-user's mental model of the data (Codd et al., 1993) (Yougworth, 1995). Based upon this approach, the interface of a tool exploring the multidimensional paradigm, such as OLAP, is usually intuitive, and the user can perform

196

analysis ranging from simple to complex, mostly by clicking on the data being organized in a meaningful way (Yougworth, 1995). This adds to the fact that the multidimensional data structure is optimized for rapid, ad hoc information retrieval (OLAP Council, 1995), which greatly facilitates the data exploration and analysis process.

b. SOLAP analysis technique for spatial data

Traditional OLAP offers good support for simultaneous usage of descriptive, temporal, and spatial dimensions, in a multidimensional analysis process. Descriptive dimensions are used to describe the data to be analyzed. The temporal ones take into account the temporal aspect of the analysis, while the spatial dimensions allow for the spatial reference of the phenomena under study. However, using traditional OLAP tools, the spatial dimensions are treated like any other descriptive dimension, without consideration for the cartographic component of the data. OLAP tools have serious limitations in the support of spatio-temporal analysis (no spatial visualization, practically no spatial analysis, no map-based exploration of data, etc.).

Data visualization facilitates the extraction of knowledge from the complexity of the spatio-temporal phenomena and processes being analyzed, as well as offering a better understanding of the structure and relationships existing within the dataset. In the context of information exploration, maps and graphics do more than visualizing data; they are active instruments in the end-user's thinking process (Rivest et al., 2001). Without a cartographic display, OLAP tools lack an essential feature, which could help spatio-temporal exploration and analysis. A SOLAP tool remedies this limitation because it supports the geometric spatial aspects of the data to be explored. These spatial aspects are visualized and explored cartographically.

A SOLAP system can be defined as a visual platform built especially to support rapid and easy spatio-temporal analysis and exploration of data. It follows a multidimensional approach that is available in cartographic displays, as well as in tabular and diagram displays (Bédard et al., 2001). This makes a SOLAP tool a good candidate to explore the outputs of our geosimulations.

197

c. Coupling the shopping behavior multiagent geosimulation and OLAP/SOLAP analysis techniques

The outputs of the shopping behavior geosimulation are obtained using software agents called *observer agents*. These data are then recorded in some files. Unfortunately, they cannot be used directly by the OLAP/SOLAP techniques, but must first be transformed and stored in a specific database structure (*data cube* or *hypercube*) in order to facilitate their exploration. The transformation of data is not easy and it is made in two steps: (1) we transform the data generated by the traffic observer agents into several files using a program that we developed for this purpose using Microsoft Visual Basic 6.0. Each file contains data about one variable (dimension) of the shopper agent (e.g., age_group, gender, etc.); (2) we create the structure of the data cube using Microsoft SQL Server 7.0; and (3) we copy the data from the files to the data cube using some SQL queries. This transformation requires some expertise concerning databases, OLAP techniques, data warehouse, etc. The content of this data cube is then explored and analyzed using the OLAP/SOLAP techniques and the results are presented to the users (see Fig. 8.16).

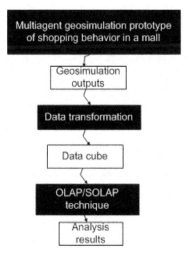

Fig. 8.16. Coupling the shopping behavior geosimulation and the OLAP/SOLAP tool.

Fig 8.17 presents a simplified view of the transformed database for the shopping behavior case study. In this database, we can distinguish two types of tables. The *fact table*, which contains measures that will be analyzed, and the *dimension tables*, which contain data about each hierarchy of data (e.g., the hierarchy of gender has one root (All_gender) and two nodes (male and female)). The database structure contains some non-spatial dimensions (age group, gender) of the shopper agents as well as a spatial dimension that contains the stores and corridors of the mall.

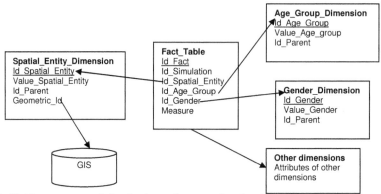

Fig. 8.17. The structure of the database that contains the simulation output data.

In the following points, we present some advantages of the OLAP/SOLAP techniques for exploring and analyzing geosmulation outputs.

- Spatial analysis:

Using the OLAP/SOLAP tool proposed by (Rivest et al., 2004), we can analyze and explore the simulation outputs of the shopping behavior geosimulation. We can perform spatial analyses and visualization of the distribution of shopper agents by store or corridor, and according to the non-spatial variables or '*dimensions*' of these agents. What is important when using the OLAP/SOLAP techniques is that the visualization is made using the geographic entities of the simulated environment. For example, the user can visualize, cartographically, the distribution of shopper agents in five major stores of Square One (Wall-

Mart, Sears, Zellers, Old Navy, and The Bay) based upon the age group and gender dimensions. Fig 8.18 shows the distribution of shopper agents that are between 51 and 65 years old, for the five major stores using the SOLAP tool. In this figure, we can only see the non-null distribution (8 for Sears and 15 for Wall-Mart).

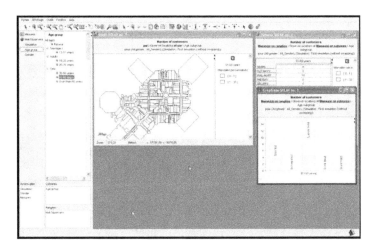

Fig. 8.18. Distribution of software shopper agents that are between 51 and 65 years old, for five major stores (Wall-Mart, Sears, Zellers, Old Navy, and The Bay).

- Multi-variables (multidimensional) analysis:

Using the OLAP/SOLAP tool we can perform multi-variables analysis. Therefore, we can analyze the combination of non-spatial variables coming from the shoppers and spatial variables belonging to the spatial simulated environment (mall). This is relevant because it gives the users ideas about the interactions of the shoppers and their environment (mall). For example, if the user wants to see which categories of shoppers visit the other stores (Zellers, Old Navy, and The Bay) in terms of the age group dimension, he/she can use the OLAP/SOLAP drill-up operation on the age group dimension, in order to see the distribution for all the ages (see Fig 8.19). The user can see that Sears and Wall-Mart are also most visited by shopper agents that are between 18 and 25 years of age (54 for Sears and 82 for Wall-Mart). One can also observe that Zellers store is visited by only one shopper agent that is between 36 and 50 years of age. In this figure, the white areas are not visited by this category

200

of shoppers (distribution is null), and colored areas correspond to the most visited ones (orange), and less visited ones (yellow).

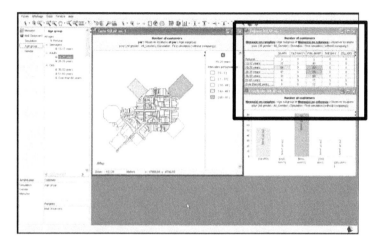

Fig. 8.19. Distribution of software shopper agents for five major stores. The table shows the number of shoppers per age group for each store. The map and bar chart show the number of shoppers that are between 18 and 25.

- Advanced exploration/visualization modes:

The OLAP/SOLAP tool offers its users advanced exploration and visualization capabilities to present the analysis results. In the following example, we present some of these capabilities.

▪ The OLAP/SOLAP tool allows the user to use the chart display in order to study the distribution based upon all the age groups (Fig 8.20). In this case, we only focus on the non-null distributions and we can represent the 6 age groups in the same bar chart.

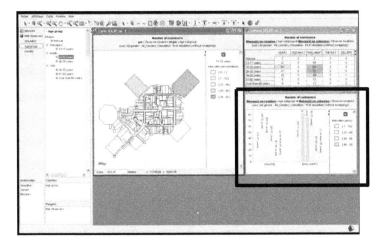

Fig. 8.20. Distribution of software shopper agents for five major stores. The bar chart shows the number of shoppers per age group for Sears and Wall-Mart.

- It can also present maps of the distribution for different dimensions such as all genders and age groups. In Fig 8.21, we show a cartographic representation, comprising two maps (one for male and another for female agents), that include superimposed pie charts to present the distribution of each age group.

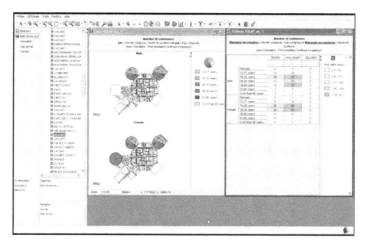

Fig. 8.21. Cartographic representation of the distribution of shopper agents, comprising two maps (one for male and another for female agents), that includes superimposed pie charts to present the distribution of each age group.

- It is also possible to show the same information, but in another way by using multimaps (one for each age group) and pie charts to represent gender (see Fig 8.22).

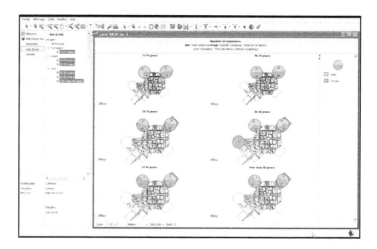

Fig. 8.22. Cartographic representation of the distribution of software agents, comprising one map for each age group, and superimposed pie charts to represent gender.

- The SOLAP tool also allows the user to visualize maps of the distribution of shopper agents that are based on combinations of members from different dimensions. Fig 8.23 shows 14 maps, each one representing the distribution of shopper agents for a combination of members from the age group and the gender dimensions (7 age groups and 2 genders).

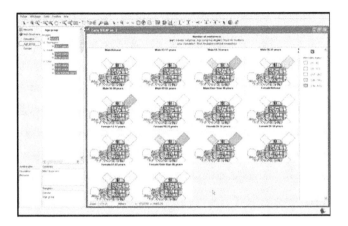

Fig. 8.23. Cartographic representation of the distribution of software agents, comprising one map for each combination of age group and gender.

■ The SOLAP tool is very flexible in terms of visualization and exploitation of spatial and non-spatial data. It can display data using maps, pie charts, histograms, or other visualization modes. Fig 8.24 offers an example of this visualization flexibility, where the same analysis is displayed using superimposed pie charts or histograms on maps.

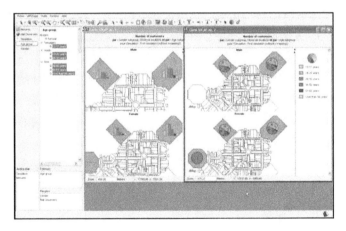

Fig. 8.24. Cartographic representation of the distribution of software agents by age group (combining pie charts or histograms on a map).

In this sub-section, we presented how we can use the OLAP/SOLAP technique to analyze multiagent geosimulations. This technique is proftable because: 1) OLAP allows users and analysts to analyze data in the way they think, simultaneously across multiple variables called *dimensions* (Codd et al., 1993); 2) the multidimensional approach of OLAP is more in agreement with the end user's mental model (Yougworth, 1995); 3) we can take into account the spatial aspect of the data to be analyzed using a recent extension of OLAP called SOLAP (Bédard et al., 1997); and 4) OLAP/SOLAP techniques present advanced visualization functionality of the analysis results. These results are presented directly on the map (GIS), with different levels of detail and in different modes. This dynamic aspect allows the user to create several displays (maps, tables, and diagrams), using the dataset without having to store each display individually.

Unfortunately, the OLAP/SOLAP technique still presents some limitations because:

- it requires a transformation of the output data generated by the geosimulation in order to create a data cube. This transformation is not obvious and requires expertise in databases, OLAP techniques, and data warehouse, etc.

- it cannot be used to analyze outputs generated by more than one simulation execution at once. What's more, for each scenario, we need to transform the data generated by the geosimulation into a data cube. Due to this limitation, the user cannot compare, simultaneously, several simulation executions in order to compare different simulation scenarios. This limitation is critical for the geosimulation users because, as we will see in Chapter 10, comparing geosimulation scenarios is the basis of the use of the geosimulation as a decision-making tool.

8.5. Discussion and conclusion

This chapter aimed to present and illustrate the method's step in which we collect and analyze output data generated from the geosimulation. In the first sub-step, we showed how we benefit from the agent technology to collect spatial and non-spatial data from the geosimulation. In the second sub-step, we presented how we can analyze the geosimulation outputs using some analysis techniques and tools. Therefore, we presented three analysis techniques and tools and illustrated them using the shopping behavior case study. These tools or techniques are: (1) classical or traditional statistical techniques, (2) our own analysis tool, and the OLAP/SOLAP techniques. For each technique or tool, we presented the advantages and limitations. Table 8.1 summarizes these advantages and limitations based upon some characteristics which must be considered in the geosimulation outputs analysis.

Characteristics	Classical analysis techniques	Our proposed tool	OLAP/SOLAP technique
Analyzing non-spatial data	**YES**: They can be used to analyze non-spatial data	**YES**: It can be used to analyze non-spatial data.	**YES**: It can be used to analyze non-spatial data.
Analyzing spatial data	**NO**: They do not take into account spatial data.	**YES**: It takes into account the spatial data generated by the geosimulation.	**YES**: Using the SOLAP extension, the technique takes into account the spatial data
Analyzing multi-variables (spatial and non-spatial)	**NO**: It cannot be used to analyze multi-variables (spatial and non-spatial) simultaneously.	**YES**: It can be used to analyze the combination of spatial and non-spatial variables. But, **the number of variables to be analyzed is limited**.	**YES**: It is efficient in the multi-variables (multi-diemensions) analysis.
Coupling with the geosimulation	**NO**: In the geosimulation, spatial data is relevant. This kind of data is not considered by these techniques.	**YES**: It is coupled with the geosimulation directly without transformation of the data to be analyzed.	**YES**: It can be coupled with the geosimulation.But, **it requires a transformtion of the data to be analyzed into data cubes**.
Exploring and manipulating the analysis results (visualization of the results)	**YES**: It allows the user to explore the analysis results of non-spatial data based upon tables, pie charts, diagrams. It does not allow spatial representation of the analyzed data.	**YES**: It enables the visualization and exploration of the analyzed data spatially with limited visualization capabilities and functionalities.	**YES**: It enables the user to visualize and explore the analyzed data spatially with advanced visualization capabilities and functionalities.
Comparing several simulation execution results at the same interface	**NO**: It cannot be used to compare the results of several geosimulation scenarios.	**YES**: It can be used to compare the results of several geosimulation scenarios.	**NO**: It cannot be used to compare the results of several geosimulation scenarios.

Table 8.1. Criteria distinguishing the analysis techniques and tools.

Based upon the results presented in Table 8.1, we can conclude that:

- OLAP/SOLAP technique can be used to manipulate and explore the outputs of one geosimulation;

- Our tool is used to analyze and exploit the geosimulation outputs with limited exploration/visualization capabilities. It also can be used to compare several scenarios simulation executions. This makes the simulation more useful for decision-making process about the phenomenon to be simulated or the simulated environment (see Chapter 10).

To summarize, in this chapter we presented a promising technique that can be used to collect spatial and non-spatial output data from a geosimulation prototype. This technique is based upon the concept of *observer agents* whose the mission is to observe some aspects of the geosimulation execution and generate data in specific files or databases. The advantages of using such a technique represents a contribution of this work to the simulation field.

This chapter also presented our new analysis technique and tool that can be used to analyze the outputs generated from the geosimulation. This technique/tool differs from the existing techniques/tools such as those presented by (Sanchez, 2001), (Kelton, 1997), (Alexopoulos et al., 1998), (Alexopoulos, 2002), and (Seila, 1992) because it takes into account the spatial aspects of the data to be analyzed, which is fundamental to a geosimulation study. Furthermore, the analysis results are presented and exploited spatially on the simulated environment which is closer to the users' mental models. The characteristics of such a technique/tool let us consider it as a contribution in the simulation field. The chapter also presented how we exploit an existing technique called OLAP/SOLAP in order to analyze and explore spatial and non-spatial data generated from geosimulation. The idea of coupling a multiagent geosimulation application and OLAP/SOLAP tools is also an original contribution to the simulation field.

The next chapter of the dissertation aims to present the next two steps of our proposed method which seeks, respectively, to (1) verify and validate the geosimulation models and (2) test and document the geosimulation. It also aims at illustrating these steps using the shopping behavior case study.

CHAPTER 9: Verify/Validate, Test and Document the Multiagent Geosimulation

In this chapter, we present two steps of our proposed method. The first step aims to verify and validate the multiagent geosimulation models, while the second aims to test and document the geosimulation. We also present how we can illustrate these steps using the shopping behavior as a case study.

9.1. Introduction and motivations

The sixth step of the proposed method aims at developing an operational geosimulation prototype that can be used by end-users (see Chapter 7). This prototype may be employed to (1) merely visualize, in 2D and 3D modes the phenomenon to be simulated in a geographic environment or (2) to make decisions about the phenomenon to be simulated, or about the simulation environment. In order to increase the users' confidence in the geosimulation models, it is important to include in our method a step designed at verifying and validating the geosimulation models. This step is the first one which is presented in this chapter.

The geosimulation prototype is intended at being used by end-users. Hence, it is relevant to test and document this prototype which represents a grood practice in computer science. The test and the documentation of the geosimulation prototype are the purpose of the second step to be presented in this chapter.

This chapter is organized as follows: Section 9.1 presents generic descriptions of the two steps aiming, respectively, at verifying and validating the geosimulation models and at testing and documenting the geosimulation. Section 9.2 illustrates these two steps using the shopping behavior simulation models. The last section of the chapter (Section 9.3) presents the conclusion.

9.2. Generic presentation of the steps of the method

9.2.1. Verification and validation of the geosimulation models

Using a simulation is a surrogate for the experimentation with a real phenomenon (existing or proposed), where experimentation with that phenomenon could be disruptive, non-cost effective, or even not feasible. Therefore, the model or simulation must be able to provide valid representations of the actual phenomenon. The verification and validation steps of a simulation insure that the simulation models accurately represent the real phenomenon to be simulated. These two steps which are theoretically distinct are closely related in practice (Arthur and Nance, 1996) (Balci, 1988). They not only insure that the model assumptions are correct, complete, and consistent, but also enhance the users' confidence in the simulation models (Anu, 1997). When we talk about simulation verification and validation, it is pertinent to keep in mind the following elements:

- The verification and validation step establish the reliability of the model and simulation of the thing being represented. Verification and validation provide a crucial piece of evidence to support the simulation model credibility for a particular simulation application.

- The ease or difficulty of the verification and validation processes depends upon the complexity of the phenomenon being modeled.

- The simulation of a complex phenomenon can only approximate the actual phenomenon, no matter how much time and money are spent on simulation construction. There is no such thing as absolute simulation validity, nor is it even desired. Indeed, a simulation model is supposed to be an abstraction and simplification of reality.

- A simulation should always be developed for a particular set of objectives (goals). Indeed, a simulation that is verified and valid for one set of objectives may not be so for another set of objectives.

209

In our method, we propose a step that takes into account the verification and validation of the geosimulation models. Because we deal with geosimulations, it is relevant to focus on the spatial aspects of the models during the verification and validation. This step contains the following sub-steps (see Fig 9.1):

(1) *Choose the verification and validation technique*: Our literature review revealed that there exist several verification and validation techniques that can be used to verify and validate a simulation model. These techniques are separated into four categories: informal, static, dynamic, and formal.

> ▪ *Informal verification and validation techniques* are among the most commonly used. They are called informal because their tools and approaches rely heavily on human reasoning and subjectivity, without stringent mathematical formalism (DMSO, 2005).

> ▪ *Static verification and validation techniques* assess the accuracy of the static model design and source code. Static techniques do not require machine execution of the model, but mental execution can be used. These techniques are very popular and widely used, and many automated tools are available to assist in the verification and validation process. Static techniques can reveal a variety of information about the structure of the model, the modeling techniques used, data and control flow within the model, and syntactical accuracy (Whitner and Balci, 1989).

> ▪ *Dynamic verification and validation techniques* require model execution; they evaluate the model, based upon its execution behavior. Most dynamic verification and validation techniques require model instrumentation, the insertion of additional code into the executable model to collect information about model behavior during execution. Dynamic verification and validation techniques are usually applied in three steps: executable models are instrumented; instrumented models are executed; and models' outputs are analyzed and dynamic models' behaviors are evaluated (DMSO, 2005).

210

■ *Formal verification and validation techniques (or formal methods)* are based upon formal mathematical proofs of correctness, and are the most thorough means of model verification and validation. The successful application of formal methods requires that the model development process must be well defined and structured. Formal methods should be applied early in the model development process in order to achieve maximum benefit. Because formal techniques require significant effort they are best applied to complex problems, which cannot be handled by simpler methods (DMSO, 2005).

The taxonomy, presented in Table 9.1, lists the majority of the verification and validation techniques of simulation models that exist in the literature. They are grouped according to the categories described above. The detail of each technique is not presented in this dissertation.

Category	Technique
Informal verification and validation techniques	• Audit
	• Desk checking/Self-inspection
	• Face validation
	• Inspection
	• Review
	• Turing test
	• Walkthroughs
Static verification and validation techniques	• Cause-Effect graphing
	• Control analysis
	• Data analysis
	• Fault/Failure analysis
	• Interface analysis
	• Semantic analysis
	• Structural analysis
	• Symbolic evaluation
	• Syntax analysis
	• Traceability assessment
Dynamic verification and validation techniques	• Acceptance testing
	• Alpha testing
	• Assertion checking
	• Beta testing
	• Bottom-up testing
	• Comparison testing
	• Compliance testing
	• Debugging
	• Execution testing
	• Fault/Failure insertion testing
	• Field testing
	• Functional testing
	• Graphical comparison
	• Interface testing
	• Object-flow testing
	• Partition testing
	• Predictive validation
	• Product testing
	• Regression testing
	• Sensitivity analysis

	• Special input testing • Statistical techniques • Structural testing • SubModel/Module testing • Symbolic debugging • Top-Down testing • Visualization/Animation
Formal verification and validation techniques (or formal methods)	• Induction • Inference • Logical deduction • Inductive assertions • Lambda calculus • Predicate calculus • Predicate transformation

Table 9.1. The taxonomy of verification and validation techniques (DMSO, 2005).

In our method, the first part of this verification and validation step aims at choosing the suited technique that can be used to verify and validate the geosimulation models. It is relevant to note that the choice of a verification and validation technique depends upon the nature of the phenomenon to be simulated.

(2) *Verify and validate the geosimulation models*: Using the technique chosen in the previous sub-step, we verify and validate the geosimulation models. In multiagent geosimulation models, we distinguish two parts: The first is related to the phenomenon to be simulated, while the second concerns the simulated environment. Hence, it is relevant to verify and validate these two parts, as well as their spatial characteristics.

(3) *Adjust the geosimulation models*: Based upon the results of the verification and validation processes, we may notice some divergence between the geosimulation models and the real phenomenon to be simulated. If this is the case, we must adjust some elements of the geosimulation models. Hence, and depending upon the required adjustments, we may return back to some steps of the method in order to adjust them.

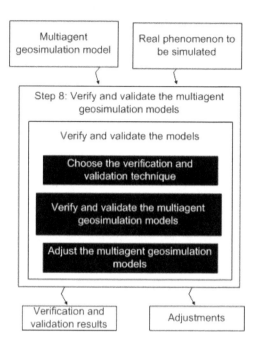

Fig. 9.1. Verify and validate the multiagent geosimulation models

9.2.2. Test and document the geosimulation prototype:

Once the geosimulation is verified and validated, it can be used by end-users. Before that, it is important to test and document the geosimulation. Hence, in our method, we propose a step that takes into account the test and documentation tasks of the geosimulation. This step contains the following sub-steps (see Fig 9.2):

(1) *Test the multiagent geosimulation*: Testing the geosimulation is a vital part of our method because testing can show the presence of problems in the geosimulation models and prototype. The step of geosimulation testing answers some questions like: Does the geosimulation prototype really work as expected? Does it meet the users' needs? Does it produce what users expect? Do the users like it? What is its performance? Is it ready for release? If we answer this kind of questions, we can: save time and money by identifying defects early, avoid or reduce development downtime, know that we've satisfied our users'

213

requirements, build a list of desired modifications and enhancement, for later versions of the geosimulation prototype, etc.

(2) *Document the multiagent geosimulation*: When the geosimulation is tested, and before it is used by end-users, it must be documented. The geosimulation documentation is an important aspect. In geosimulation, we should write documents, describing the process of the geosimulation development from the users' needs identification to the final step. We also need to provide documents describing the analysis results of the simulation, as well as the geosimulation prototype. The main documents that can be generated during the documentation step are:

- *Documenting the users' needs (users' requirements document URD)*: This document describes the problems from the users' point of view. After the problem description, we describe what the users would like the geosimulator to do. Briefly, in this document, we find: a user's view of the problem, a brief description of the problem, a complete description of the problem, what is expected from the simulator (the solution), and what is not expected from the simulator.

- *Documenting the geosimulation models*: In this document, we describe the geosimulation models. It contains the detailed design of the geosimulation, as well as any architectural information.

- *Documenting the simulation data*: This document presents the detail of data collected to feed the geosimulation models, as well as the technique used to collect this data.

- *Documenting the program code, or the used platforms/tools/languages*: In this document, we must document the program code or the platform/tool/language used to execute the geosimulation models (user guide). If we use our own code for the simulation, we are expected to fully document this code.

- *Documenting the simulation results*: In this document, we need to write out the details of the simulation results (simulation outputs, analysis results of these outputs, etc.).

- *Documenting the verification, validation results*: In this document, we present the techniques used for the verification and validation of the geosimulation models and prototype.

- *Testing documentation*: The testing documentation describes how we tested the geosimulation prototype in order to prove that it works adequately. We should include testbeds for the prototype. We should provide test datasets where applicable.

- *User documentation*: In this document, we present how users can use the geosimulation prototype. We have two styles of user documentation: 'instruction' or 'tutorial' style, useful for the new user, and 'reference' style, useful for the more experienced user who needs information on specific topics. These two styles are often known as the 'User guide' and the 'Reference manual'.

  ❐ *A user guide (or introductory manual)*: Is an instructional document, giving step-by-step procedures and explanations for accomplishing specific tasks when using the geosimulation prototype. It is not necessary to cover, in detail, all the geosimulation prototype features in this document, but it must provide enough information for all but the most experienced users. This document should be designed to 'teach' new users how to use the geosimulation application, so worked examples of useful operations should also be included. As with other kind of documents, the most important principle in designing user guides is to write with readers in mind. How will readers use the geosimulation application? Will they install the geosimulation prototype themselves? Will they need to transfer the prototype from one computer environment to another?

❏ *A reference manual*: It contains the basic operations, facts and key definitions, ordered for easy reference (e.g., alphabetically). The aim of this document is to allow an experienced user to look up terms and procedures, as simply and rapidly as possible. This document should be more rigorous, formal, and exhaustive than the user guide.

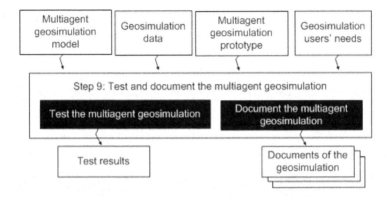

Fig. 9.2. Test and document the multiagent geosimulation

In the remaining part of the chapter, we illustrate these steps using the customers' shopping behavior in a mall as case study.

9.3. The illustration of the steps using the shopping behavior case study

9.3.1. Verify and validate the shopping behavior geosimulation models:

In Chapter 5, we presented the details of the shopping behavior multiagent geosimulation models. These models are composed of two main parts: the first is related to the simulation environment (the mall), while the second concerns the main actor of the geosimulation (the shopper). If we want to verify and validate the shopping behavior geosimulation models, it is relevant to take into account these two parts of the models. In the following points, we present the verification and the validation of some elements of the two parts of the shopping behavior geosimulation models.

a. The verification/validation of the geosimulation environment model (the mall)

In order to verify and validate the shopping mall model (mall) we propose to use the face validation technique. This technique is defined as follows: '*Face validation technique is an informal technique in which certain persons, such as the simulation projects team members, potential users of the simulation model, and subject matter experts, review simulation outputs (e.g., numerical, results, graphics, animation, etc.) for reasonableness. They use their estimates and intuition to compare model and the* phenomenon to be simulated subjectively, in addition to judging whether the model and its results are reasonable' (Hermann, 1967). We propose such technique, because it is based upon the visualization and animation modes to verify and validate the simulation models. These modes are efficient to represent the spatial characteristics of the simulated environment in a geosimulation. Hence, the persons carrying out the verification/validation processes, can use this technique to compare the geographic features of the real mall (on the plans) (see Fig 9.3) with those of the virtual mall, presented in 2D (in the GIS) (Fig 9.4) and 3D (Fig 9.5) models. The validation of the geosimulation environment model (mall) depends on the geographic data coming from the GIS of the mall and which fed the environment model.

Fig. 9.3. A real plan of the first floor of Square One mall.

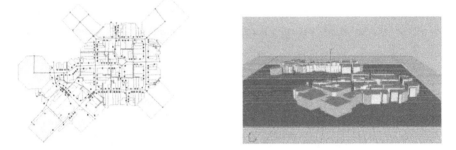

Fig. 9.4. The 2D model of the virtual mall.   Fig. 9.5. The 3D model of the virtual mall.

b. The verification and validation of the shopper model

In order to verify and validate the shopper model we propose to use the visualization/animation technique. This technique is defined as follows: '*Visualization/Animation technique is a dynamic technique. Visualization and animation of a simulation greatly assist in a model's verification and validation. Seeing the model in action is very useful for uncovering errors* (Sargent, 1992)'. We chose this technique for the following reasons:

218

- It allows us to verify and validate the model when it is in action during the simulation. Unlike the environment model, the shopper model is active during the simulation (it has a behavior) and it is relevant to verify and validate its actions;

- The visualization and animation aspects of the technique are efficient to verify and validate the spatial aspects of the shopper model which are relevant when dealing with geosimulations.

As mentioned in (DMSO, 2005), verification and validation of human behaviors are extremely complex: '*Verifying and validating human behavior (such as the shopping behavior) is very different from the other behaviors of non-human systems. What differentiates human behavior simulation from other kinds of behaviors comes primarily from their highly inherent complexity. Human behavior arises from numerous nonlinear relationships all interacting chaotically over many different orders of magnitude. Also, the verification and validation of human behavior is extremely difficult. Advances in information system technology make the construction of fine-grained simulations of human behavior, for a variety of situations, more feasible and practical. Developers have built many primarily cognitive simulations of human behavior, and the sophistication and fidelity of these systems continue to improve. However, the technology for the verification and validation of human behavior has not kept pace with these advances, despite facing particularly vexing problems since their very first applications. Human behavior manifests an intricate fabric of effects, coupled over many orders of magnitude, a property shared by complex chaotic systems. Small situational changes often create greatly different responses in the same system. Thus, verification and validation of human behaviors, even for simple tasks, can prove extremely difficult because of the large number of behavioral paths that must be explored for any given purpose. The lack of well-established techniques to support the verification and validation of human behaviors further exacerbates the difficulty of these problems. At the most abstract level, verification and validation of a human behavior involves comparing human behavior capabilities to the model, and simulation requirements for human behaviors in order to determine its fitness for the purpose represented by those requirements. Usually, defining human behavior capabilities involves testing the human behavior within the simulated environment, in which it will be used and determined if the behaviors manifested in test results are sufficient'* (DMSO, 2005).

The complexity of the behavior to be verified and validated (the shopping behavior in a mall) leads us to make some choices and define some limits concerning the shopper model's elements to be verified and validated. First, we are more interested to validate the shopper agent's decision-making process. Furthermore, we focus on the spatial aspects of the decision-making process (movement decisions of the shopper agent inside the virtual environment). Second, we focus on some specific shopping situations in order to evaluate the movement decisions made by the shopper agent. Finally, since the shopping behavior is composed of several patterns (see Chapter 7), we focus on some shopping behavior patterns. To sum up, our verification and validation of the shopper model is based upon the evaluation of the shopper agent's spatial decision-making process, of some shopping patterns, during specific shopping situations. In the following points, we present some results of this verification and validation step. At each point, we focus on a specific shopping behavior pattern, we put the shopper agent in a specific shopping situation (where some variables and factors (internal or external) are defined), and we evaluate the spatial decisions made by the shopper agent.

- *Go to a shop*:

Deciding about which shop to visit is influenced by several factors: internal variables (shopping list, preferences, etc.), knowledge (via the memorization process), in addition to external variables (the geographic characteristics and the knowledge of the environment) via the shopper agent's perception process, and the priority of the objectives. In order to verify and validate this shopping pattern, we try to put the shopper agent in specific shopping situations (based upon the factors mentioned above) and observe how it behaves and makes decisions. In the following points, we present some of these situations.

- *Situation 1: Evaluate the influence of distance on the decision-making process*: This situation aims at evaluating how the shopper agent makes decisions taking into account the distance factor. This situation is described by the following elements: the two shopper agents,

A and B, enter the virtual mall by the doors A and B, respectively (see Fig 9.6). These agents' starting points are presented in red in Figs 9.7 and 9.8. The shopping lists and memories' contents of these agents are presented in Table 9.2.

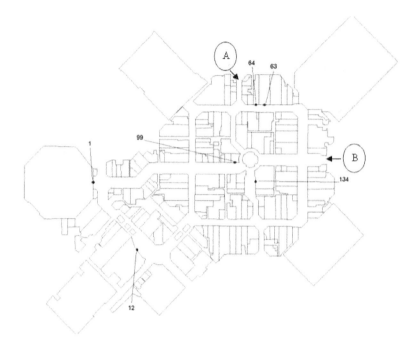

Fig. 9.06. The positions of agents A and B in the simulation environment (Situation 1).

Agent A	Agent B
Shopping list:	**Shopping list:**
Shopper_List_Shop_Shop1 = 134	Shopper_List_Shop_Shop1 = 134
Shopper_List_Shop_Shop2 = 64	Shopper_List_Shop_Shop2 = 64
Shopper_List_Shop_Shop3 = 99	Shopper_List_Shop_Shop3 = 99
Shopper_List_Shop_Shop4 = 63	Shopper_List_Shop_Shop4 = 63
Shopper_List_Shop_Shop5 = 1	Shopper_List_Shop_Shop5 = 1
Shopper_List_Shop_Shop6 = 12	Shopper_List_Shop_Shop6 = 12
Shopper_List_Shop_Shop7 = 0	Shopper_List_Shop_Shop7 = 0
Shopper_List_Shop_Shop8 = 0	Shopper_List_Shop_Shop8 = 0
Shopper_List_Shop_Shop9 = 0	Shopper_List_Shop_Shop9 = 0
Shopper_List_Shop_Shop10 = 0	Shopper_List_Shop_Shop10 = 0
Memory:	**Memory:**
Agent 64	Agent 64
Agent 134	Agent 134

Table 09.2. The shopping lists and memories' contents of the agents (Situation 1).

During the simulation we can verify that agent A visits shop 64 (the second element in its shopping list) and agent B visits shop 134. This shows that the agents are rational about distance and visit the shop nearest to them.

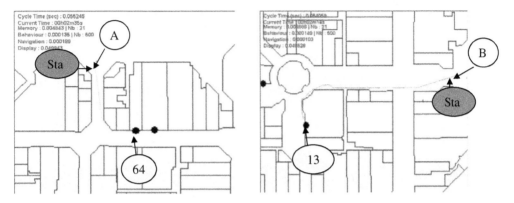

Fig. 09.7. Agent A visits shop 64.   Fig. 9.8. Agent B visits shop 134.

- *Situation 2: Evaluate the influence of perception on the decision making process*: This situation aims at evaluating how the shopper agent makes decisions based upon its perception capability. This situation is described by the following elements: The locations of shopper agents A and B are presented in Fig 9.9. These positions are presented in red in Fig 9.10. The shopping lists and the agents' memories contents are presented in Table 9.3.

Fig. 9.9. The locations of agents A and B in the simulation environment (Situation 2).

Agent A	Agent B
Shopping list:	**Shopping list:**
Shopper_List_Shop_Shop1 = 134	Shopper_List_Shop_Shop1 = 99
Shopper_List_Shop_Shop2 = 1	Shopper_List_Shop_Shop2 = 1
Shopper_List_Shop_Shop3 = 0	Shopper_List_Shop_Shop3 = 0
Shopper_List_Shop_Shop4 = 0	Shopper_List_Shop_Shop4 = 0
Shopper_List_Shop_Shop5 = 0	Shopper_List_Shop_Shop5 = 0
Shopper_List_Shop_Shop6 = 0	Shopper_List_Shop_Shop6 = 0
Shopper_List_Shop_Shop7 = 0	Shopper_List_Shop_Shop7 = 0
Shopper_List_Shop_Shop8 = 0	Shopper_List_Shop_Shop8 = 0
Shopper_List_Shop_Shop9 = 0	Shopper_List_Shop_Shop9 = 0
Shopper_List_Shop_Shop10 = 0	Shopper_List_Shop_Shop10 = 0
Memory:	**Memory:**
Agent 1	Agent 1

Table 9.3. The shopping lists and the agents' memories contents (Situation 2).

During the simulation presented in Fig 9.10 we can verify that agent A does not visit shop 134, even though it is on its shopping list. This happens because the agent A does not perceive the shop 134 (this shop is not in the perception field of agent A). On the other hand, shop 99 is in agent B' perception field, therefore, agent B visits shop 99 once it perceives it.

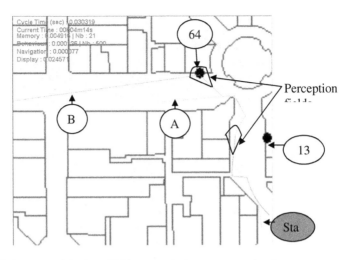

Fig. 09.10. Agent A does not visit shop 134 because it does not perceive it.

- Situation 3: Evaluation of the influence of the memorization process on agent's decision-making process: This situation aims at evaluating how the shopper agent makes spatial decisions based upon its memorization process. In this situation, the positions of agents A and B are presented in Fig 9.11. The agents' shopping lists and their memories contents are presented in Table 9.4.

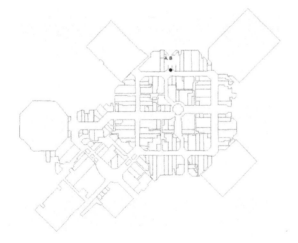

Fig. 9.11. The positions of agents A and B in the simulation environment (Situation 3).

Agent A	Agent B
Shopping list:	**Shopping list:**
Shopper_List_Shop_Shop1 = 63	Shopper_List_Shop_Shop1 = 63
Shopper_List_Shop_Shop2 = 1	Shopper_List_Shop_Shop2 = 1
Shopper_List_Shop_Shop3 = 0	Shopper_List_Shop_Shop3 = 0
Shopper_List_Shop_Shop4 = 0	Shopper_List_Shop_Shop4 = 0
Shopper_List_Shop_Shop5 = 0	Shopper_List_Shop_Shop5 = 0
Shopper_List_Shop_Shop6 = 0	Shopper_List_Shop_Shop6 = 0
Shopper_List_Shop_Shop7 = 0	Shopper_List_Shop_Shop7 = 0
Shopper_List_Shop_Shop8 = 0	Shopper_List_Shop_Shop8 = 0
Shopper_List_Shop_Shop9 = 0	Shopper_List_Shop_Shop9 = 0
Shopper_List_Shop_Shop10 = 0	Shopper_List_Shop_Shop10 = 0
Memory:	**Memory:**
Agent 1	Agent 1
Agent 63	

Table 9.4. The agents' shopping lists and memories' contents (Situation 3).

During the simulation execution presented in Fig 9.12 we can verify that agent A visits shop 63 because it is in its memory (agent A knows this shop). This is not the case with agent B. Shop 63 is on agent B' shopping list, but this agent does not know it, therefore, it moves closer to the known shop which is shop 1.

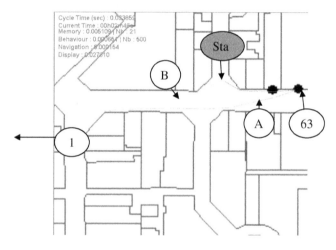

Fig. 9.12. Agent A visits shop 63, but agent B does not (agent B does not know shop 63).

• *Go to a restroom*:

In order to verify and validate this pattern, we illustrate it with a specific situation. This situation aims to evaluate how the shopper agent's dynamic variables can influence their decisions in the virtual mall. In particular, we show how the agent can change its destination in order to satisfy a need having a greater priority (the need to use the restroom has more priority than the need to visit a shop). Fig 9.13 shows this situation which presents the positions of two agents A and B. It also shows the location of the restroom in the virtual mall. Moreover, the shopping lists, the agents' memories, and the coefficient of variation of the agents' dynamic states are presented in Table 9.5. In this table, we can see that the dynamic state of agent A in relation with its need to use the restroom varies more quickly than that for agent B. Therefore, agent A feels the need to use the restroom before agent B.

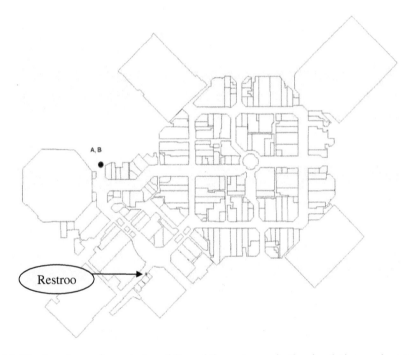

Fig. 9.13. The locations of agents A and B, and the restroom in the simulation environment.

Agent A	Agent B
Shopping list:	**Shopping list:**
Shopper_List_Shop_Shop1 = 1	Shopper_List_Shop_Shop1 = 1
Shopper_List_Shop_Shop2 = 99	Shopper_List_Shop_Shop2 = 99
Shopper_List_Shop_Shop3 = 0	Shopper_List_Shop_Shop3 = 0
Shopper_List_Shop_Shop4 = 0	Shopper_List_Shop_Shop4 = 0
Shopper_List_Shop_Shop5 = 0	Shopper_List_Shop_Shop5 = 0
Shopper_List_Shop_Shop6 = 0	Shopper_List_Shop_Shop6 = 0
Shopper_List_Shop_Shop7 = 0	Shopper_List_Shop_Shop7 = 0
Shopper_List_Shop_Shop8 = 0	Shopper_List_Shop_Shop8 = 0
Shopper_List_Shop_Shop9 = 0	Shopper_List_Shop_Shop9 = 0
Shopper_List_Shop_Shop10 = 0	Shopper_List_Shop_Shop10 = 0
Memory:	**Memory:**
Agent 1	Agent 1
Agent 9	Agent 9
Agent 3 (Restroom)	Agent 3 (Restroom)
Coefficient :	**Coefficient :**
1 by simulation cycle	0.01 by simulation cycle

Table 9.5. Shopping lists, agents' memories, and the coefficient of the dynamic states related to the agents' needs to use the restroom

During the executed situation in the MAGS platform, presented in Fig 9.14, we can verify that agents A and B visit shop 1. When they move to agent 99 (next destination), agent A feels the need to use the restroom. Agent B continues it way to shop 99 and agent A changes its direction to go to the restroom. When agent A satisfies its need of using the restroom, it visits shop 99 as planned before it felt the need to visit the restroom (see Fig 9.15).

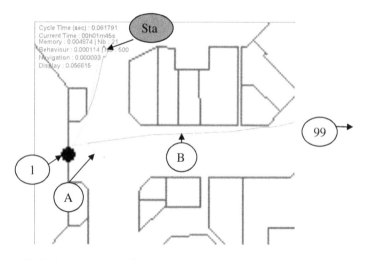

Fig. 9.14. Agent A feels the need to use the restroom, but not agent B (B goes to shop 99).

227

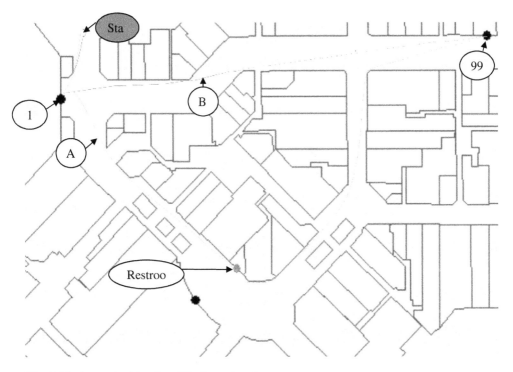

Fig. 9.15. Agent A visits shop 99 after using the restroom.

▪ *Leave the mall*:

In order to verify and validate this pattern, we consider the situation presented in Fig 9.16. Based on this figure, we can verify that the agent visited store 1 and decided to visit store 99. When it moves to store 99, it is aware that it reaches the time limit of its shopping trip and decides to leave the mall. Thus, the agent leaves the mall by the closest door.

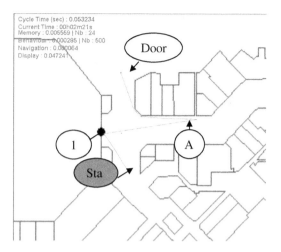

Fig. 9.16. Agent A reaches its shopping time limit and decides to leave the mall

The verification and validation of the shopper agent's decision-making process, which is presented above, is simple because:

- we verify and validate the spatial decision-making process of the shopper agents;

- some patterns of the shopping behavior; and

- in very limited shopping situations.

These limitations are due to a lack of the gathered data concerning the shopper in Square One mall. We recall that in our questionnaire we did not gather data concerning the decision-making process of the shoppers (their choices, their decisions, etc.). In order to improve the verification and validation processes, we can:

▪ elaborate a survey whose the purpose is to gather data concerning the shopping decisions made by the shoppers during their shopping trip;

▪ conduct this survey;

▪ simulate the shopping behavior in the MAGS platform using the collected data; and

229

• compare the shopping decisions made by the shopper agents (during the simulation) with those of the real shoppers in order to calibrate the geosimulation and to verify and validate the models.

9.3.2. Test and document the shopping behavior geosimulation:

A first attempt to test the shopping behavior geosimulation was made in our lab. Hence, we tested the user-interface of the geosimulation prototype, as well as the geosimulation outputs analysis tool. Unfortunately, these modules have not been yet tested from an end-user's view point.

Concerning documentation of the shopping behavior geosimulation we can consider this dissertation as the most important document because:

- it describes the steps that we followed to develop the multiagent geosimulation.

- it illustrates each step using the customer's shopping behavior prototype. Thus, each chapter of this dissertation can represent one independent document that can be generated for the shopping behavior geosimulation's end-users.

Beside this document, we wrote several other technical documents describing in detail:

- the input and output geosimulation data;

- the analysis results of this data;

- the use of the MAGS platform to create and execute the shopping behavior geosimulation models;

- the tool which is developed to digitalize the geosimulation input data;

- the tool which is used to analyze the collected data generated from the geosimulation;

Unfortunately, these technical documents cannot be included in this dissertation because of space limitation.

9.4. Conclusion

In this chapter we presented two important steps of our generic method. The first step aims to verify and validate the geosimulation models. The verification and validation of the simulation models are important (1) to insure that the simulation models represent the real phenomenon to be simulated, and (2) to enhance the users' confidence in the simulation models. The second step aims to test and document the geosimulation prototype and results.

After the verification, validation, test, and documentation of the shopping behavior geosimulation models, the shopping behavior geosimulation prototype can be used by end-users (mall managers) to make efficient decisions about the shoppers' behavior, or about the configuration of their mall. In the next chapter, we present the last step of our proposed method which consists in the use of the geosimulation by the end-users. We also illustrate it using the shopping behavior as a case study.

CHAPTER 10: Use the Shopping Behavior Multiagent Geosimulation as a Spatial Decision-Making Tool

In this chapter, we present the description of the last step of our method. This step shows how end-users can use multiagent geosimulations to support spatial decision-making. It also illustrates this step using the shopping behavior case study. Therefore, it demonstrates how mall managers may use the shopping behavior multiagent geosimulation prototype to make some decisions about their mall configuration.

10.1. Introduction and motivations

Simulation is generally used to analyze what-if scenarios (or alternatives). It can be used to study and compare alternative designs, or troubleshoot existing systems (Simon, 1960). This allows users to determine the impact of changing key variables in simulation models and processes. Using simulation models, we are free to imagine how an existing system might perform if altered, or imagine, and explicitly visualize, how a new system might behave before the prototype is even completed. The ability to easily construct and execute models, as well as generate statistics and animations about results, has always been one of the main attractions of simulation applications. The nature of simulation makes it a good tool to support decision-making. Furthermore, if we deal with the spatial decision-making process, it is appropriate to use simulation that deals with spatial and geographic data, such as geosimulation. In the literature, the decision making processes that include spatial information are known as *spatial or geographic decision-making processes*. They are generally more complex than the classical decision-making processes, which do not involve spatial data (Densham, 1991). This kind of spatial decision is also called *Spatial Decision Problem (SDP)*, which is characterised by the following features (Simon, 1960):

- A large number of decision alternatives;

- The outcomes or consequences of the decision alternatives are spatial variables;

- Each alternative is evaluated on the basis of multiple criteria;

- Some of the criteria may be qualitative, while others may be quantitative;

- There is typically more than one decision-maker involved in the decision-making process;

- The decisions are often surrounded by uncertainty.

In this chapter, we present the last step of our proposed method. This step concerns the use of the geosimulation by end-users. It presents how geosimulation can help them to make decisions related to a phenomenon's behavior or to assess the configuration of a geographic environment. This chapter also presents the illustration of this step using the shopping behavior case study.

This chapter is organized as follows: Section 10.1 presents a generic description of the step. In Section 10.2, we present the illustration of the step using the shopping behavior case study. Therefore, we show how mall managers can use the shopping behavior geosimulation prototype to make decisions about spatial configurations in their malls. Section 10.3 then discusses the chapter in relation to other works. Finally, Section 10.4 concludes the chapter.

10.2. Generic presentation of the step:

Before presenting the details of the step, let us define some basic concepts:

- Configuration: It is defined in the Oxford English Dictionary as follows: '*Arrangement of parts or elements in a particular form or figure; the form, shape, figure, resulting from such arrangement; conformation; outline, contour (of geographical features, etc.).*' (http://www.oed.com/).

- Environment configuration: It is the spatial arrangement of the elements belonging to this environment (their geographic features, shapes, positions, etc.).

During this step, a user can use the geosimulation in order to explore various spatial configurations of a simulated environment. For each simulation scenario involving new configuration, of the environment, the user can launch the geosimulation, collect the generated outputs, and then analyze them. By comparing these results, he can make informed decisions about the impact of spatial changes in the environment. This step contains the following sub-steps (see Fig 10.1):

(1) *Prepare some simulation scenarios*: In this sub-step, a user prepares some simulation scenarios. In each scenario, the user can change the spatial configuration of the simulation environment. For example, he/she can change the position of an entity belonging to this environment, the spatial configuration of this entity, etc.

(2) *Launch the geosimulation application using the scenarios*: In this sub-step, a user can launch the simulation for each scenario.

(3) *Generate simulation outputs and analyze data for each scenario*: In this sub-step, a user generates and analyzes data gathered from each simulation scenario, and stores the output data in files or databases related to each scenario.

(4) *Compare the simulation scenarios*: In this sub-step, a user compares the results of the analyses of the scenarios. Based upon this comparison, a user can decide about the best scenario and may apply it in the real environment.

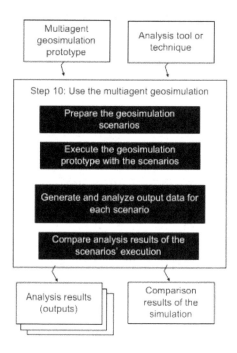

Fig. 10.1. Use the multiagent geosimulation.

This step is illustrated in the next section (Section 10.2) using the customers' shopping behavior in a mall.

10.3. How can Mall_MAGS help the mall manager in the decision-making process?

This section aims to illustrate the last step of our method using the shopping behavior case study. In this illustration, we demonstrate how mall managers use of Mall_MAGS prototype for the spatial decision-making process. Before presenting this illustration, it is relevant to present, in detail, why these managers need this geosimulation tool of shopping behavior in a mall.

10.3.1. Why mall managers need the shopping behavior geosimulation tool?

The world of shopping malls has been changing dramatically in the last decade, buffeted by, among other things, the introduction of electronic commerce, the saturation of locations, and changes in customers' shopping behavior (Ruiz et al., 2004). According to (Wakelfield et al., 1998), there are essentially three factors which explain the mall's declining role. First, consumers are increasingly busy, have less time for shopping, and therefore, reduce the frequency of their visits to the mall. Next, too many malls are alike, and customers will go to the shopping center that offers the most product and service variety, as well as the most comfortable atmosphere. Finally, (Wakelfield et al., 1998) emphasize the fact that fewer consumers are going to the mall in order to "enjoy their shopping experience". These factors lead mall managers to develop strategies to differentiate their malls from the competition, in order to enhance customer loyalty.

In a mall, the interaction between people and the environment is an important issue (Norman 1988). The environment can be characterized by its degree of complexity, mystery, coherence, and legibility (Kaplan and Kaplan 1989). Perception plays a key role in customers' activities in a mall (Sheridan, 2002). Spatial legibility may be thought of as a way for mall managers and tenants to communicate information to customers. Hence, the importance of stores' locations, the perception of products, or shopping opportunities, when customers walk through the mall's corridors. Public buildings that are not legible often induce frustration and negative reactions on busy people who cannot easily find their way. In shopping malls, spatial legibility is of great importance, and one of the important related issues is the mall layout (Garling et al. 1982). Indeed, people have different methods of finding their ways in complex spatial environments such as memorizing particular locations and routes in information-rich environments, like malls. One important property of a legible space is to facilitate the creation of mental maps of its layout by the individuals who frequent this space. Hence, the importance of adequately locating stores in a mall (Hernandez and Biasiotto, 2001). During a shopping trip in a mall, a customer may have a precise idea of where he or she wants to purchase given items. However, discovering unexpected shopping opportunities also influences a customer's decision–making, and may result in a buying decision if the opportunity fits with the customer's needs and preferences. Creating buying opportunities for a large proportion of customers is an important goal for mall managers and tenants. To this end, mall managers must find a location for every store that will optimize the chances for customers to be attracted to this store and by the buying opportunities it may offer. Managers know very well the importance of '*anchor stores*', such as Wall Mart which attract certain types of customers and favor '*proximity shopping*' in stores that are located in corridors converging toward the anchor stores (Konishi and Standfort, 2001).

Changing a mall configuration is a very important and expensive decision in terms of money and time. In order to guarantee the success of such a decision, mall managers should be able to better understand customers' behaviors, and the way they may react to the changes in the mall's configuration. Certain traditional techniques may help mall managers to understand how customers interact with the mall environment. For example, they can use *questionnaires* to collect information about customers and analyze the collected data in order to try to understand how customers use the mall. Although surveys can help mall managers to understand how customers appreciate the current mall configuration (and it is well known that most customers are not keen on filling out questionnaires), they are not very useful for anticipating the reactions of customers to future changes in the mall's configuration. Hence, managers lack tools to anticipate customers' reactions to changes in the mall's configuration.

Indeed, optimizing the location of stores in a mall is a complex problem if a manager wants to take into account the factors that influence the customers' shopping and buying decisions in relation to the mall's spatial layout: 1) relative locations of stores; 2) store's location in relation to corridors, entrances, and other services; 3) customers' preferences in relation to their needs and socio-economic profiles; 4) Customers' perception of buying opportunities in the mall in an environment that is rapidly changing. Traditional statistical and data analysis methods are not able to take into account so many factors, and cannot encompass the spatial and perceptual characteristics of people's shopping behaviors.

An ideal solution would be to enable mall managers to try various mall configurations by changing the locations of certain stores and to carry out surveys in order to determine the impact of these changes on customers. Obviously, such a solution is not practical in a real setting because: 1) changing a store's location is a costly activity that cannot be done often; 2) it is not possible to try several locations for a store and to assess the reactions of customers for each of these locations before making a final decision about the store's location. An alternative solution would be to simulate on a computer the customers' behaviors in a virtual mall and enable managers to explore various scenarios by changing stores' locations in the virtual mall and by observing the reactions of customers to these changes. Until recently, such an approach was not feasible; however, thanks to recent progress in the areas of geosimulation (Benenson and Torrens 2004) and multiagent systems simulation (Moss and Davidson, 2001) and more specifically, multi-agent geo-simulations (Moulin et al. 2003), simulating the behaviors of a large number of virtual agents in a georeferenced virtual world is now possible.

10.3.2. How mall managers can use Mall_MAGS prototype?

To illustrate the use of the shopping behavior geosimulation tool we used two simulation scenarios. In the first, we launched a simulation with a given configuration of the shopping mall (Fig 10.2), and with a population of 390 shoppers. The simulation generated output data regarding shoppers' itineraries during their shopping trips. In scenario 2, we switched the locations of a two department stores: *Wal-Mart* and *Zellers* (Fig 10.3). The simulation was once again launched, and generated the output data for the shopper agents' itineraries once again. By comparing the output data from the two scenarios, we noticed the divergence between the paths taken by the shopper agents in order to reach the department stores. The simulation analysis showed that corridor X was less frequented in scenario 2 than it was in scenario 1 (Fig 10.2). However, corridor Y was more often used in scenario 2 than in scenario 1 (Fig 10.3). In these figures, the flow of the shoppers agents passing through a corridor is represented by a line, attached to the corridor. The width and color of the line are proportional to the flow of shopper agents that use the walkway. If the flow increases, the width of the line grows, in addition to its color becoming darker. Through a data analysis of the shopper agents' characteristics, we can see that in scenario 2, most of the agents going through corridor Y are female, and they go to the mall primarily to visit female clothing stores. If the mall manager chooses the mall's configuration portrayed by scenario 2, he may consider renting the spaces along corridor Y to female clothing stores.

Determining store locations in a mall is widely recognized as the most decisive factor in defining retail success or failure. As it has been observed over many years, good locations are 'the keystone to profitability' (Hernandez and Biasiotto, 2001). They represent an aspect of major investment that must be managed. Once made, poor location decisions are difficult to remedy, and it is these factors that, in theory, 'compel the retailer to make the decision carefully' (Hernandez and Biasiotto, 2001). Due to increasing competition, the pressure placed upon retailers to make 'good' decisions has grown markedly, as the consequences of 'bad' decisions have escalated. For these reasons, retailers, such as mall managers or store managers, who need to make decisions about their locations, need to be supported in these decisions by efficient tools.

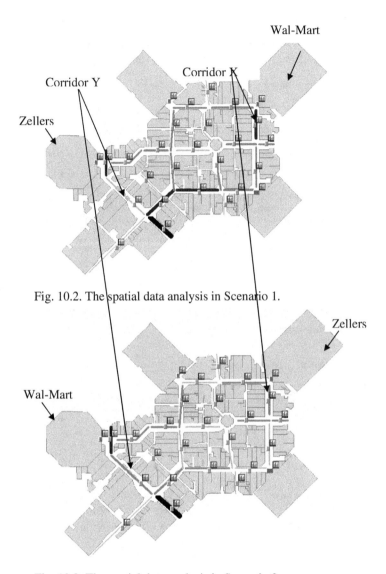

Fig. 10.2. The spatial data analysis in Scenario 1.

Fig. 10.3. The spatial data analysis in Scenario 2.

10.4. Discussion and related works

The main objective of a simulation tool is to aid users in their decision-making process with regards to a phenomenon, or to help solve problems related to this phenomenon. When we deal with a spatial phenomenon (i.e., which behaves in spatial environment) the decision-making process is generally more complex than that of the classical decision-making process, given that it involves spatial data (Densham, 1991). If we look at simulation applications proposed in the literature to simulate human behaviors in spatial environments (Raubal, 2001), (Dijkstra, 2001), (Koch, 2000), and (Moulin et al., 2003), we note that they are used only to visualize the simulation course. Thus, they are not used to compare simulation scenarios, nor to generate results about the comparisons of these scenarios. This represents a noteworthy gap in the usage of simulation. In order to fill this gap, we developed a multiagent geosimulator of shopping behavior that can be used to compare several simulation scenarios. This prototype generates analysis results related to these comparisons, and can be applied by users (mall managers) in order to make efficient decisions about the phenomenon to be simulated, or about the simulation environment.

To sum up, our shopping behaviour geosimulation tool stands out from other human behavior simulation tools because it can be used by end-users to make spatial decisions about the configurations of the simulated environment. This can be considered as a good contribution in the field of simulation.

10.5. Conclusion

This chapter presented and illustrated the last step of our method which is the use of the geosimulation by its end-users. First, we presented why it is appropriate to use geosimulation tools in order to aid users in their decision-making process. We focuzed on the importance of using the geosimulation as a spatial decision-making tool for spatialized behaviors in geographic environments. Then, we illustrated the step using the customers' shopping behavior in a mall as a case study. Hence, we showed why and how users, mainly mall managers, can use our shopping behavior geosimulation in order to try various mall configurations, by changing the locations of certain stores. As mentioned in this chapter, we can see that the shopping behavior prototype can satisfy the main users' needs set in the first step of our method (Chapter 4). The users (mall managers) of the shopping behavior prototype, can visualize the flows of shopper agents in several simulation scenarios. Using our analysis tool and the OLAP/SOLAP one they can visualize in a graphical form the characteristics of these shopper agents and combine them and compute and compare several indicators of interest. What's more, mall managers can exchange the positions of certain stores and observe how virtual shoppers react to these configuration changes, etc. They can again use the analysis and OLAP/SOLAP tools to asses the different scenarios and compare them. We think that this prototype can help mall managers to make better decisions about the mall configuration (store locations), as well as the impact of changes on customers' shopping behavior. Let us mention that we presented the simulation prototype to mall managers of another mall, *Place De La Cité* in Quebec City, and they showed a great interest in using our simulation tool. They asked us to develop, as soon as possible, a simulation prototype for their mall, using the data collected during our 2004 survey about shoppers attending *Place De La Cité* mall.

CHAPTER 11: General Conclusion and Future Work

In this chapter, we give a general conclusion about the research done in this dissertation. We then present the major contributions of our work. Finally, we propose various directions for future research works.

11.1. General discussion

In this dissertation, we proposed a generic method that can be followed to develop 2D and 3D multiagent geosimulation applications of phenomena in georeferenced virtual environments. One of the advantages of this method lies in the fact that it captures recent progress in two promising domains, multiagent based simulation and geographic information systems. This method contains ten steps, which are summarized as follows:

The first three steps of the method aim to (1) define the geosimulation users' needs, (2) identify the characteristics of the phenomenon to be simulated, as well as its environment, and (3) create the geosimulation models using the multiagent paradigm. The fourth step aims at selecting the simulation tool/environment/language that is used to develop the geosimulation. In step five, we collect the data which feed the geosimulation models. In this step, we analyzed the collected information in order to define some patterns of the behaviors of the phenomenon to be simulated. In the sixth step, we develop the geosimulation prototype, on the selected simulation platform, using the collected data. In step seven, we collect information about the course of the simulation, once again using the multiagent paradigm. In this step, we deal with the non-spatial and spatial data, generated by the simulation using several analysis techniques: Classical or traditional analysis techniques, our own analysis technique/tool, and the OLAP (On Line Analytical Processing) and SOLAP (Spatial On Line Analytical Processing) technique. In order to ensure the correctness of the simulation models, as well as to enhance the confidence of the simulation users, we need to verify and validate the simulation models. The verification and validation are the purpose of the eighth step of our method. In the ninth step, we test and document the simulation, while in the last step users can use the multiagent geosimulator in order to make efficient spatial decisions about the phenomenon to be simulated or about the configuration of the simulation environment.

Our method is illustrated throughout this dissertation, using the customers shopping behavior in a mall as a case study. The information used in the simulator has been collected from a survey on customers' behavior of Square One mall, in the Toronto area.

As shown all along this dissertation, our method is suited to develop 2D-3D geosimulation of phenomenon in georeferenced environments. This method is intended to be generic; even it has been illustrated using the shopping behavior case study. This illustration makes it a promising method that can be followed to develop other geosimulation applications of similar phenomena in different geographic environments. The main advantage of the method with respect to the other methods and approaches existing in the literature, is that it takes into account and focusses on the spatial characteristics of the phenomena to be simulated and the geographic features of the simulated environments. The characteristics of the method's steps, as discussed all along this dissertation, make is easily applicable to simulate other phenomena in various geographic environments.

Our method has currently a limitation which: it is intended to simulate phenomena in geographic environments represented at only one level (e.g., simulation of shopping behavior in one floor of the mall). It would be interesting to improve it in order to take into account the multi-level aspects of simulated geographic environments.

11.2. Contributions (original points)

In this thesis, we presented a generic method that can be used to develop multiagent geosimulations of spatial phenomena in geographic environments. Based on our literature review, we can mention a noteworthy absence of methods or approaches to develop simulation applications in the geosimulation field. Our proposal of such a method can be considered as a significant contribution since geosimulations are becoming increasingly useful in several different domains, and a method to systematically develop and use geosimulations is a step forward to help users from different fields to take advantage of theis powerful approach.

In order to illustrate this method, we used as a case study the human shopping behavior in a mall. Studying and simulating such behavior required that we carried out in-depth studies in several disciplines: this which gives a multi-disciplinary flavor to our research work. The results of this work, which have been presented in this dissertation make our research findings as original in the computer simulation field as in the other fields we have investigated.

The main scientific contributions of this dissertation are the following:

- The main contribution of this thesis is the proposition of a new generic method that can be followed to develop 2D-3D multiagent geosimulations of phenomena in georeferenced virtual environments. What distinguishes our method from those proposed by (Drogoul et al., 2002) and (Ramanath and Gilbert, 2003), is that it focusses on the spatial characteristics of the phenomenon to be simulated and the geographic features of the simulated environment. What's more, our method contains some steps which are useful, but are often neglected by other methods and approaches. As examples, we can cite: the step in which we collect and analyze input data aiming to feed the geosimulation and the step aiming to analyze the outputs generated by the geosimulation. Since geosimulation is considered as a new field, our method can be considered as original. This method was published in (Ali and Moulin, 2005a) and (Ali and Moulin, 2005b).

- In this thesis, we illustrated our method using the shopping behavior case study. In this illustration, we created some useful models. As an example, we created a model of the individual's shopping behavior based upon the models of consumer behavior proposed by (Engel et al., 1968), (Howard and Sheth, 1969), and (Nicosa, 1966). In this model, we integrated some factors (variables) that influence the shopping behavior, as well as some processes that compose the shopping behavior. These factors and processes were not presented in the models presented by the

245

aforementioned authors. We also proposed an agent-based model of the individual's shopping behavior in a mall. This model stands out from those proposed by (Dijkstra et al., 2001) and (Timmermans et al., 2003) and (Ben Said et al., 2001) because it is not limited to presenting the shopping behavior in a mall as a pedestrian activity, but it presents it as a whole behavior containing several activities which can be spatial, social, cultural, etc. In addition, in our agent-based model, the shopping behavior contains some spatial and knowledge-based processes such as perception, memorization, decision-making, etc. Finally, based upon our literature review, we can affirm that there are no research papers involving the simulation of shopping behavior of group in a mall. The majority of works that deal with groups and collective decision-making are restricted to social psychology. In our work, we propose a simple model to represent a group of shoppers. We also proposed a simple model representing a crowd of shoppers in the mall.

▪ Without data, computer simulation does not work (Anu, 1997). Since we deal with geosimulation, the spatial aspect of the simulation data is a very relevant one. In our method, we introduced two steps that take into account this data. The first step deals with the simulation input data, while the second concerns the data generated as outputs. These steps were presented in (Ali and Moulin, 2005a) and (Ali and Moulin, 2005b).

❐ *For the input data*: We presented a step in which we collected and analyzed data before using it to feed the geosimulation models. This step is, generally, neglected by research works dealing with simulation methods and approaches such as (Anu, 1997), (Fishwick, 1995), (Allen et al., 2001), (Groumpos and Merkuryev, 2002), (Drogoul et al., 2002), (Ramanath and Gilbert, 2003), etc. The introduction of such a step in our method can be considered as an original work in the field of simulation. What's more, (1) developing a software to digitalize non-spatial and spatial simulation data at once and (2) analyzing these two kinds of data can also be considered as original work. We also presented a survey method to collect spatial and non-spatial real data about a

246

phenomenon for geosimulation. This method which is illustrated using the shopping behavior case study can be considered as a contribution, because we did not find any similar method or technique that can be used to collect spatial empirical data about a specific phenomenon which operates in a geographic context.

❐ *For the output data*: we presented a promising technique that can be used to collect spatial and non-spatial output data from a geosimulation prototype. This technique is based upon the concept of *observer agents* whose mission is to observe some aspects of the geosimulation execution and generate data in specific files or databases. The advantages of using such a technique represent a contribution of this work to the simulation field. We also presented our new analysis technique and tool that can be used to analyze the outputs generated by the geosimulation. This technique/tool differs from the existing techniques/tools such as those presented by (Sanchez, 2001), (Kelton, 1997), (Alexopoulos et al., 1998), (Alexopoulos, 2002), and (Seila, 1992) because it takes into account the spatial aspects of the data to be analyzed. We emphasized the fact that the spatial data is fundamental to a geosimulation study. What's more, the analysis results are presented and exploited spatially on the simulated environment which is closer to the users' mental models. The characteristics of such a technique/tool let us consider it as a contribution in the simulation field. We also presented how we exploited an existing technique called OLAP/SOLAP in order to analyze and explore spatial and non-spatial data generated from geosimulation. The idea of coupling a multiagent geosimulation application and a SOLAP tool is also original in the simulation field.

▪ In this thesis we illustrated our method by developing a geosimulation prototype that simulates the shopping behavior in a mall. This prototype stands out from the simulation prototypes existing in the literature by its 'realism' and 'usefulness':

247

❏ A more *'realistic'* prototype: In the simulation, the shopper agents are equipped with advanced spatial knowledge-based capabilities which can increase the realism of the behavior simulation. What's more, the simulation is presented in 2D and 3D modes. It is known, that simulating in 3D mode increases the realism of the visualization of the simulation. In the literature, we did not find any geosimulation prototypes exhibiting, simultaneously, these characteristics. Our prototype was presented in (Ali and Moulin, 2005c).

❏ A more 'useful' prototype: If we look at simulation applications proposed in the literature to simulate human behaviors in spatial environments (Raubal, 2001), (Dijkstra, 2001), (Koch, 2000), and (Moulin et al., 2003), we note that they are used only to visualize the simulation course. Thus, they are not used to compare simulation scenarios, nor to generate results about the comparisons of these scenarios. This represents a noteworthy gap in the usage of a simulation. In order to fill this gap, we developed a multiagent geosimulator of shopping behavior that can be used to compare several simulation scenarios. This prototype generates analysis results related to these comparisons, and can be applied by users (mall managers) in order to make efficient decisions about the phenomenon to be simulated, or about the simulation environment. To sum up, our shopping behavior geosimulation tool stands out from other human behavior simulation tools because it can be used by end-users to make spatial decisions about the configurations of the simulated environment. Hence, our shopping behavior geosimulation prototype can be considered as a contribution to the field of computer simulation, and especially, to the field of multiagent based-simulation.

In this thesis, we reached the following objectives:

- *'To propose a generic method that can be followed to develop 2D-3D multiagent geosimulation of phenomena in geographic environments. This method will be illustrated by developing a prototype that simulates the human shopping behavior in a mall'*:

Even if it is illustrated using the customers' shopping behavior case study, our method is intended to be generic and can be followed to develop geosimulations for other phenomena in different geographic environments.

- *'To design the simulation models: the models for the environment (shopping mall) and those for the shopper'*:

In this thesis, we developed several models that are used by the shopping behavior geosimulation. For example, we developed: an initial version of the shopping behavior model based upon a large literature review, an initial version of the multiagent model which is independent of the tool used to execute the simulation, and an agent-based model created according to the selected platform used to develop the geosimulation. All these models are related to the individual shoppers and to the simulated environment representing the mall.

- *'To develop, using empirical data, a multiagent geosimulation prototype that simulates human shopping behavior in a mall'*:

This led us to the development of a 2D-3D multiagent geosimulation prototype of the shopping behavior in a mall. Unfortunately, this prototype does not simulate the shopping behavior of groups of shoppers due to a lack of data ccollected in the surveyx and related to groups.

- *'To propose an analysis technique to efficiently exploit (in terms of easiness and rapidity) the data generated by the multiagent geosimulation prototype'*:

In this thesis we proposed and developed an analysis technique and tool that can be coupled with the geosimulation in order to analyze its outputs. These techniques and tools focus on the spatial aspect of the output data generated by the shopping behavior geosimulation. We also tested the use of an existing technique called OLAP/SOLAP which is coupled with the geosimulation. This technique was then, compared with our proposed technique/tool.

11.3. Directions for future works

As future works, we intend:

1. To apply our method in order to simulate the shopping behavior in other geographic environments. We plan to use our method to simulate the shopping behavior in a large scale environment, such as a city (in the shopping streets), and to simulate the shopping behavior inside a store.

2. To develop a simulation prototype that simulates the shopping behavior in several floors of a mall.

3. To use the method in order to simulate other phenomena and behaviors in different geographic environments.

4. To develop a simulation prototype for the shopping behavior in a Quebec City's mall, called Place De La Cite. We have already conducted a survey in this mall in 2004 and gathered data, just as we did at Square One. We would then be able to compare the shopping behavior of Toronto residents with that of Quebec City customers. This comparison can be interesting in order to understand the differences or common points between the shopping habits and behaviors of Toronto residents and those of Quebec City residents. Understanding these differences or common points can be relevant to (1) retailers (stores or others) in both Toronto and Quebec City (e.g., The Bay, Wal-Mart, Old Navy, etc.) and to (2) companies that own shopping malls in the two areas (e.g., OMERS that owns Square One mall in Toronto and Place Laurier mall in Quebec City).

5. To conduct a new survey concerning the groups of shoppers using an enhanced version of the questionnaire already developed for groups. This would enable us to simulate group behaviors in our geosimulation environment and to study the effects of this kind of behavior on the customers' shopping patterns.

Bibliography

(Akhter et al., 1994) Akhter S.H., Craig A.J., and Srinivas D., 1994, Retail Store Envirnment's Influence on Brand -Related Judgement, *Journal or Retailing and Consumer Services*, Vol. 01, p. 67-76.

(Alba and Marmorstein, 1987) Alba J.W., and Marmorstein H., 1987, The effects of frequency knowledge on consumer decision making. *Journal of Consumer Research,* Vol. 14, p. 14-25.

(Alexopoulos, 1998) Alexopoulos C., 1998, Advanced methods for simulation output analysis, *Proc. of the 1998 Winter Simulation Conference*, December 13-16, Washington DC, USA, p. 113-120.

(Alexopoulos, 2002) Alexopoulos C., 2002, Output data analysis for simulations, *Proc. of the 2002 Winter Simulation Conference*, December 8-11, San Diego California, USA, p. 85-96.

(Ali and Moulin, 2005a) Ali W., and Moulin B., 2005, Towards a generic approach to develop 2D-3D multiagent geosimulation, *Agent Directed Simulation (ADS 05)*, San Diego, California, USA, 3-7 April 2005.

(Ali and Moulin, 2005b) Ali W., and Moulin B., 2005, Developing 2D-3D agent-based simulation in geographic environment: An approach and its application to simulate shopping behavior in a mall, *Agent Based Simulation (ABS 6)*, Erlangen, Bavaria, Germany, 12-14 September 2005.

(Ali and Moulin, 2005c) Ali W., and Moulin B., 2005, 2D-3D multiagent geosimulation with knowledge-based agents of customers' shopping behavior in a shopping mall, *Conference On Spatial Information Theory (COSIT 05)*, Ellicottville, New York, USA, 14-18 September 2005.

(Anastassakis et al., 2001) Anastassakis G., Panayiotopoulos T., and Ritchings T., 2001, Virtual Agent Societies with the mVITAL Intelligent Agent System, *Proc. of Intelligent Virtual Agents*, September 10-11, Madrid, Spain, p. 112-125.

(Anthony et al., 2004) Anthony S., Chee S.Y., and Rajkumar B., 2004, A taxonomy of computer-based simulations and its mapping to parallel and distributed systems simulation tools, *Software – Practice and experience*, p. 653-673.

(Anu, 1997) Anu M., 1997, Introduction to modeling and simulation, *Proc. of the 29th conference on Winter simulation*, December 07-10, Atlanta Georgia, USA, p. 7-13.

(Arentze and Timmermans, 1998) Arentze T.A., and Timmermans H.J.P., 1998, Using Models of Consumer Spatial Shopping Behavior for Developing Retail Networks, *Casebook to Accompany Retailing*, Third Edition, Lusch R.F, and Dunne P. (Eds.), The Dryden Press, Harbourt Brace College Publishers, USA, p. 98-109.

(Arentze and Timmermans, 2001) Arentze T.A., and Timmermans H.J.P., 2001. Deriving Performance Indicators from Models of Multipurpose Shopping Behaviour, *Journal of Retailing and Consumer Services*, Vol. 8, p. 325-334.

(Arentze et al., 1997) Arentze T.A., Oppewal H., and Timmermans H.J.P., 1997, A Multipurpose Destination Choice Model For Shopping Trips: Some Empirical Results, *4th Recent Advances in Retailing and Services Science Conference*, Scottsdal Arizona, USA.

(Aronson, 1978) Aronson E., 1978, The Theory of Cognitive Dissonance: A Current

Perspective in Cognitive Theories in Social Psychology, *Academic Press*, Berkowitz L. (Eds.).

(Arthur and Nance, 1996) Arthur J.D., and Nance R., 1996, Independent verification and validation: a missing link in simulation methodology?, Proceedings of the 28th conference on Winter simulation, Coronado, California, United States, p. 230-236.

(Arthur and Nance, 1996) Arthur J.D., and Nance R.E., 1996, Independent verification and validation: a missing link in simulation methodology?, *Proc. of the 28th conference on Winter simulation*, December 8-11, Coronado California, USA, p. 230-236.

(Asawari et al., 2005) Asawari S., Abhijit C., and Dionisios G. V., 2005, Multiscale Stochastic Simulations of the Mitogen Activated Protein (Map) Kinase Cascade, *AICHE: American Institute of Chemical Engineers*.

(Assael, 1997) Assael H., 1997, Consumer Behaviour and Marketing Action, Sixth Editions, International Thomson Publishing Company.

(Axelrod, 1997) Axelrod R., 1997, Advancing the Art of Simulation in the Social Sciences, *Simulating Social Phenomena*, Conte R., Hegselmann R., and Terna P. (Eds.), Vol. 456, Berlin, p. 21–40.

(Baianu and Lin, 1986) Baianu I.C., and Lin H.C., 1986, Computer simulation and computability of biological systems, Mathematical Modelling, Vol. 7, p.1513-1577.

(Baker et al. 1988) Baker J., Berry L.L., and Parasuraman A., 1988, The marketing impact of branch facility design, Journal of Retail Banking, Vol. 10, No. 2, p.33-42.

(Baker et al., 1994) Baker J., Dhruv G., and Parasuraman A., 1994, The Effect of Store Atmosphere on Customer Quality Perceptions and Store Image, *Journal of the Academy of Marketing Science*, Vol. 22, p. 22-42.

(Balci, 1998) Balci O., 1998, Verification, validation, and accreditation, *Proc. of the 30th conference on Winter simulation*, IEEE Computer Society Press, p. 41-49.

(Bandi and Thalmann, 2000) Bandi S., and Thalmann D., 2000, Path Finding For Human Motion In Virtual Environments, *Journal of Computational Geometry: Theory and Applications*, Vol. 15, No. 1, p. 103-127.

(Bandini et al., 2002) Bandini S., Manzoni S., and Simone C., 2002, Enhancing Cellular Spaces by Multilayered Multi Agent Situated Systems, *Lecture Notes in Computer Science*, Vol. 2493, p. 156-167.

(Bandyopadhyay et al., 2001) Bandyopadhyay S., Vieragama M., and Khuller R., 2001, The missing piece in the puzzle: How retail atmospherics can improve merchandise and store promotions, *The Journal of Marketing*, Vol 146, No. 5, p. 141-159.

(Batty and al., 2001) Batty M., Chapman D., Evans S., Haklay M., Kueppers S., Shiode N., Smith A., and Torrens P.M., 2001, Visualizing the city: communicating urban design to planners and decision-makers, *Planning Support Systems: Integrating Geographic Information Systems, Models, and Visualization Tools*, Brail R.K., and Klosterman R.E. (Eds.), Redlands, CA and New Brunswick, NJ, ESRI Press, and Center for Urban Policy Research Press, p. 405-443.

(Bawa and Ghosh, 1999) Bawa K., and Ghosh A., 1999, A Model of Household Grocery Shopping Behavior, *Marketing Letters*, Vol. 10, No. 2, p. 149-160.

(Bayard and O'Mara, 1998) Bayard M., and O'Mara W.P., 1998, Shopping center development handbook, Urban Land Institute, USA.

(Bayton, 1958) Bayton J. A., 1958, Motivation, cognition, learning: Basic factors in consumer behaviour, *Journal of Marketing*, Vol. 22, No. 3, p. 282-289.

(Bazzan et al., 1999) Bazzan A.L.C., Wahle J., and Klügl F., 1999, Agents in Traffic Modelling - From Reactive to Social Behaviour, *Lecture Notes in Computer Science*, Vol. 1701, p. 303-306.

(Beatty and smith, 1987) Beatty S., and Smith S., 1987, External Search Effort: An Investigation Across Several Product Categories, *Journal of Consumer Research*, Vol. 14, p. 83-95.

(Bédard et al., 1997) Bédard Y., 1997, Spatial OLAP, 2ème forum annuel sur la R-D, Géomatique VI: Un monde accessible, 13-14 Novembre, Montréal.

(Bédard et al., 2001) Bédard Y., Rivest S., and Marchand P., 2001, Toward better support for spatial decision making: Defining the characteristics of Spatial On-Line Processing (SOLAP), *Geomatica, the Journal of the Canadian Institute of Geomatics*, Vol. 55, No. 4, p. 539-555.

(Belk, 1974) Belk R.W., 1974, An Exploratory Assessment of Situational Effects in Buyer Behavior, *Journal of Marketing Research*, Vol. 11, p.156-163.

(Ben Said et al., 2001) Ben Said L., Bouron T., Drogoul A., 2001, Multi-Agent Based Simulation of Consumer Behaviour: Towards a New Marketing Approach, *Proc. of the International Congress On Modelling and Simulation (MODSIM)*, Canberra, Australia.

(Benenson and Portugali, 1997) Benenson I., and Portugali J., 1997, Agent-based simulations of a city dynamics in a GIS environment, *Spatial Information Theory: A Theoretical Basis for GIS*, Hurtle S.C., and Frank A.U. (Eds.), Berlin, p. 501-502.

(Benenson and Torrens, 2003) Benenson, I., and Torrens P.M., 2003, Geographic Automata Systems: A New Paradigm for Integrating GIS and Geographic Simulation, *Proc. of GeoComputation Conference*, p. 24-30.

(Benenson and Torrens, 2004) Benenson, I., and Torrens P.M., 2004, Geosimulation: object-based modeling of urban phenomena, *Computers, Environment and Urban Systems*, Vol. 28, No. 1, p. 1-8.

(Benenson and Torrens, 2004) Benenson, I., and Torrens P.M., 2004, Geosimulation: Automata-Based Modeling of Urban Phenomena, John Wiley and Sons, London.

(Benenson and Torrens., 2004) Benenson, I., and Torrens P.M., 2004, A Minimal Prototype for Integrating GIS and Geographic Simulation through Geographic Automata Systems, *Geodynamics*, Atkinson P., and Wu F. (Eds.), CRC Press.

(Benenson., 1998) Benenson I., 1998, Multi-Agent Simulations of Residential Dynamics in the City, *Computers, Environment and Urban Systems*, Vol. 22, No. 1, p. 25-42.

(Benenson., 1999) Benenson I., 1999, Modeling population dynamics in the city: from a regional to a multi-agent approach, *Discrete Dynamics in Nature and Society*, Vol. 3, p. 149-170.

(Berlets and Boman, 2001) Bertels K., and Boman M., 2001, Agent-Based Social Simulation in Markets, *Electronic Commerce Research*, Vol. 1, No. 1, p. 149-158.

(Bettman and park, 1980) Bettman J.R., and Park C.W., 1980, Effects of Prior Knowledge and Experience and Phase of the Choice Process on Consumer Decision Processes: A Protocal Analysis, *Journal of Consumer Research*, Vol. 7, p. 234-248.

(Bettman et al., 1991) Bettman J., Johnson E., and Payne J., 1991, Consumer Decision Making, *Handbook of Consumer Behavior*, Robertson T., and Kassarjian H. (Eds.),

Englewood Cliffs, and NJ: Prentice-Hall.

(Bettman, 1979) Bettman J.R., 1979, An Information Processing Theory of Consumer Behavior, *Reading*, M.A.: Addison-Wesley.

(Bishop and Myers, 1974) Bishop G., and Myers D.G., 1974, Informational influence in group discussion, *Organizational Behavior and Human Performance*, Vol. 12, p. 92-104.

(Bitner, 1992) Bitner M.J., 1992, Servicescapes: The impact of physical surrounding on consumers and employees, *Journal of Marketing*, Vol. 56, No. 2, p. 57-71.

(Blaisdell et al., 1992) Blaisdell W.E., and Haddock J., 1992, SIMSTAT: A tool for simulation analysis, *Proc. of the 1992 Winter Simulation Conference*,

(Bloch et al., 1994) Bloch P.H., Nancy M.R., and Scott A. D., 1994, The Shopping Mall as a Consumer Habitat, *Journal of Retailing*, Vol. 70, p. 23–42.

(Böge and Koch, 2004) Böge M., and Koch A., 2004, A Processor for Artificial Life Simulation, *Lecture Notes in Computer Science*, Vol. 1673, p. 495-500.

(Borgers et al., 1997) Borgers A.W.J., Schaijk E., Waerden P.J.H.J., and Timmermans, H.J.P., 1997, The Potentials of Shopping Shuttles in Downtown Areas: A Stated Choice Experiment, RSAI North American Meeting, Buffalo, USA.

(Borgers et al., 1998) Borgers A.W.J., Waerden P.J.H.J., and Timmermans H.J.P., 1998, Micro Shopping Behaviour in Veldhoven: a Before-After Study, *5th Recent Advances in Retailing and Services Science Conference*, Baveno, Italy.

(Boulic and Hegron, 1997) Boulic R., and Hegron G., 1997, Computer Animation and Simulation 96, Springer Verlag, Wien.

(Bousquet et al. , 1998) Bousquet F., Bakam I., Proton H., and LePage C., 1998, Cormas: COmmon-pool Resources and Multi-Agent Systems, *Proc. of the 11th International Conference on Industrial and Engineering Applications of Artificial In telligence and Expert Systems*, Springer-Verlag, p. 826-837.

(Bousquet et al., 2003) Bousquet F., Davidsson P., and Sichman J., 2003, Report on the Multi-Agent Based Simulation (MABS) 2002 workshop, *Journal of Artificial Societies and Social Simulation*, Vol. 6, No. 2.

(Box, 2000) Box P.W., 2000, Specialized aspects of GIS and spatial analysis, *Journal of Geographical Systems*, Vol. 2, No. 1, p. 49-54.

(Brucks, 1985) Brucks M., 1985, The Effects of Product Class Knowledge on Information Search Behavior, *Journal of Consumer Research*, Vol. 12, p. 1-16.

(Burford et al., 1999) Burford G., Pennell J., and MacLeod S., 1999, Family group decision making, *Social work processes (6th Eds.)*, Compton B.R., and Galaway B., Pacific Grove, CA: Brooks/Cole, p. 278-283.

(Burrough, 2001) Burrough P.A., 2001, GIS and geostatistics: Essential partners for spatial analysis, *Environmental and Ecological Statistics*, Vol. 8, No. 4, p. 361-377.

(Campari and Levi, 2002) Campari E.G., and Levi G., 2002, A Realistic Simulation for Highway Traffic by the Use of Cellular Automata, *Lecture Notes in Computer Science*, Vol. 2329, p. 763.

(Campari et al., 2004) Campari E.G., Levi G., and Maniezzo V., 2004, Cellular Automata and Roundabout Traffic Simulation, *Lecture Notes in Computer Science*, Vol. 3305, p. 202-210.

(Cao and Frada, 1999) Cao P.P., and Frada B., 1999, An Asynchronous Group Decision

Support System Study for Intelligent Multicriteria Decision Making, *Proc. of the Thirty-Second Annual Hawaii International Conference on Systems Sciences, IEEE.*

(Capin and Thalmann, 1999) Capin T.K., and Thalmann D., 1999, A Taxonomy of Networked Virtual Environments, *Proc. of IWSNHC3DI'99*, Santorini, Greece.

(Capon and Kuhn, 1982) Capon N., and Kuhn D., 1982, Can Consumers Calculate Best Buys?, *Journal of Consumer Research*, Vol. 8, No. 4, p. 449-53.

(Carmon, 1991) Carmon Z., 1991, Recent studies of time in consumer behaviour, *Advances in Consumer Research*, Vol. 18, p. 7.3-7.5.

(Caron, 1998) Caron P.Y., 1998, Etude du potentiel de OLAP pour supporter l'analyse spatio-temporelle, *Mémoire de M. Sc.*, Département des sciences géomatiques, Faculté de foresterie et géomatique, Université Laval, p. 132.

(Carver, 1991) Carver S.J., 1991, Integrating multi-criteria evaluation with geographical information systems, *International Journal of Geographical Information Systems*, Vol. 5, No. 3, p. 321-339.

(Castelfranchi and Müller, 1993) Castelfranchi C., and Müller J.P., From Reaction to Cognition, 5th European Workshop on Modelling an Agent in a Multi-Agent World - MAAMAW'93, p. 3-9.

(Castelfranchi and Müller, 1995) Castelfranchi C., and Müller J.P., 1995, From Reaction to Cognition, Castelfranchi C., and Müller J.P., (editors), LNAI 957, Springer Verlag.

(Cellier, 1986) Cellier F.E., 1986, Combined continuous/discrete simulation: applications, *Proc. of the 18th conference on Winter simulation*, ACM Press, techniques and tools, p. 24–33.

(Cellier, 1991) Cellier F.E., 1991, Qualitative modeling and simulation: promise or illusion, *Proceedings of the 23rd conference on Winter simulation*, IEEE Computer Society, p. 1086–1090.

(Chaturvedi et al., 2004) Chaturvedi A., Chi J., Mehta S., Dolk D., 2004, SAMAS: Scalable Architecture for Multi-resolution Agent-Based Simulation, *Lecture Notes in Computer Science*, Vol. 3038, p. 779-788.

(Cheng and Masser, 2002) Cheng J., and Masser I., 2002, Cellular Automata Based Temporal Process Understanding of Urban Growth, *Lecture Notes in Computer Science*, Vol. 2493, p. 325-336.

(Choffray and Lilien, 1980) Choffray J.M., and Lilien G.L., 1980, Industrial market segmentation by the structure of the purchasing process, *Industrial Marketing Management,* Vol. 9, p. 331-342.

(Church et al., 1992) Church R.L., Loban S.R., and Lombard K., 1992, An interface for exploring spatial alternatives for a corridor location problem, *Computers and Geosciences*, Vol. 8, No. 9, p. 1095-1105.

(Clark and Smith, 1979) Clark, W.A.V., and Smith T.R., Modeling Information Use in a Spatial Context, *Annals of Association of American Geographers*, Vol. 69, p. 575-588.

(Clark, 1990) Clark T., 1990, International Marketing and National Character: A Review and Proposal for an Integrative Theory, *Journal of Marketing*, Vol. 54, No. 4, p. 66-79.

(Codd et al., 1993) Codd E.F., and Salley C.T., 1993, Providing OLAP (On-Line

Analytical Processing) to user-analysts: An IT Mandate, *Hyperion white papers*, p. 20.

(Cole and Balasubramanian, 1993) Cole C.A., and Balasubramanian S.K., 1993, Age Differences in Consumers' Search for Information, *Journal of Consumer Research*, Vol. 20, No. 1, p. 157-169.

(Collier, 2002) Collier N., 2002, RePast: the REcursive Porous Agent Toolkit, http://repast.sourceforge.net/.

(Conde and Thalmann, 2004) Conde T., and Thalmann D., 2004, An Artificial Life Environment for Autonomous Virtual Agents with multi-sensorial and multi-perceptive features, *Computer Animation and Virtual Worlds*, Vol. 15, No. 3, John Wiley.

(Conte and Gilbert, 1995) Conte R., and Gilbert N., 1995, Introduction: Computer Simulation for Social Theory, In Gilbert N., and Conte R. (Eds.), *Artificial Societies: the Computer Simulation of Social Life*, UCL Press.

(Conte et al., 1998) Conte R., Gilbert N., and Sichman J.S., 1998, MAS and Social Simulation: A Suitable Commitment, *Proc. of the First International Workshop on Multi-Agent Systems and Agent-Based Simulation*, Springer-Verlag, p. 1–9.

(Conte et al., 2001) Conte R., Edmonds B., Scott M., R. and Sawyer R.K., 2001, Sociology and Social Theory in Agent Based Social Simulation: A Symposium, *Computational and Mathematical Organization Theory*, Vol. 7, No. 3, p. 183-205.

(Corfmanand Lehmann, 1987) Corfman K.P., and Lehmann D.R., 1987, Models of Cooperative Group Decision-Making and Relative Influence: An Experimental Investigation of Family Purchase Decisions, *Journal of Consumer Research* Vol. 14, p.1-13.

(Cosmas, 1982) Cosmas S.C., 1982, Life Style and Consumption patterns, *The Journal of Consumer Research*, Vol. 8, No. 4, p. 453-455.

(Craik and Watkins, 1973) Craik F.I.M., and Watkins M.J., 1973, The Role of Rehearsal in Short Term Memory, *Journal of Verbal Learning and Verbal Behaviour*, Vol. 12, p. 599-607.

(Crossland et al., 1995) Crossland M.D., Perkins W.C., and Wynne B.E., 1995, Spatial decision support systems: an overview of technology and a test efficiency, *Decision Support Systems*, Vol. 14, No. 3, p. 219-235.

(Crowder, 1976) Crowder R., 1976, The Effects of Repetition on Memory, *Principles of Learning and Memory*, Hillsdale, NJ: Lawrence Erlbaum Associates.

(Czogalla et al., 2002) Czogalla O., Hoyer R., and Ulrich J., 2002, Modelling and Simulation of Controlled Road Traffic, *Lecture Notes in Control and Information Sciences*, Vol. 279, p. 419-436.

(Dahr and Nowlia, 1999) Dhar R., and Nowlis S.M., 1999, The effect of time pressure on consumer choice deferral, *The Journal of Consumer Research*, Vol. 25, No. 4, p. 369-384.

(Davidsson and Boman, 2000) Davidsson P., and Boman M., 2000, A Multi-Agent System for Controlling Intelligent Buildings, *Proc. of the Fourth International Conference on Multi-Agent Systems (ICMAS '2000), IEEE*.

(Davidsson and Gustavsson, 1998) Davidsson P., and Gustavsson R., 1998, Societies of Computation, *In AgentLink News*, Vol. 1, No. 1, p. 15-16,

(Davidsson et al., 2005) Davidsson P., Logan B., and Takadama K., 2005, Multi-Agent Based Simulation IV, *LNAI series*, Vol. 3415.

(Davidsson, 2000) Davidsson P., 2000, Multi Agent Based Simulation of "Socio-Technical" Systems, *In Second International Workshop on Multi Agent Based Simulation (MABS'2000)*.

(Davidsson, 2000) Davidsson P., 2000, Multi Agent Based Simulation: Beyond social simulation, *In Multi Agent Based Simulation, Lecture Notes in Computer Science*, Vol. 1979, Springer Verlag, p 97.

(Davidsson, 2001) Davidsson P., 2001, Categories of Artificial Societies, *In Engineering Societies in the Agents World II*, Springer Verlag, *Lecture Notes in Computer Science* series, Vol. 2203.

(Davidsson, 2002) Davidsson P., 2002, Agent Based Social Simulation: A Computer Science View, *Journal of Artificial Societies and Social Simulation*, Vol. 5, No. 1.

(Davila and Tucci, 2000) Davila J., and Tucci K., 2000, Towards a logic-based, multi-agent simulation theory, *In International Conference on Modeling, Simulation and Neural Networks MSNN'2000, IEEE*.

(Davila and Uzcagegui, 2000) Davila J., and Uzcagegui M., 2000, GALATEA: A Multi-agent, simulation platform, *In International Conference on Modeling, Simulation and Neural Networks MSNN'2000*.

(Davis and Rigaux, 1974) Davis H.L., and Rigaux B.P., 1974, Perception of marital roles in decision processes, *Journal of consumer research*, Vol. 1, p. 51-62.

(Davis, 1976) Davis H.L., 1976, Decision making within the household, *Journal of consumer research*, Vol. 2, p. 241-260.

(De Sevin et al., 2001) De Sevin E., Kallmann M., and Thalmann D., 2001, Towards Real Time Virtual Human Life Simulations, *Proc. Computer Graphic International (CGI 2001)*, Hong Kong, p.31-37.

(Deborah and Whan, 1991) Deborah J.M., and Whan C.P., 1991, The Differential Role of Characteristics of Music on High- and Low- Involvement Consumers' Processing of Ads, *The Journal of Consumer Research*, Vol. 18, No. 2, p. 161-173.

(Dellaert et al., 2003) Dellaert B.G.C., Borgers A.W.J., Louviere J.J., and Timmermans, H.J.P., 2003, Using conjoint choice experiments to model consumer choices of product component packages, *Conjoint Measurement*, Gustafsson A., Hermann A., and Huber F. (Eds.), New York: Springer Publishing Company.

(Demazeau and Müller, 1991) Demazeau Y., and Müller J.P., 1991, From Reactive to Intentional Agents, *Decentralized A.I. 2*, Y.Demazeau & J.P. Müller Eds, Elsevier.

(Densham and Goodchild, 1989) Densham P.J., and Goodchild M.F., 1989, Spatial decision support systems: A research agenda, *Proc. of GIS/LIS'89*, Orlando, USA, p. 707-716.

(Densham, 1991) Densham P.J., 1991, Spatial decision support systems, *Geographical information systems: principles and applications*, Maguire D.J., Goodchild M.S., and Rhind D.W. (Eds.), London: Longman, p. 403-412.

(Dijkstra and Timmermans, 1999) Dijkstra J., and Timmermans H.J.P., 1999, Towards a Multi-Agent Model for Visualizing Simulated USer Behavior to Support the Assessment of Design Performance, *Media and Design Proces*, ACADIA '99, Ataman O., and Bermúdez J. (Eds.), p.226-237.

(Dijkstra and Timmermans, 1999) Dijkstra J., and Timmermans H.J.P., 1999, Simulating Movement in Shopping Centres, *Proc. of the 6th International Conference on Recent Advances in Retailing and Services Science*, 18-21 July, Croabas.

(Dijkstra and Timmermans, 2000) Dijkstra J., and Timmermans H.J.P., 2000, A Multi-Agent Systems Approach for Visualizing Simulated Behavior to Support the Assessment of Design Performance, *Proc. of the 4th International Conference on Autonomous Agents*, 03-07 June, Barcelona, Spain.

(Dijkstra and Timmermans, 2001) Dijkstra J., and Timmermans H.J.P., 2001, A Multi-Agent System for Visualising Simulated Consumer Behaviour With the Retail Environment, *The Recent Advances in Retailing and Consumer Services Science Conference*, 06-18 August, Vancouver, Canada.

(Dijkstra et al., 2000) Dijkstra J., Timmermans H.J.P., and Jessurun A.J., 2000, A Multi-Agent Cellular Automata System for Visualising Simulated Pedestrian Activity, *Proc. of the 4th International Conference on Cellular Automata for Research and Industry: Theoretical and Practical Issues on Cellular Automata*, Karlsruhe, p. 29-36.

(Dijkstra et al., 2000) Dijkstra J., Timmermans H.J.P., and Vries B., 2000, Towards a Multi-Agent Model for Visualising Simulated User Behaviour within th Built Environment, *Design and Decision Spupport Systems in Urban Planning*, Timmermans H.J.P., and Vries B. (Eds.), Eindhoven: EIRASS.

(Dijkstra et al., 2001) Dijkstra J., Jessurun A.J., and Timmermans H.J.P., 2001, A Multi-agent cellular automata model of pedestrian movement, *Pedestrian and Evacuation Dynamics*, Springer-Verlag, p. 173-181.

(Dijkstra et al., 2003) Dijkstra J., Jessurun A.J., and Timmermans H.J.P., 2003, Simulating Pedestrian activity Scheduling Behaior and Movement Patterns Using A Multi-Agent Cellular Automata Model, *Proc. of the Transportation Research Board Conference*,

(Dijkstra et al., 2003) Dijkstra J., Leeuwen J.P., and Timmermans H.J.P., 2003,. Evaluating Design Alternatives Using Conjoint Experiments in Virtual Reality, *Environment and Planning B: Planning and Design*, Vol. 30, p. 357-367.

(Dijskstra and Timmermans, 2002) Dijkstra J., and Timmermans H.J.P., 2002, Towards a Multi-Agent Model for Visualizing Simulated User Behavior to Support the Assesment of Design Performance, *Automation in Construction*, p. 135-145.

(Dijsktra et al., 2001) Dijsktra J., Harry J.P., and Bauke U., 2001, Virtual reality-based simulation of user behavior within the build environment to support the early stages of building design, *Pedestrian and Evacuation Dynamics*, Schreckenberg M., and Sharma S.D. (ed.): Springer-Verlag, Berlin, p. 173-181.

(DMSO, 2005) Defense Modeling and Simulation Office., 2005, VV&A Recommended practices guide, (http://vva.dmso.mil/Default.htm).

(Drogoul and Ferber, 1992) Drogoul A., and Ferber J., 1992, Multi-Agent Simulation as a Tool for Modeling Societies: Application to Social Differentiation in Ant Colonies, *Proc. of MAAMAW'92*, Viterbo.

(Drogoul et al., 1992) Drogoul A., Ferber J., Corbara B., and Fresneau D., 1992, A Behavioral Simulation Model for the Study of Emergent Social Structures, *Towards a Practice of Autonomous Systems*, MIT Press, Cambridge, p. 161-170.

(Drogoul et al., 2002) Drogoul A., Vanbergue D., and Meurisse T., 2002, Multi-Agent Based Simulation: Where are the Agents?, *Multi-Agent-Based Simulation II*, Sichman J.S., Bousquet F., and Davidsson P. (Eds.), Proceedings of MABS 2002, Third International Worshop, p. 89-104.

(Drogoul et al., 2003) Drogoul A., Vanbergue D., and Meurisse T., 2003, Simulation Orientée Agent: où sont les agents?, *Actes des Journées de Rochebrune*, Rencontres interdisciplinaires sur les systèmes complexes naturels et artificiels, Megève, France.

(Drogoul, 1995) Drogoul A., 1995, When ants play chess, in From reaction to cognition, lecture notes in AI, No. 957, Castelfranchi C., and Müller J.P., (Eds), Springer-Verlag, Berlin-Heidelberg, p. 13-27.

(Drogu Erkip) Dogu U., and Erkip F., 2000, Spatial factors affecting wayfinding and orientation: A case study in a shopping mall, *Environment and Behavior*, Vol. 32, No. 6, p. 731-755.

(Duboz, 2004) Duboz R., 2004, Intégration de modèles héetérogènes pour la modélisation et la simulation de systèmes complexes, *Application à la modélisation multi-échelles en écologie marine*, Thèse de Doctorat, Université du Littoral, Cote d'Opale, Calais.

(Duhaime et al., 1996) Duhaime A., Kindra M., Laroche L., and Muller M., 1996, Le comportement du consommateur, 2ème édition. Gaétan Morin, éditeur.

(Duncan and Olshavsky, 1982) Duncan C. P., and Olshavsky R.W., 1982, External Search: The Role of Consumer Beliefs, Journal of Marketing Research, Vol. 19, No. 3, p. 32-44.

(Eastman et al., 1993) Eastman J.R., Kyem P.A., Toledano J., and Jin W., 1993, GIS and decision making, Geneva: UNITAR.

(Eliashberg et al., 1986) Eliashberg J., LaTour S.A., Rangaswamy A., and Stern L.W., 1986, Assessing the Predictive Accuracy of Two Utility-Based Theories in a Marketing Channel Negotiation Context, *Journal of Marketing Research,* Vol. 23, p. 101-110.

(Engel et al, 1995) Engel J.F., Blackwell R.D., and Miniard P.W., 1995, Consumer behavior (8th ed), Forth Worth, TX: The Dryden Press.

(Engel et al., 1973) Engel J.F., Kollat D.T, and Blackwell. R.D., 1973, Consumer Behavior, 1st ed. New York: Holt, Rinehart and Winston.

(Engel et al., 1973) Engel J.F., Kollat D.T, and Blackwell. R.D., 1973, Consumer Behavior, 2nd ed. New York: Holt, Rinehart and Winston.

(Engel et al., 1995) Engel J.F., Blakwell R.D., and Miniard P.W., 1995, Consumer behaviour, 8th (Eds.), Forth Worth, TX: The Dryden Press.

(Engel, 2002) Engel T.P., 2002, Computer Simulation Techniques, *Journal of Clinical Monitoring and Computing*, Vol. 17, No. 1, p. 3-9.

(Epstein and Axtell, 1996) Epstein J.M., and Axtell R.L., 1996, Growing Artificial Societies, Brookings Institution Press, Washington D.C.

(Eroglu and Gilbert, 1986) Eroglu S.A., and Gilbert D.H., 1986, Retail Crowding: Theoretical and Strategic Implications, *Journal of Retailing*, Vol. 62, p. 346-363.

(Ettema and Timmermans, 1997) Ettema D.F., and Timmermans H.J.P., 1997, Theories and Models of Activity Patterns, *Activity-Based Approaches to Travel Analysis*,

Ettema D.F., and Timmermans H.J.P. (Eds.), Oxford: Pergamon Press, p. 1-36.

(Evans et al., 1996) Evans M.J., Moutinho L., and Raaij W.F., 1996, Applied Consumer Behaviour, Addison-Wesley.

(Faihe and Müller) Faihe Y., and Müller J.P., 1997, Analysis and Design of Robot's Behavior: Towards a Methodology, EWLR 1997, p. 46-61.

(Farenc and Thalmann, 2001) Farenc N., and Thalmann D., 2001, Simulation de la Vie dans une Ville Virtuelle, *Vermessung and Photogrammetrie Kulturtechnik, special issue on visualization*, Vol.7, p.477-479.

(Farenc et al., 1999) Farenc N., Boulic R., and Thalmann D., 1999, An Informed Environment Dedicated to the Simulation of Virtual Humans in Urban Context, *Proc of Eurographics '99*, Milano, Italy, p.309-318.

(Farenc et al., 1999) Farenc N., Raupp S.M., Schweiss E., Kallmann M., Aune O., Boulic R., and Thalmann D., 1999, A Paradigm for Controlling Virtual Humans in Urban Environment Simulations, *Applied Artificial Intelligence Journal*,

(Feng and Liang, 2003) Feng L., and Liang R., 2003, Intelligent Crowd Simulation, *Lecture Notes in Computer Science*, Vol. 2667, p. 462-471.

(Ferber and Drogoul, 1992) Ferber J., and Drogoul A., 1992, Using Reactive Multi-Agent Systems in Simulation and Problem Solving, *Distributed Artificial Intelligence: Theory and Praxis*, ECSC-EEC-EAEC, Bruxelles et Luxembourg, p. 53-80.

(Ferber and Müller, 1996) Ferber J., and Müller J.P., 1996, Influences and Reaction: a Model of Situated Multiagent Systems, ICMAS'96, Kyoto, December 1996.

(Ferber et al., 1997) Ferber J., Labbani O., J.P.Müller J.P., and Bourjault A., 1997, Formalising emergent collective behaviours: preliminary report, *DAIMAS'97*, St-Petersbourg, June 1997.

(Ferber et al., 2000) Ferber J., Gutknecht O., Jonke C.M.r, Jan Treur, and Müller J.P., 2000, Organization Models and Behavioral Requirements Specification for Multi-Agent Systems, ICMAS 2000, p. 387-388.

(Ferber, 1999) Ferber J., 1999, Multi-agent Systems: An Introduction to Distributed Artificial Intelligence, Addison Wesley Longman, England.

(Fishwick, 1995) Fishwick P.A., 1995, Simulation Model Design and Execution: Building Digital Worlds, Prentice Hall, p. 450.

(Fishwick, 1997) Fishwick P.A., 1997, Computer simulation: growth through extension, *Transactions of the Society for Computer Simulation International*, Vol. 14, No. 1, p. 13–23.

(Fortuno et al., 2004) Fortino G., Garro A., and Russo W., 2004, From Modeling to Simulation of Multi-agent Systems: An Integrated Approach and a Case Study, *Lecture Notes in Computer Science*, Vol. 3187, p. 213-227.

(Fotheringham, 1988) Fotheringham A.S., 1988, Consumer Store Choice and Choice Set Definition, *MarketingScience,* Vol. 7, No. 3, p. 299-310.

(Fotheringham, 1998) Fotheringham A.S., 1998, Consumer store choice and choice set definition, *Marketing science*, Vol. 7, No. 4, p. 137-144.

(Foxall, 1996) Foxall G., 1996, Consumers in Context: The BPM Process, International Thomson Business Press.

(Frank and al., 2001) Frank A.U., Bittner S., and Raubal M., 2001, Spatial and Cognitive Simulation with Multi-agent Systems, *Spatial Information Theory-Foundations of*

Geographic Information Science, Montello D. (Ed.), Proc. of COSIT 2001, Morro Bay, CA, USA, p. 124-139.

(Fritzsche et al., 2004) Fritzsche S., Haberlandt R., Vörtler H.L., 2004, Modeling and Simulation of Structure, *Thermodynamics, and Transport of Fluids in Molecular Confinements, Lecture Notes in Physics*, Vol. 634, p. 1-88.

(Frolova and Korobitsin, 2002) Frolova J., and Korobitsin V., 2002, Simulation of Gender Artificial Society: Multi-agent Models of Subject-Object Interactions, *Lecture Notes in Computer Science*, Vol. 2329, p. 226.

(Gardner, 1985) Gardner M.P., 1985, Mood states and consumer behavior: A critical review, *The Journal of Consumer Research*, Vol. 12, No. 3, p. 281-300.

(Garling et al., 1982) Garling T., Book A., and Ergezen N., 1982, Memory of the spatial layout of the everyday physical environment, *Scandinavian Journal of Psychology*, Vol. 23, p. 23-35.

(Garling et al., 1982) Garling T., Book A., and Ergezen N., 1982, Memory of the spatial layout of the everyday physical environment, *Scandinavian Journal of Psychology*, Vol. 23, p. 23-35.

(Gat and Müller, 1992) Gat Y., and Müller J.P., 1992, Reactive Navigation based on Simple World Modeling, *Proc. of 9th Israeli Symposium on Artificial Intelligence*, 1992.

(Gilbert and kahl, 1992) Gilber D., and Kahl J.A., 1982, The American Class Structure: A New Synthesis, Homewood, IL: Dorsey Press.

(Gilbert and Troitzsch, 1999) Gilbert N., and Troitzsch, K.G., 1999, Simulation for the Social Scientist, Open University Press.

(Gloor et al., 2004) Gloor C., Stucki P., and Nagel K., 2004, Hybrid Techniques for Pedestrian Simulations, *Lecture Notes in Computer Science*, Vol. 3305, p. 581-590.

(Goncalvez et al., 2002) Goncalvez L.M.G., Kallmann M., and Thalmann D., 2002, Defining Behaviors for Autonomous Agents based on Local Perception and Smart Objects, *Computer Grahics Forum*, Vol. 21, No 4, p. 767-776.

(Gordon et al., 1996) Gordon D.B.C., and Gordon I.D.D., 1996, PARAMICS-Parallel microscopic simulation of road traffic, *The Journal of Supercomputing (Historical Archive)*, Vol. 10, No. 1, p. 25-53.

(Grether and Wilde, 1983) Grether D.M., and Wilde L.L., 1983, Consumer choice and information: New experimental evidence. Information Economics and Policy, Vol. 1, p. 115-144.

(Grether et al., 1985) Grether D.M., Schwartz A., and Wilde L.L., 1985, The irrelevance of Information Overload: An analysis of search and Disclosure, Southerne California Law Review, Vol. 59, p. 277-303.

(Grier, 1992) Grier A.D., 1992, Graphical techniques for output analysis, *Proc. of the 1992 Winter Simulation Conference*,

(Grönroos, 1984) Grönroos C., 1984, A Service Quality Model and its Marketing Implications," *European Journal of Marketing*, Vol. 18, No. 4, p. 36-44.

(Grönroos, 1993) Grönroos C., 1993, Toward a Third Phase in Service Quality Research: Challenges and Future Directions," *Advances in Services Marketing and Management*, Vol. 2, p. 49-64.

(Groumpos and Merkuryev, 2002) Groumpos P.P., and Merkuryev Y., 2002, A methodology of Discrete-Event Simulation of Manufacturing Systems: an overview, *Studies in Informatics and Control: with emphasis on useful applications of advanced technology*, Vol. 11, No. 1, p. 103-110.

(Guermond et al., 2004) Guermond Y., Delahaye D., Dubos-Paillard E., and Langlois P., 2004, From modelling to experiment, *GeoJournal*, Vol. 59, No. 3, p. 171-176.

(Guessoum, 2000) Guessoum Z., 2000, A multi-agent simulation framework, *Transactions of the Society for Computer Simulation International*, Vol. 17, No. 1, p. 2–11.

(Gunter and Furnham, 1992) Gunter B., and Furnham A., 1992, Consumer Profiles: An Introduction to Psychographics, International Thomson Business Press.

(Hare, 1976) Hare A.P., 1976, Handbook of small group research, New York: free Press.

(Harrell and Hutt, 1975) Harrell G.D., and Hutt M.D., 1975, Buyer behavior Under Conditions of Crowding: An Initial Framework.

(Hassay and smith, 1996) Hassay D.N., and Smith M.C., 1996, Compulsive buying: An examination of the consumption motive, *Psychology and Marketing*, Vol. 13, p. 741-752.

(Havlena and Holbrook, 1986) Havlena W.J., and Holbrook M.B., 1986, The Varieties of Consumption Experience, *Journal of Consumer Research*, Vol. 13, No. 3, p. 394-404.

(Haynes et al., 1994) Haynes J.L., Pipkin A.L., Black W.C., and Cloud R.M., 1994, Application of a choice sets model to assess patronage decision styles of high involvement consumers.

(Heinze et al., 2000) Heinze C., Papasimeon M., and Goss S., 2000, Specifying Agent Behaviour with Use Cases, *Lecture Notes in Computer Science*, Vol. 1881, p. 128.

(Helgeson et al., 1984) Helgeson J.G., Kluge E.A., Mager J., and Taylor C., 1984, Trends in Consumer Behavior Litareature: A content analysis, *The Journal of Consumer Research*, Vol. 10, No. 4, p. 449-454.

(Hempel and Jain, 1978) Hempel D.J., and Jain S.C., 1978, House Buying Behavior, *Journal of the American Real Estate and Urban Economics Association*, Vol. 6, p. 1-21.

(Hermann, 1967) Hermann C.F., 1967, Validation problems in games and simulations with special reference to models of international politics, *Behavioral Science, Vol.* 12, No. 3, p. 216–231.

(Hernandez and Biasiotto, 2001) Hernandez T., and Biasiotto M. 2001, Retail location Decision-making and Store Portfolio management, *Canadian Journal of Regional Sciences*, Vol. XXIV, No. 3.

(Herr and Fazio, 1993) Herr P., and Fazio R., 1993, The Attitude-to-Behavior Process: Implications for Consumer Behavior, *Advertising, Exposure, Memory, and Choice*, Mitchell A. (Eds.), (Hillsdale, N.J.: Lawrence Erlbaum Associates).

(Hilmer and Dennis, 2000) Hilmer K.M., and Dennis A., 2000, Stimulating Thinking in Group Decision Making, *Proc. of the Thirty-Third Annual Hawaii International Conference on Systems Sciences*,

(Hirschmann, 1991) Hirschman E.C., 1981, American Jewish Ethnicity, Its Relationship to Some Selected Aspects of Consumer Behavior, *Journal of Marketing*, Vol. 45, p. 102-110.

(Homans, 1950) Homans G., 1950, The human group. New York: Harcourt.

(Howard and Sheth, 1969) Howard J.A., and Sheth J.N., 1969, The Theory of Buyer Behavior, New York: John Wiley and Sons.

(Howard and Sheth, 1978) Howard J.A., and Sheth J.N., 1978, The Theory of Buyer Behavior, NX: Wiley, Huff, J.0., and W.A.V.Clark, Cumulative Stress and Cumulative Inertia, Environment and Planning A.

(Iglehart and Shedler, 1984) Iglehart D.L., Shedler G.S, 1984, Simulation output analysis for local area computer networks, *Acta Informatica (Historical Archive)*, Vol. 21, No. 4, p. 321-338.

(Ingalls, 2001) Ingalls R.G., 2001, Introduction to simulation, *Proc. of the 33nd conference on Winter simulation*, IEEE Computer Society, p. 7–16,

(Ioan et al., 2001) Ioan A.L., Craciun F., and Zoltan K., 2001, Towards Validation of Specifications by Simulation, *Lecture Notes in Computer Science*, Vol. 1887, p. 293.

(Iz, 1992) Iz P.H., 1992, An Experimental Assessment of Preference Aggregation in a Group Decision Support System Based on Multiple Criteria Optimization, *Proc. of the Twenty-Fifth Annual Hawaii International Conference on Systems Sciences*,

(Jager, 2000) Jager W., 2000, Modelling consumer behavior, Ph.D. thesis, Universal Press, Veenendaal.

(Janiszewski, 1995) Janiszewski C., 1995, Increasing the Effectiveness of In-Store Displays, Stores, RR1-RR4.

(Jankowski et al., 1997) Jankowski P., Nyerges T.L., Smith A., Moore T.J., and Horvath E., 1997, Spatial group choice: a SDSS tool for collaborative spatial decision-making, International Journal of Geographical Information Systems, Vol. 11, No. 6, p. 566-602.

(Janssen and Jager, 1999) Janssen M.A., and Jager W., 1999, An integrated approach to simulating behavioural processes: A case study of the lock-in of consumption patterns. Journal of Artificial Societies and Social Simulation, Vil. 2, No. 2. Online at http://jasss.soc.surrey.ac.uk/2/2/2.html.

(Jennings and Wooldridge, 1998) Jennings N.R., and Woolridge M., 1995, Applying agent technology, *Journal of Applied Artificial Intelligence*, Vol. 9, No. 4, p. 351-369.

(Jennings, 2000) Jennings N.R., 2000, On agent-based software engineering, *Artificial Intelligence,* Vol. 117, p. 277-296.

(Jonker et al., 2002) Jonker C.M., Treur J., and Wijngaards W.C.A., 2002, Temporal Languages for Simulation and Analysis of the Dynamics within an Organisation, *Lecture Notes in Computer Science*, Vol. 2296, p. 151.

(Jordan and al., 1998) Jordan T., Raubal M., Gartrell B., and Egenhofer M., 1998, An Affordance-Based Model of Place in GIS, *8th Int. Symposium on Spatial Data Handling, SDH'98*, Poiker T., and Chrisman N. (Eds.), Vancouver, Canada, p. 98-109.

(Kahn and Schmittlein, 1989) Kahn B.E., and Schmittlein D.C., 1989, Shopping trip behavior: An empirical investigation, *Marketing Letters (Historical Archive)*, Vol.1, No. 1, p. 55-69.

(Kallmann et al., 2000) Kallmann M., Monzani J.S., Caicedo A., and Thalmann D., 2000, A Common Environment for Simulating Virtual Human Agents in Real Time, *Proc. of the Workshop on Achieving Human-Like Behavior in Interactive Animated*

Agents, AGENTS, Barcelona, Spain

(Kallmann et al., 2001) Kallmann M., De Sevin E., and Thalmann D., 2001, Constructing Virtual Human Life Simulations, *Deformable Avatars*, Kluwer Publ., p.240-247.

(Kalyanam and Pulter, 1997) Kalyanam K. and Pulter D.S., 1997, Incorporating Demongraphic Variables in Brand ChoiceModels: An Indivisible Alternative Framework, *Marketing Sciences*, Vol. 16, No. 2, p.166-181.

(Kamara et al., 2003) Kamara L., Artikis A., Neville B., and Pitt J., 2003, Simulating Computational Societies, *Lecture Notes in Computer Science*, Vol. 2577, p. 53-67.

(Kaplan and Kaplan, 1989) Kaplan R., and Kaplan S., 1989. The Experience of Nature: A Psychological Perspective, Cambridge University Press.

(Kassarjian, 1971) Kassarjian H.H., 1971, Personality and Consumer Behavior: A Review, *The Journal of Marketing Research*, Vol. 8, No. 4, p. 409-418.

(Keiki et al., 2003) Takadama K., Suematsu Y.L., Sugimoto N., Nawa N.E., and Shimohara K., 2003, Towards Verification and Validation in Multiagent-Based Systems and Simulations: Analyzing Different Learning Bargaining Agents, *Lecture Notes in Computer Science*, Vol. 2927, p. 26-42.

(Kelton, 1983) Kelton W.D., 1983, Simulation analysis, Proc. of the 15th conference on Winter simulation, Arlington, Virginia, United States, p.159-168.

(Kelton, 1997) Kelton D.W., 1997, Statistical analysis simulation output, *Proc. of the 1997 Winter Simulation Conference*,

(Klabbers and Timmermans, 1999) Klabbers M.D., and Timmermans H.J.P., 1999, Measuring Consumer Shopping Decision-Making Using ESCAPE, *6th International Conference on Recent Advances in Retailing and Services Science*, 18-21 July, Las Croabas, Puerto Rico.

(Klügl et al., 2005) Klügl F., Fehler M., and Herrler R., 2005, About the Role of the Environment in Multi-agent Simulations, *Lecture Notes in Computer Science*, Vol. 3374, p. 127-149.

(Koch, 2001) Koch A., 2001, Linking Multi-Agent Systems and GIS- Modeling and simulating spatial interactions-, Department of Geography RWTH Aachen. Angewandte Geographische Informationsverarbeitung XII, Beiträge zum AGIT-Symposium Salzburg 2000, Hrsg.: Strobl/Blaschke/Griesebner, Heidelberg, p. 252-262.

(Konishi and Standfort, 2001) Konishi H., and Standfort M., 2001, Anchor Stores. *Journal of Urban Economics*, Vol. 53, p. 413-435.

(Konishi and Standfort, 2001) Konishi H., and Standfort M., 2001, Anchor Stores, *Journal of Urban Economics*, Vol. 53, p. 413-435.

(Kotler, 1973) Kotler P., 1973, Atmosphere as a Marketing Tool, *Journal of Retailing*, Vol.18, p. 25-26.

(Kriewall, 1980) Kriewall M.O., 1980, Modeling multi-person decision processes on major consumption decision, Unpublished dissertation, Department of marketing. Stanford university. Stanford, CA 94305.

(Kurose et al., 1998) Kurose S., Borgers A.W.J., and Timmermans H.J.P., 1998, Predicting Pedestrian Shopping Behaviour Using Choice Heuristics, *5th Recent Advances in Retailing and Services Science Conference*, Baveno, Italy.

(Kurose et al., 2001) Kurose S., Borgers A.W.J., and Timmermans H.J.P., 2001,

Classifying Pedestrian Shopping Behaviour According To Implied Heuristic Choice Rules, *Environment and Planning B: Planning and Design*, Vol. 28, p. 405-418.

(Labbani-Igbida et al., 1998) Labbani-Igbida O., Müller J.P., and Bourjault A., 1998, *Cirta*: An Emergentist Methodology to Design and Evaluate Collective Behaviors in robots' colonies, CRW 1998, p. 72-84.

(Lamm and Myers, 1978) Lamm H., and Myers D.G., 1978, Group induced polarization of attitudes and behaviour, *Advances in Experimental Social Psychology*, Berkowitz L. (Ed.), Vol. 11, New York: Academic Press, p. 145-195.

(Lee and Sternthal, 1999) Lee A., and Sternthal B., 1999, The Effects of Positive Mood on Memory, *Journal of Consumer Research*, Vol. 26, p. 115-127.

(Lees et al., 2005) Lees M., Loga B., Minson R., Oguara T., and Theodoropoulos G, 2005, Distributed Simulation of MAS, *Lecture Notes in Computer Science*, Vol. 3415, p. 25-36.

(Lees et al., 2005) Lees M., Loga B., Minson R., Oguara T., and Theodoropoulos G, 2005, Modelling Environments for Distributed Simulation, *Lecture Notes in Computer Science*, Vol. 3374, p. 150-167.

(Lemoine, 2001) Lemoine J.F., 2001, Comment tenir compte des emotions du consommateur. *Revue Française de Gestion*, Vol. 134, p. 47-60.

(Lewison, 1994) Lewison D.M., 1994, Retailing (5th ed.). New York: Macmillan College Publishing Company.

(Lombardo et al., 2004) Lombardo S., Petri M., and Zotta D., 2004, Intelligent Gis and Retail Location Dynamics: A Multi Agent System Integrated with ArcGis, *Lecture Notes in Computer Science*, Vol. 3044, p. 1046-1056.

(Loudon and Della, 1993) Loudon, D., and Della B.J.A., 1993, Consumer Behaviour: Concepts and Applications, 4/e, McGraw-Hill.

(Luengo and Iglesias, 2004) Luengo F., and Iglesias A., 2004, Framework for Simulating the Human Behavior for Intelligent Virtual Agents. *Part II: Behavioral System*, Lecture Notes in Computer Science, Vol. 3039, p. 237-244.

(Magnenat Thalmann and Thalmann, 2004) Magnenat-Thalmann N., and Thalmann D., 2004, Handbook of Virtual Humans, John Wiley, 2004.

(Magnenat-Thalmann and Thalmann, 1999) Magnenat-Thalmann N., and Thalmann D., 1999,Computer Animation and Simulation 99, Springer Verlag, Wien.

(Maier and Grobler, 1998) Maier F.H., and Grobler A., 1998, What are we talking about? - A taxonomy of computer simulations to support learning, *System Dynamics Review*, Vol.16, No. 2, p. 135-148.

(Maitland, 1990) Maitland B., 1990, The new architecture of the retail mall, Architecture Design and Technology Press, London.

(Mandl, 2000) Mandl P., 2000, Geo-Simulation- Experimentieren und Problemlösen mit GIS-Modellen. *Angewandte Geographische Informationsverarbeitung XII*, Hrsg.: Strobl/Blaschke/Griesebner, Wichmann Heidelberg, p. 345-356.

(Marcenac and Giroux, 1998) Marcenac P., and Giroux S., 1998, GEAMAS: A Generic Architecture for Agent-Oriented Simulations of Complex Processes, *Applied Intelligence*, Vol. 8, No. 3, p. 247-267.

(Marcenac and Giroux, 1998) Marcenac P., and Giroux S., 1998, GEAMAS : A Generic

Architecture for Agent-Oriented Simulations of Complex Processes, *International Journal of Applied Intelligence, Neural Networks, and Complex Problem-Solving Technologies*, Kluwer Academic Publishers, Vol. 8, No. 3, p. 247-267.

(Marcus et al., 2003) Marcus G. E., MacKuen M., Wolak J., and Keele L., 2003, The measure and mismeasure of emotion. *Shambaugh Conference on Affect and Cognition in Political Action*,

(Marietto et al., 2003) Marietto M.B., David N., Sichman J.S, and Coelho H., 2003, Requirements Analysis of Agent-Based Simulation Platforms: State of the Art and New Prospects, *Lecture Notes in Computer Science*, Vol. 2581, p. 125-141.

(Marmorstein et al., 1992) Marmorstein H., Grewal D., and Fishe R., 1992, The Value of Time Spent in Price-Comparison Shopping: Survey and Experimental Evidence, *Journal of Consumer Research*, Vol. 19, p. 52-61.

(Maslow, 1954) Maslow A., 1954, Motivation and Personality, 2nd ed., Harper and Row.

(Matthew and Graem, 1999) Matthew M. H., Graem A.R., 1999, Actors and Agents, *Lecture Notes in Computer Science*, Vol. 1630, p. 139.

(McConnell, 1996) McConnell S., 1996, Software Quality at Top Speed.

(McGuire, 1976) McGuire W., 1976, Some internal psychological factors influencing consumer choice, *The Journal of Consumer Research*, Vol. 2, No. 4, p. 302-319.

(Mehrabian and Russel, 1974) Mehrabian A., and Russel J.A., 1974, An approach to environmental psychology, Cambridge, MA: MIT Press.

(Mehrabian, 1995) Mehrabian A., 1995, Framework for a comprehensive description and measurement of emotional states, *Genetic, Social, and General Psychology Monographs*, Vol. 121, p. 339-361.

(Mehrabian, 1998) Mehrabian A., 1998, Manual for a comprehensive system of measures of emotional states: The PAD Model. Albert Mehrabian, 1130 Alta Mesa Road, Monterey, CA, USA 93940.

(Meurisse and Vanbergue, 2001) Meurisse T., and Vanbergue D., 2001, Et maintenant à qui le tour? Aperˏcu de Problématiques de Conception de Simulations Multi-Agents. *Actes de la conf´erence Agents Logiciels, Coopration, Apprentissage et Activités humaines ALCAA'01*.

(Meyer et al., 2003) Meyer D., Karatzoglou A., Leisch F., Buchta C., and Hornik K., 2003, A Simulation Framework for Heterogeneous Agents, *Computational Economics*, Vol. 22, No. 2, p. 285-301.

(Michel et al., 2003) Michel F., Abdelkader G., and Ferber J., 2003, Weak Interaction and Strong Interaction in Agent Based Simulations. *Multi-Agent-Based Simulation III, Proceedings of MABS 2003, Fourth International Worshop*, Hales D., Edmonds B., Norling E., and Rouchier J. (Eds.), p. 43–56.

(Michel, 2000) Michel F., 2000, Une approche m´ethodologique pour l'analyse et la conception de simulateur multi-agents, *Cinquièmes rencontres des Jeunes Chercheurs en Intelligence Artificielle*, AFIA, p. 269–279.

(Michel, 2001) Michel F., 2001, Le mod`ele Influence/R´eaction pour la Simulation Multi-Agents. *Actes des 1ères Journées Francophones des Modèles Formels de l'Interaction, MFI' 01*, Chaib-draa B., and Enjalbert P. (Eds.), Vol. 3, p. 391–406.

(Michon et al., 2005) Michon R., Chebat J.C., and Turley L.W., 2005, Mall atmospherics: the interaction effects of the mall environment on shopping behavior. *Journal of*

Business Research, Vol. 58, p. 576-583.

(Miller, 1998) Miller D., 1998, A Theory of Shopping, Cornell University Press.

(Millman, 1982) Millman R.E., 1982, Using Background Music to Affect the Behavior of Supermarket Shoppers, *Journal of Marketing*, Vol. 46, p. 86-91.

(Minar et al., 1996) Minar N., Burkhart R., Langton C., and Askenazi M., 1996, The Swarm Simulation System: A Toolkit for Building Multi-Agent Simulations, Santa Fe Institute Working Paper #96-06-042.

(Mohan, 1995) Mohan M., 1995, The Influence of Marital Roles in Consumer Decision Making, *Irish Marketing Review-Dublin*, Vol. 8, p. 97-106.

(Moreno et al., 2003) Moreno A., Valls A., and Marín M., 2003, Multi-agent Simulation of Work Teams, *Lecture Notes in Computer Science*, Vol. 2691, p. 281.

(Morris, 1956) Morris C., 1956, Varieties of Human Value. Chicago: University of Chicago Press.

(Morris, 1988) Morris M., 1988, Things to Do in Shopping Centers. Feminist Cultural Criticism (Eds.), Sheridan S., New York: Verso, p. 193-225.

(Moschis, 1992) Moschis G.P., 1992, Marketing to older consumers: A handbook of information for strategy development, Westport, Connecticut: Quorum Books.

(Moss and Davidson, 2000) Moss S., and Davidsson P., 2000, Multi-Agent-Based Simulation, *Proc. of the 2nd International Workshop MASB 2000*, Springer Verlag, LNAI, No.1979.

(Moss et al., 1998) Moss S., Gaylard H., Wallis S., and Edmonds B., 1998, SDML: A Multi-Agent Language for Organizational Modelling, *Computational and Mathematical Organization Theory*, Vol. 4, No. 1, p. 43–69.

(Moss, 1999) Moss A.M., 1999, What's new in store fixtures, *Furniture Design and Manufacturing*, Vol. 71, No. 7, p. 46-52.

(Moulin et al., 2003) Moulin B., Chaker W., Perron J., Pelletier P., and Hogan J., 2003, MAGS Project: Multi-agent geosimulation and crowd simulation. *Proc. of the COSIT'03 Conference*, Kuhn W. and Timp F. (Eds.), Spatial Information Theory, Springer Verlag *Lecture Notes in Computer Science*, Vol. 2825, p. 151-168.

(Müller, 1993) Müller J.P., 1993, Systèmes multiagents appliqués aux problèmes complexes, INFAUTOM'93, Aerospace Engineer School, Toulouse.

(Müller, 2003) Müller J.P., 2003, Emergence of Collective Behaviour and Problem Solving, ESAW, p. 1-21.

(Murray, 1938) Murray H. A., 1938, Explorations in Personality. *New York: Oxford University Press*.

(Musse and Thalmann, 1997) Musse S.R., and Thalmann D., 1997, A Model of Human Crowd Behavior, Computer Animation and Simulation '97, Eurographics workshop, Budapest, Springer Verlag, Wien, p.39-51.

(Musse and Thalmann, 2000) Musse S.R., and Thalmann D., 2000, From One Virtual Actor to Virtual Crowds: Requirements and Constraints, *Proc. Agents 2000*, p. 52-53.

(Musse and Thalmann, 2001) Musse S.R., and Thalmann D., 2001, A Behavioral Model for Real Time Simulation of Virtual Human Crowds, *IEEE Transactions on Visualization and Computer Graphics*, Vol.7, No. 2, p.152-164.

(Musse et al., 1998) Musse S.R., Babski C., Capin T., and Thalmann D., 1998, Crowd

Modelling in Collaborative Virtual Environments, ACM VRST /98, Taiwan.

(Myers and Kaplan, 1976) Myers D.G., and Kaplan M.F., 1976, Group-induced polarization in simulated juries. *Personality and Social Psychology Bulletin*, Vol. 2, p. 63-66.

(Myers and Lamm, 1975) Myers D.G., and Lamm H., 1975, The polarizing effects of group discussion. *American Scientist*, Vol. 63, p. 297-303.

(Myers and Lamm, 1976) Myers D.G., and Lamm H., 1976, The group polarization phenomenon, *Psychological Bulletin*, Vol. 83, p. 602-627.

(Myers et al., 1974) Myers D.G., Bach P.J., and Schreiber B.V., 1974, Normative and informational effects of group interaction, *Sociometry*, Vol. 37, p. 275-286.

(Myers, 1975) Myers D.G., 1975, Discussion-induced attitude polarization, *Human Relations*, Vol. 28, p. 699-714.

(Myers, 1978) Myers D.G., 1978, Polarizing effects of social comparison, *Journal of Experimental Social Psychology*, Vol. 14, p. 554-563.

(Myers, 1979) Myers D.G., 1979, How groups intensify decisions, *Human Nature*, Annual Editions: Psychology 80/81, 81/82 and in Readings in Social Psychology, p. 34-39.

(Myers, 1982) Myers D.G., 1982, Polarizing effects of social interaction. Brandstätter H., Davis J.H., and Stocker-Kreichgauer G. (Eds.), Group Decision Making. London: Academic Press, p. 125-161.

(NCGIA, 1990) NCGIA., 1990, Spatial decision support systems, Initiative 6 NCGIA Technical Paper 90-5, UC Santa Barbara.

(Nicosa, 1966) Nicosa F.M., 1966, Consumer Decision Processes, Englewood Cliffs, N.J.: Prentice-Hall, Okoruwa, A. A. and G. D. Jud, Buyer Satisfaction with Residential Brokerage Services, Journal of Real Estate Research, Vol. 10, p. 15-21.

(Norling et al., 2000) Norling E., Sonenberg L., and Rönnquist R., 2000, Enhancing Multi-Agent Based Simulation with Human-Like Decision Making Strategies, *Lecture Notes in Computer Science*, Vol. 1979, p. 214.

(Norman, 1988) Norman D.A., 1988, The Psychology of Everyday Things (1st edition), New York, Basic Books Inc.

(Nuno et al. , 2002) Nuno D., Sichman J.S., and Coelho H., 2002, Towards an Emergence-Driven Software Process for Agent-Based Simulation, *Multi-Agent-Based Simulation II, Proceedings of MABS 2002, Third International Worshop*, Sichman J.S., Bousquet F., and Davidsson P. (Eds.), LNAI, Vol. 2581, Springer-Verlag 2003, p. 89–104.

(Nuno et al., 2000) David N., Sichman J.S, and Helder H., 2000, Agent-Based Social Simulation with Coalitions in Social Reasoning, *Lecture Notes in Computer Science*, Vol. 1979, p. 244.

(Nuno et al., 2003) David N., Sichman J.S, Helder and H., 2003, Towards an Emergence-Driven Software Process for Agent-Based Simulation, *Lecture Notes in Computer Science*, Vol. 2581, p. 89.

(Obst and Rollmann, 2004) Oliver Obst O., and Rollmann M., 2004, Spark-A Generic Simulator for Physical Multi-agent Simulations, *Lecture Notes in Computer Science*, Vol. 3187, p. 243-257.

(Odell et al. , 2002) Odell J.P., H. Van D.H., Fleischer M., and Breuckner S., 2002, Modeling Agents and their Environment. *Agent-Oriented Software Engineering*

(AOSE) III, Giunchiglia F., Odell, J.P., and Weiss G. (Eds.), *Lecture Notes on Computer Science*, Vol. 2585, Springer, Berlin, p. 16-31.

(Odell et al., 2000) Odell J., Parunak H.V., and Bauer B., 2000, Extending UML for Agents, In Proc. of the *Agent-Oriented Information systems Workshop* at 17th National conference on Artifical Intelligence, Austin, TX.

(Oechslein et al., 2002) Oechslein C., Klügl F., Herrler R., and Puppe F., 2002, UML for Behavior-Oriented Multi-agent Simulations, *Lecture Notes in Computer Science*, Vol. 2296, p. 217.

(Okuyama et al., 2005) Okuyama F.Y., Bordini R.H., and Carlos A.R.C., 2005, ELMS: An Environment Description Language for Multi-agent Simulation, *Lecture Notes in Computer Science*, Vol. 3374, p. 24–33.

(Oliver, 1981) Oliver R., 1981, A Cognitive Model of the Antecedents and Consequences of Satisfaction Decisions, *Journal of Marketing Research*, Vol. 17, p. 460-469.

(Olivier, 1997) Oliver R., 1997, Satisfaction: A Behavioural Perspective on the Consumer, McGraw-Hill.

(OMERS, 2001) OMERS Realty Corporation, 2001. Square One shopping center, Calss handout.

(Onkvisit and Shaw, 1997) Onkvisit S., and Shaw J.J., 1994, Consumer Behaviour: Strategy and Analysis, Macmillan College Publishing Company.

(OPCS, 1980) OPCS, 1980, Classification of Occupations, London: HMSO.

(Oppewal and Timmermans, 1997) Oppewal H., and Timmermans H.J.P., 1997, Perception of Public Space in Shopping Areas, *Proc. of the Australia - New Zealand Marketing Educators' Conference*. Reed P.W. et al (Eds.), Monash University, Melbourne, p. 485-486.

(Oppewal and Timmermans, 1999) Oppewal H., and Timmermans H.J.P., 1999, Modeling Consumer Perception of Public Space in Shopping Centers. *Environment and Behavior*, Vol. 31, p. 45-65.

(Oppewal et al., 1997) Oppewal H., Timmermans H.J.P., and Louviere J.J., 1997, Modelling the Effects of Shopping Centre Size and Store Variety on Consumer Choice Behaviour, *Environment and Planning. Part A*, International Journal of Urban and Regional Research, Vol. 29, p. 1073-1090.

(O'Sullivan and Torrens., 2000) O'Sullivan D., and Torrens P.M., 2000, Research issues in cellular automata, *Cellular Automata in Spatial Modelling: A Seminar to Evaluate the State of the Art*, Spatial Analysis Group, Cardiff University, and Centre for Advanced Spatial Analysis, University College London, London.

(Palan, 2001) Palan K.M., 2001, Gender identity in consumer behavior research: A literature review and research agenda, *Academy of Marketing Scence Review*, Vol. 6, No. 10.

(Palm, 1976) Palm R., 1976, Real Estate Agents and Geographical Information, *Geographical Review*, Vol. 66, p. 266-80.

(Panangadan and Dyer, 2001) Panangadan A., and Dyer M.G., 2001, Construction by Autonomous Agents in a Simulated Environment, *Lecture Notes in Computer Science*, Vol. 2130, p. 963.

(Park et al., 1994) Park C., Mothersbaugh D., and Feick L., 1994, Consumer Knowledge and Assessment, *Journal of Consumer Research*, Vol. 21, p. 71-82.

(Parker, 2001) Parker M.T., 2001, What is Ascape and Why Should You Care?, *The Journal of Artificial Societies and Social Simulation JASSS*, Vol. 4, No. 1.

(Parunak and Odell, 2002) Parunak H.D., and Odell J., 2002, Representing social structures in UML, Agent-Oriented Software Engineering II, *Lecture notes in computer science*, Vol. 2222. Springer, p. 1-16.

(Parunak et al. , 1998) Parunak H.D., Savit R., and Riolo R.L., 1998, Agent-Based Modeling vs. Equation-Based Modeling: A Case Study and Users' Guide. *Proc. of the 1st Workshop on Modelling Agent Based Systems, MABS'98*, Schiman J.S., Conte R., and Gilbert N. (Eds.), Vol. LNAI 1534, Lecture Notes in Artificial Intelligence LNAI, Springer-Verlag, Berlin.

(Pellet, 1990) Pellet J., 1990, The Power of Lighting, *Direct Marketing*, p. 71-74.

(Pendse, 2000) Pendse N., 2000, Glossary, the OLAP report, http://www.olapreport.com/fasmi.htin.

(Peres and Bergmann, 2005) Peres J., and Bergmann U., 2005, Experiencing AUML for MAS Modeling: A Critical View, in Proc. of *Software Engineering for Agent-Oriented Systems* (SEAS), p. 11-20.

(Perner, 2005) Perner L., 2005, The psychology of consumers: consumer behavior and marketing. Teaching resources, http://www.consumerpsychologist.com/ and http://www.larsperner.com/.

(Perram and Müller, 1996) Perram J.W., and Müller J.P., 1996, Distributed Software Agents and Applications, 6th European Workshop on Modelling Autonomous Agents, MAAMAW '94, Odense, Denmark, August 3-5.

(Perron and Moulin, 2004) Perron J., and Moulin B., 2004, Un modèle de mémoire dans un système multi-agent de géo-simulation, *Revue d'Intelligence Artificielle*, Hermes.

(Petrof, 1978) Petrof V.J., 1978, Comportement du consommateur et Marketing, Les Presses de l'Université Laval.

(Pols et al., 1997) Pols E., Koelemeijer K., Oppewal H., Timmermans H.J.P., and Verhallen T., 1997, Assortments and the Process of Deciding Where to Shop and What to Purchase. *4th Recent Advances in Retailing and Services Science Conference*, Scottsdale, Arizona, USA.

(Ponje et al., 1999) Ponje M.M.W., Borgers A.W.J., and Timmermans H.J.P., 1999, Shopping Behavior in the Context of Activity Patterns, *6th International Conference on Recent Advances in Retailing and Services Science*, 18-21 July, Las Croabes, Puerto Rico.

(Popkowski and Timmermans, 1997) Popkowski L.P.T.L., and Timmermans H.J.P., 1997, Store-Switching Behavior. *Marketing Letters*, Vol. 8, p. 193-204.

(Popkowski and Timmermans, 2001) Popkowski L.P.T.L., and Timmermans H.J.P., 2001, Experimental Choice Analysis of Shopping Strategies, *Journal of Retailing*.

(Popkowski et al., 2000) Popkowski L.P.T.L., Sinha A., and Timmermans H.J.P., 2000, Consumer Store Choice Dynamics, *Marketing Science Conference*, Los Angeles, US.

(Portugali, 1999) Portugali J., 1999, Self-Organization and the City, Heidelberg: Springer-Verlag.

(Praehofer et al. , 1993) Praehofer H., Auering F., and Reisinger G., 1993, An Environment for DEVS-Based Multi-Formalism Simulation in Common

Lisp/CLOS. *Discrete Event Dynamic Systems: Theory and Applications*, Vol. 3, No. 2, p. 119–149.

(Prandy, 1990) Prandy K., 1990, The Revised Cambridge Scale of Occupations, *Sociology*, Vol. 24, No. 4, p. 629-655.

(Qualls, 1982) Qualls W.J., 1982, Changing Sex Roles: Its Impact upon Family Decision Making, In *Advances in Consumer Research*, Vol. 9. Ed. Andrew Mitchell. St. Louis, MO: Association for Consumer Research, p. 267-270.

(Ramanath and Gilbert, 2003) Ramanath A.M., and Gilbert N., 2003, Towards a Methodology for Agent-based Social Simulation Research, Agent-based Social simulation SIG, Barcelona.

(Raney et al., 2002) Raney B., Voellmy A., Cetin N., Vrtic M., and Nagel K., 2002, Towards a Microscopic Traffic Simulation of All of Switzerland, *Lecture Notes in Computer Science*, Vol. 2329, p. 371.

(Rao and Steckel, 1991) Rao V.R., and Steckel J.H., 1991, A polarization model for describing group preferences, *The Journal of consumer research*, Vol. 18, No. 1, p. 108-118.

(Ratneshwar and Allan, 1991) Ratneshwar D., and Allan D. S., 1991, Substitution in Use and the Role of Usage Context in Product Category Structures, Journal of Marketing Research, Vol. 28, p. 281-295.

(Raubal and al., 1997) Raubal M., Egenhofer M., Pfoser D., and Tryfona N., 1997, Structuring Space with Image Schemata: Wayfinding in Airports as a Case Study, *Proc. of the 1st Workshop on Modelling Agent Based Systems, MABS'98, Proc. of the 1st Workshop on Modelling Agent Based Systems, MABS'98*, Hirtle S., and Frank A. (Eds.), Laurel Highlands, PA. Lecture Notes in Computer Science 1329, Springer-Verlag, Berlin, p. 85-102.

(Raubal and Egenhofer, 1998) Raubal M., and Egenhofer M., 1998, Comparing the complexity of wayfinding tasks in built environments, *Environment and Planning B*, Vol. 25, No. 6, p. 895-913.

(Raubal and Winter, 2002) Raubal M., and Winter S., 2002, Enriching Wayfinding Instructions with Local Landmarks, *Geographic Information Science - Second International Conference GIScience 2002*, Egenhofer M., and Mark M. (Eds.), Boulder, CO, USA, September 2002, Lecture Notes in Computer Science 2478, Springer, Berlin, p. 243-259.

(Raubal and Worboys, 1999) Raubal M., and Worboys M., 1999, A Formal Model of the Process of Wayfinding in Built Environments, *Spatial Information Theory - Cognitive and Computational Foundations of Geographic Information Science, International Conference COSIT '99*, Freksa C., and Mark D. (Eds.), Stade, Germany, p. 381-399.

(Raubal, 2001) Raubal M., 2001, Agent-Based Simulation of human wayfinding. A perceptual model for unfamiliar building, *PhD thesis*, Vienna University of Technology, Faculty of Sciences and Informatics.

(Raubal, 2001) Raubal M., 2001, Human wayfinding in unfamiliar buildings: a simulation with a cognizing agent, *Cognitive Processing*, Vol 2, No. 3, p. 363-388.

(Raubal, 2001) Raubal M., 2001, Ontology and epistemology for agent-based wayfinding simulation, *International Journal of Geographical Information Science*, Vol. 15,

No. 7, p. 653-665.

(Raubal, 2002) Raubal M., 2002, Wayfinding in Built Environments: The Case of Airports. Verlag Natur and Wissenschaft, Solingen, Germany.

(Raubal., 2000) Raubal M., 2000, Human wayfinding in unfamiliar buildings: a simulation with cognizing agents, *International Conference on Spatial Cognition: Scientific Research and Applications (ICSC 2000), Cognitive Processing - special issue 2000*, Belardinelli M. (Ed.), Rome, Italy, p. 66.

(Raubal., 2001) Raubal M., 2001, Agent-based Simulation of Human Wayfinding: A Perceptual Model for Unfamiliar Buildings, *Ph.D Thesis*, Vienna University of Technology, Vienna.

(Reynolds et al., 2002) Reynolds K.E., Ganesh J., and Luckett M., 2002, Traditional malls vs factory outlets: comparing shopper typologies and implications for retail strategy, *Journal of Business Research*, Vol. 55, p. 687-696.

(Richardson-Klavehn and Bjork, 1988) Richardson-Klavehn A., and Bjork R., 1988, Measures of Memory, *Annual Review of Psychology*, Vol. 39, p. 475-543.

(Richins, 1997) Richins M., 1997, Measuring Emotions in the Consumption Experience, *Journal of Consumer Research*, Vol. 24, p. 127-146.

(Richins, 1997) Richins M.L., 1997, Measuring emotions in the consumption experience, *The Journal of Consumer Research*, Vol. 24, No. 2, p. 127-146.

(Rivest et al., 2001) Rivest S., Bédard Y., and Marchand P., 2001, Toward Better Support for spatial decision making: Defining the characteristics of spatial on-line analytical processing (SOLAP), *Geomatica*, Vol. 55, No 4, p.539-555.

(Rivest et al., 2004) Rivest S., Gignac P., Charron J., and Bédard Y., 2004, Développement d'un système d'exploration spatio-temporelle interactive des données de la Banque d'information corporative du ministère des Transports du Québec, *Proc. Geomatics 2004*, Conference of the Canadian Institute of Geomatics, October 28-29, Montreal Section.

(Roberts and Merrilees, 2001) Roberts J., and Merrilees G., 2001, Shopping centre evolution: An historical analysis of the Australian experience. *Proc. of ANZMAC (Autralian and New Zealand Marketing Academy) conference*,

(Rodriguez et al., 1994) Rodriguez M., Erard P.J., and.Müller J.P., 1994, *Virtual Environments for Simulating Artificial Autonomy*, in *Artificial Life and Virtual Reality*, N. Thalmann Ed., Wiley, 1994.

(Rogers, 1951) Rogers C.R., 1951, Client-centered therapy: Its current practice, implications and theory, Boston: Houghton Mifflin.

(Rokeach, 1960) Rokeach M., 1960, The nature of human values, New York: Free Press.

(Rokeach, 1973) Rokeach M., 1973, The nature of human values, New York, Free Press.

(Rossides, 1997) Rossides D.W., 1997, Social Stratification: The Interplay of Class, Race, and Gender, Englewood Cliffs NJ: Prentice Hall.

(Ruiz et al., 2004) Ruiz J.P., Chebat J.C., and Hansen P., 2004, Another trip to the mall: A segmentation study of customers based on their activities, *Les cahiers du GERAD*.

(Ruth, 2003) Ruth B., 2003, Population Ecology: an Introduction to computer simulations John Wiley & Sons, p. 170.

(Sanchez, 2001) Sanchez S.M., 2001, ABC's of output analysis. *Proc. of the 2001 Winter Simulation Conference*,

(Sargent, 1992) Sargent R.G., 1992, Validation and verification of simulation models, *Proc. of the 1992 Winter Simulation Conference*, Swain J.J., Goldsman D., Crain R.C., and Wilson J.R. (Eds.), IEEE, Piscataway, NJ, p. 104–114.

(Sargent, 2001) Sargent R.G., 2001, Verification and validation: some approaches and paradigms for verifying and validating simulation models, *Proc. of the 33nd conference on Winter simulation*, IEEE Computer Society, p. 106–114.

(Sato, 2003) Tetsuya Sato T., 2003, The Earth Simulator, *Holistic Simulation and Science Evolution*, Vol. 58, No. 2, p. 79-85.

(Schadschneider et al., 2002) Schadschneider A., Kirchner A., Nishinari K., 2002, CA Approach to Collective Phenomena in Pedestrian Dynamics, *Lecture Notes in Computer Science*, Vol. 2493, p. 239–248.

(Schiffman et al., 1997) Schiffman G.L., Bednall D., Watson, J., and Kanuk L., 1997, Consumer Behaviour, 1/e, Prentice-Hall.

(Schmitz, 1999) Schmitz S., 1999, Gender Differences in Acquisition of Environmental Knowledge Related to Wayfinding Behavior, *Spatial Anxiety and Self-Estimated Environmental Competencies, Sex Roles*, Vol. 41, No. 1, p. 71-93.

(Schruben, 1980) Schruben L.W., 1980, Establishing the credibility of simulations, *Simulation*, Vol. 34, No. 3, p. 101-105.

(Schüle et al., 2004) Schüle M., Herrler R., and Klügl F., 2004, Coupling GIS and Multi-agent Simulation – Towards Infrastructure for Realistic Simulation, *Lecture Notes in Computer Science*, Vol. 3187, p. 228-242.

(Schweiss et al., 1999) Schweiss E., Musse S.R., Garat F., and Thalmann D., 1999, An Architecture to Guide Crowds Using a Rule-Based Behaviour System, *Proc. Agents 99*.

(Scott, 2000) Scott M., 2000, Editorial Introduction: Messy Systems - The Target for Multi Agent Based Simulation, *Lecture Notes in Computer Science*, Vol. 1979, p. 1.

(Servat et al., 1998) Servat D., Edith P., Treuil J.P, and Drogoul A., 1998, When Agents Emerge from Agents: Introducing Multi-Scale Viewpoints in Multi-Agent Simulations, *Proc. of the workshop MABS'98*, LNAI, No. 1534, Springer-Verlag, Berlin, p. 183-198.

(Shannon, 1976) Shannon R.E., 1976, Simulation modeling and methodology, *Proc. of the 76 Bicentennial conference on Winter simulation*, p. 9–15.

(Shannon, 1998) Shannon R.E., 1998, Introduction to the art and science of simulation, *Proc. of the 30th conference on Winter simulation*, IEEE Computer Society Press, p. 7–14.

(Sheridan, 2002) Sheridan M., 2002, Securing the mall, *Retail Traffic Magazine* (http://retailtrafficmag.com).

(Sheth et al., 1999) Sheth J.N., Mittal B., and Newman B.I., 1999, Customer Behaviour: Consumer Behaviour and Beyond, Dryden Press.

(Shiode, 2000) Shiode N., 2000, 3D urban models: Recent developments in the digital modelling of urban environments in three-dimensions, *GeoJournal*, Vol. 52, No. 3, p. 263-269.

(Sichman et al., 2003) Sichman J., Bousquet F., and Davidsson P., 2003, Multi-Agent Based Simulation II, *Lecture Notes in Computer Science*, Vol. 2581, Springer Verlag.

(Sila, 1992) Seila A.F., 1992, Advanced output analysis for simulation, *Proc. of the 1992 Winter Simulation Conference.*

(Silk and Kalwani, 1982) Silk A., and Kalwani M., 1982, Measuring influence in organizational purchase decisions, Journal of Marketing Research, Vol. 19, p. 165-181.

(Simon, 1960) Simon H.A., 1960, The new science of management decision, New York, NY: Harper and Row.

(Sirgy, 1982) Sirgy M.J., 1982, Self-Concept in consumer behavior: Acritical review, *The Journal of Consumer Research*, Vol. 9, No. 3, p. 287-300.

(Solomon, 1996) Solomon M.R., 1996, Consumer Behavior, Third edition, Englewood Cliffs, N.J.: Prentice-Hall.

(Solomon, 1999) Solomon M.R., 1999, Consumer Behaviour: Buying, Having and Being, 4/e, Allyn and Bacon.

(Soulié, 2001) Soulié J.C., 2001, Vers une approche multi-environnements pour les agents. *Thèse de Doctorat*, Université de la Réunion.

(Soulies et al., 1998) Soulies J.C., Marcenac P., Calderoni S., Courdier R., 1998, GEAMAS v2.0 : An Object Oriented Platform for Complex Systems Simulations, *in Proceedings of the 26th International Conference on Technology of Oriented-Object Languages and Systems (TOOLS USA'98)*, Eds. Singh M., Meyer B., Gil J., and Mitchell R., IEEE Computer Society Press, Santa Barbara, USA, p. 230-242.

(Srinivasan, 1987) Srinivasan T.C., 1987, An Integrative Approach to Consumer Choice, *Advances in Consumer Research*, Wallendorf M., and Anderson P. (Eds.), Provo, U.T.: Association for Consumer Research.

(Srivastava et al., 1981) Srivastava R.K., Mark I.A., and Allan D.S., 1981, A Customer-Oriented Approach for Determining Market Structures, *Journal of Marketing*, Vol. 48, p. 32-45.

(Stafford and Stafford, 1986) Stafford M.R., and Stafford T.F., 1986, Situational dimensions, shopping motives and patronage behavior: A conceptual model, *Proc. of the Southern Marketing Association*, p. 63-66.

(Stone, 1954) Stone G.P., 1954, City shoppers and urban identification: Observations on the social psychology of city life, *The American Journal of Sociology*, p. 36-45.

(Swap, 1983) Swap W., 1983, How groups make decisions: A social psychological perspective, *Group Decision Makingm*, Swap W. (Eds.), Beverly Hills, CA: Sage, p. 45-68.

(Swinyard, 1993) Swinyard W.R., 1993, The effects of mood, involvement, and quality of store experience on shopping intentions, *The Journal of Consumer Research*, Vol. 20, No. 2, p. 271-280.

(Szarowicz and Forte, 2003) Szarowicz A., and Forte P., 2003, Combining Intelligent Agents and Animation, *Lecture Notes in Computer Science*, Vol. 2829, p. 275–286.

(Tauber, 1972) Tauber E.M., 1972, Why Do people shop?, *Journal of Marketing*, Vol. 36, p. 46–59.

(Taylor and Baker, 1994) Taylor S.A., and Baker T.L., 1994, An Assessment of the Relationship between Service Quality and Customer Satisfaction in the Formation of Consumers' Purchase Intentions, *Journal of Retailing*, Vol. 70, p. 163-178

(Teklenburg et al., 1998) Teklenburg J.A.F., Borgers A.W.J., Waerden P.J.H.J., and

Timmermans H.J.P., 1998, The Use of Pedestrian Exits in A Suburban Shopping Centre, *15th IAPS conference 'Shifting Balances: Changing Roles in Policy, Research and Design*, Eindhoven.

(Thalmann et al., 1995) Thalmann D., Boulic R., Huang Z., and Noser H., 1995, Virtual and Real Humans Interacting in the Virtual World, *Proc. International Conference on Virtual Systems and Multimedia'95*, Gifu, Japan, p.48-57.

(Thalmann et al., 1996) Thalmann D., Noser H., and Huang Z., 1996, How to Create a Virtual Life?, *Interactive Computer Animation*, Prentice Hall, p.263-291.

(Thalmann et al., 2000) Thalmann D., Musse S.R., and Kallmann M., 2000, From Individual Human Agents to Crowds, *Informatik/Informatique*, No1.

(Thalmann, 2000) Thalmann D., 2000, Virtual Humans: From Individual to Social and Crowd Behaviors, *Proc. International Workshop on Human Modeling and Animation*, Seoul, Korea (invited paper).

(Thalmann, 2001) Thalmann D., 2001, The Foundations to Build a Virtual Human Society, *Proc. Intelligent Virtual Actors (IVA) 2001* (invited paper), Madrid, Spain, Springer-Verlag, p. 1.

(Theodoropoulos and Logan, 1999) Theodoropoulos G., and Logan B., 1999, A framework for the distributed simulation of agent-based systems, *Modelling and Simulation: a tool for the next millenium, Proc. of the 13th European Simulation Multiconference (ESM'99)*, Szczerbicka H. (Eds.), SCS, Vol. 1, Society for Computer Simulation International, p. 58–65.

(Thomsen et al., 1999) Thomsen E., Spofford G., and Chase D., 1999, Microsoft OLAP solutions, John Wiley and Sons (Eds.), p. 495.

(Timmermans et al., 2001) Timmermans H.J.P., Arentze T.A., and Joh C.H., 2001, Analyzing Space-time behaviour: New approaches to Old Problems, Progress in Human Geografy.

(Timmermans, 1999) Timmermans H.J.P., 1999, Modeling complex shopping patterns, Key note.

(Timmermans, 2000) Timmermans H.J.P., 2000, Theories and Models of Activity Patterns, *ALBATROSS: A Learning Based Oriented Simulation System*, Arentze A.T., and Timmermans H.J.P. (Eds.), Eindhoven: European Institute of Retailing and Services Studies, p. 6-70.

(Timmermans, 2003) Timmermans H.J.P., 2003, Application of stated preference to retail site selection, *Proc. of South African Transport Conference*.

(Torrens and Benenson, 2005) Torrens P.M., and Benenson I., 2005, Geographic Automata Systems, *International Journal of Geographic Information Science*, (In press.).

(Torrens and Benenson., 2003) Torrens P.M., and Benenson I., 2003, Geographic Automata Systems, *Special session: Geographical Perspectives on Complexity Theory and Complex Systems 2, 99th Annual Meeting of the Association of American Geographers*, New Orleans.

(Torrens and O'Sullivan., 2000) Torrens P.M., and O'Sullivan D., 2000, Cities, cells, and cellular automata: developing a research agenda for urban geocomputation, *Proc. of the Fifth Annual Conference on GeoComputation. Manchester*, GeoComputation CD-ROM.

(Torrens., 2000) Torrens P.M., 2000, GeoComputation, complexity, and urban systems simulation. *Meeting of Special Interest Group 1 (Transport and Spatial Development) of the World Conference on Transportation Research*, Portland, OR.

(Torrens., 2001) Torrens P.M., 2001, A hybrid geocomputation model for operational land-use and transport simulation, *97th Annual Meeting of the Association of American Geographers*, New York.

(Torrens., 2001) Torrens P.M., 2001, Advanced simulation technologies at the Centre for Advanced Spatial Analysis, *Presentation to the International Institute for Aerospace Survey and Earth Sciences*, London.

(Torrens., 2001) Torrens P.M., 2001, Can geocomputation save urban simulation?, *Winter Colloquium*, Department of City and Regional Planning, Cornell University, Ithaca, New York.

(Torrens., 2001) Torrens P.M., 2001, Simulating complex urban systems, Presentation to Bartlett School of Planning, University College London, London.

(Torrens., 2002) Torrens P.M., 2002, Advanced geographical analysis, *Seminar given at Trinity College Dublin*, Department of Geography, Dublin.

(Torrens., 2002) Torrens P.M., 2002, Review of Dynamics in Human and Primate Societies: Agent-Based Modeling of Social and Spatial Processes, *Environment and Planning B 29*, Kohler T.A., and Gumerman G.J. (Eds.), Oxford University Press, New York, p. 632-633.

(Torrens., 2002) Torrens P.M., 2002, Urban simulation: a primer, *Seminar given to the Urban Design Master's course*, Bartlett School, University College London, London.

(Torrens., 2004) Torrens P.M., 2004, Emerging trends in spatial simulation, IGERT, New York: State University of New York at Buffalo.

(Torrens., 2004) Torrens P.M., 2004, Geosimulation and transport modeling, *Handbooks in Transport 5: Transport Geography and Spatial Systems*, Stopher P., Button K., Haynes K., Hensher D. (Eds.), London: Pergamon/Elsevier Science.

(Troitzch, 1997) Troitzsch K.G., 1997, Social science simulation - Origin, prospects, purposes, in. Conte R., and Hegselmann P.T. (eds.) *Simulating social phenomena*, Heidelberg: Springer.

(Uhrmacher and Schattenberg, 1998) Uhrmacher, A.M., and Schattenberg B., 1998, Agents in Discrete Event Simulation, *10TH European Simulation Symposium "Simulation in Industry – Simulation Technology: Science and Art" (ESS'98)*, Bargiela A., and Kerckhoffs E. (Eds.), Nottingham, UK: SCS Publications, Ghent, for The Society for Computer Simulation International (SCS), p. 129-136.

(Ulicny and Thalmann, 2001) Ulicny B., and Thalmann D., 2001, Crowd simulation for interactive virtual environments and VRtraining systems, *Proc. Eurographics Workshop on Animation and Simulation*, Springer-Verlag, p. 163-170.

(Ulicny and Thalmann, 2002) Ulicny B., and Thalmann D., 2002, Crowd simulation for virtual heritage, *Proc. First International Workshop on 3D Virtual Heritage*, Geneva, p. 28-32.

(Ulicny and Thalmann, 2002) Ulicny B., and Thalmann D., 2002, Towards Interactive Real-Time Crowd Behavior Simulation, *Computer Graphics Forum*, Vol. 21, No. 4, p. 767-775.

(Urbao., 2001) URBAO Magazine, 2001, Automates cellulaires et systèmes multi-agents:

mettez de la vie dans vos SIGs, *Urbao: L'information Numérisée pour Aménager, Construire, Gérer*, Vol. 4, p. 34-38.

(Vanbergue and Drogoul, 2002) Vanbergue D., and Drogoul A., 2002, Approche multi-agent pour la simulation urbaine, *Actes des Journées Cassini*, Brest, France.

(Vanbergue et al., 2000) Vanbergue D., Treuil J.P., and Drogoul A., 2000, Modelling urban phenomena with cellular automata. *Advances in Complex Systems*, Vol. 3, p. 127–140.

(Vosinakis and Panayiotopoulos, 2001) Vosinakis S., and Panayiotopoulos T., 2001, SimHuman: A Platform for Real-Time Virtual Agents with Planning Capabilities, *Lecture Notes in Computer Science*, Vol. 2190, p. 210.

(Waerden et al., 1997) Waerden P.J.H.J., and Timmerman, H.J.P., 1997, Parking Simulation using a Geographical Information System, *Decision Support Systems in Urban Planning*, Timmermans H.J.P. (Ed.), Londen: E and FN Spon, p. 310-322.

(Waerden et al., 1998) Waerden P.J.H.J., Borgers A.W.J., and Timmermans H.J.P., 1998, Modelling Store Choice Behaviour Using Features of a Geographical Information System, *4th Design and Decision Support Systems in Architecture and Urban Planning Conference*, Maastricht.

(Waerden et al., 1998) Waerden P.J.H.J., Borgers A.W.J., and Timmermans H.J.P., 1998, Shopping Centre Development and Parking Behaviour, *5th Recent Advances in Retailing and Services Science Conference*, Baveno, Italy.

(Waerden et al., 2001) Waerden P.J.H.J., Borgers A.W.J., and Timmermans H.J.P., 2001, Shopping Activities as Part of Activity Chains, *The Recent Advances in Retailing and Consumer Services Science Conference*, 16-19 August.

(Wagner and Tulba, 2003) Wagner G., and Tulba F., 2003, Agent-Oriented Modeling and Agent-Based Simulation, *Lecture Notes in Computer Science*, Vol. 2814, p. 205-216.

(Wagner, 2004) Wagner G., 2004, AOR Modelling and Simulation: Towards a General Architecture for Agent-Based Discrete Event Simulation, *Lecture Notes in Computer Science*, Vol. 3030, p. 174-188.

(Wakefield and Baker, 1998) Wakefield K.L., and Baker J., 1998, Excitement at the mall: determinants and effects on shopping response, *Journal of retailing*, Vol. 74, No. 4, p. 515-539.

(Wakelfield and Baker, 1998) Wakelfield K.L., and Baker J., 1998, Excitement at the mall: Determinants and effects on shopping response. *Journal of Retailing*, 74(4). P. 515-539.

(Walters and Bergiel, 1989) Walters C.G., and Bergiel J.B., 1989, Consumer Behaviour: A Decision-Making Approach, South-Western Publishing Co.

(Ward et al., 2003) Douglas P.W., Alan T.M., Stuart R.P., 2003, Integrating spatial optimization and cellular automata for evaluating urban change, *The Annals of Regional Science*, Vol. 37, No. 1, p. 131-148.

(Warlop and Ratneshwar, 1993) Warlop L., and Ratneshwar S., 1993, The Role of Usage Context in Consumer Choice: A Problem Solving Perspective, *Advances in Consumer Research*, Vol. 20, No. 1, p. 377-382.

(Webster and Wind, 1972) Webster F.E., and Wind Y., 1972, Organizational Buying Behaviour. Prentice Hall, Englewood Cliffs, New Jersey.

(Weiss, 1999) Weiss G., 1999, Multiagent systems: A modern approach to distributed artificial intelligence,. Cambridge, MA: MIT Press.

(Weiss, 2000) Weiss G., 2000, Multiagent systems: a modern approach to distributed artificial intelligence, *MIT Press*,

(Weyns et al., 2005) Weyns D., Parunak H., Michel F., Holvoet T., and Ferber J., 2005, Environments for Multiagent Systems: State-of-the-Art and Research Challenges, p. 1–47.

(Whitner and Balci, 1989) Whitner R.B., and Balci O., 1989, Guidelines for selecting and using simulation model verification techniques, *Proc. of the 1989 Winter Simulation Conference*, MacNair E.A, Musselman K.J., and Heidelberger P. (Eds.), IEEE, Piscataway, NJ, p. 559–568.

(Wickenberg and Davidsson, 2003) Wickenberg T., Davidsson P., 2003, On Multi Agent Based Simulation of Software Development Processes, *Multi-Agent Based Simulation II, LNAI*, Vol. 2581, Springer, p. 171–180.

(Wilkie, 1995) Wilkie L.W., 1995, Consumer Behaviour, 3/e, John Wiley and Sons Inc.

(Woods, 1960) Woods W.A., 1960, Psychological dimensions of consumer decision, *Journal of Marketing*, Vol. 24, No 3, p. 15-19.

(Wooldridge and Ciancarini, 2000) Wooldridge M., and Ciancarini P., 2000, Agent-Oriented Software Engineering: The State of the Art, *First Int. Workshop on Agent-Oriented Software Engineering*, Ciancarini P., and Wooldridge M. (Eds.), Springer-Verlag, vol. 1957, Berlin, p. 1–28.

(Wooldridge and Jennings, 1995) Wooldridge M., and Jennings N.R., 1995, Intelligent agents: Theory and practice, *The Knowledge Engineering Review*, Vol. 10, No. 2, p. 115–152.

(Wooldridge, 2000) Wooldridge M., 2000, Intelligent agents, *Multiagent systems: a modern approach to distributed artificial intelligence*, Weiss G. (ed), 2000, MIT Press, p. 27–77.

(Wu, 1999) Wu F., 1999, GIS-based simulation as an exploratory analysis for space-time processes, Journal of Geographical Systems, Vol. 1, No. 3, p. 199-218.

(Yalch and Spangenberg, 1990) Yalch R., and Spangenberg E., 1990, Effects of Store Music on Shopping Behavior, *Journal of Consumer Marketing*, Vol. 7, No. 2, p. 55-63.

(Yougworth, 1995) Yougworth P., 1995, OLAP spells success for users and developers, Data Based Advisor, p. 38-49.

(Zeigler and Oren, 1986) Zeigler B.P., and Oren T.I., 1986, Multifaceted, multiparadigm modeling perspectives: tools for the 90's, *Proc. of the 18th conference on Winter simulation (WSC 86)*, Wilson J., Henrickson J., and Roberts S. (Eds.), ACM Press, p. 708–712.

(Zeigler et al. , 2000) Zeigler B.P., Kim T.G., and Praehofer H., 2000, Theory of Modeling and Simulation, Academic Press Inc.

(Zeigler, 1972) Zeigler B.P., 1972, Toward a Formal Theory of Modeling and Simulation: Structure Preserving Morphisms, *Journal of the ACM (JACM)*, Vol. 19, No. 4, p. 742–764.

(Zhang et al., 2000) Zhang D.M., Alem L., Yacef K., 2000, Using Multi-agent Approach for the Design of an Intelligent Learning Environment, *Lecture Notes in Computer*

Science, Vol. 1441, p. 220.

(Zhao et al., 2002) Zhao Z., Belleman R.G, Albada G.D., and Sloot P.M.A., 2002, AG-IVE: An Agent Based Solution to Constructing Interactive Simulation Systems, *Lecture Notes in Computer Science*, Vol. 2329, p. 693.

Annexe A: The Questionnaire (Individual and Group)

This annex presents the questionnaire, which is elaborated and used to collect data about the shoppers in Square One mall in Toronto area. The questionnaire contains two main parts: the first is for the individual shoppers, while the second is for the groups. Each part contains several sections that contain many questions. This questionnaire is presented, in detail, in the rest of this annex. It is important to notice that it exists a french version of this questionnaire, which is conducted in Place De La Cité mall in Québec City. Unfortunately, the french version of the questionnaire is not presented in this annex.

A.1. Individual questionnaire

A.1.1. Section 0: Identification and instructions

This section contains the following elements:

- *The head*: It contains the identification information of the individual questionnaire, such as the station's number where the questionnaire is conducted, the administrator number, the questionnaire or the shopper number, the date/hour of the interview, and the group number (if the interviewed shopper belongs to a group).

```
KIOSK NO_____
ADMINISTRATOR NO_____
SUBJECT (SHOPPER) NO_____
DATE-HOUR_____
GROUP NO_____
```

- *Project description*: This element gives a brief description of the project related to the questionnaire. This element must be read by the questionnaire administrator for the respondent before starting the interview.

> The project related to this questionnaire consists in creating a computer tool which simulates the human shopping behavior in a shopping mall. This tool aims to help the mall's managers to configure their mall in order to make it more confortable for the shoppers.

- *Confidentiality*: By reading this element of the questionnaire, the administrator assures the respondent about the confidentiality of the gathered information.

> All the information collected using this questionnaire is confidential and will be used only for the purposes of the project described above.

- *Recompense and reward*: In order to encourage the shopper to fill the questionnaire we reserved an amount of the budget to recompense the respondents. This recompense is a 5 dollars gift certificate.

> If, after your shopping trip, you complete to fill the questionnaire, we give you a 5 dollars gift certificate.

- *Instructions*: This element informs the respondent about the general instructions of the questionnaire.

> Please read attentively the question and answer whatever's best of your knowledge. Some questions have one or some instructions before; this or these instruction-s are applied only for this question.

280

A.1.2. Section 1: General questions

This section is filled by the respondent. It contains some general and demographic questions. In this section, we find the following questions:

- The gender:

ARE YOU MALE OR FEMALE?
☐ Female
☐ Male
☐ Refusal

- The age group:

2. TO WHICH AGE GROUP DO YOU BELONG?
☐ 13-17 years   ☐ 51-65 years
☐ 18-25 years   ☐ 66 years and over
☐ 26-35 years   ☐ Refusal
☐ 36-50 years

- The occupations:

IDENTIFY THE OCCUPATIONS THAT MOST RESEMBLES YOURS.
☐ Full-time worker (at least 30 hours)   ☐ Student
☐ Part-time worker (less than 30 hours)   ☐ Retired
☐ Work at home   ☐ Other: _____
          ☐ Refusal

- The sectors of employment:

Instructions: If you work, answer questions 4a and 4b. If you are a student, answer question 4c.
4a. WHICH SECTOR OF EMPLOYMENT MOST RESEMBLES YOURS?
☐ Commission Sales/Service   ☐ Professional
☐ Administration/Management   ☐ Health
☐ Machinery/Technical/Industry/Construction   ☐ Other: _____
☐ Teacher/Education   ☐ Refusal

4b. MORE PRECISELY, WHERE DO YOU WORK?
☐ Location of work: _____
☐ Refusal

4c. WHERE DO YOU ATTEND SCHOOL?
☐ University   ☐ Refusal
☐ College
☐ High-school
☐ Grade-school
☐ Other: _____

- The marital statuses:

WHAT IS YOUR MARITAL STATUS?
☐ Single   ☐ Widow(er)
☐ Married   ☐ Other: _____
☐ Partnered   ☐ Refusal
☐ Divorced

- The life modality:

DO YOU LIVE...

281

Alone	☐ With your parents
☐ As a couple	☐ Other: _____
☐ With one or more roommates	☐ Refusal

- The persons whom live with…

IF YOU DON'T LIVE ALONE, INDICATE THE NUMBER OF PEOPLE WHO LIVE WITH YOU WHO BELONG TO EACH OF THESE AGE GROUPS.
- ☐ 0 – 4 years: _____   ☐ 18 – 25 years: _____
- ☐ 5 – 12 years: _____   ☐ People over the age of 25: _____
- ☐ 13-17 years: _____   ☐ Refusal

- The postal code:

WHAT IS YOUR POSTAL CODE?
Postal code: _____
☐ Refusal

- The frequency of mall's visit:

HOW OFTEN DO YOU COME TO THE MALL?

Frequency of visit	Square One
- Once per month	☐
- Twice per month	☐
- Once a week	☐
- More than once a week	☐
- Once a day	☐
- Other :	
specify :	
- Refusal	☐

- The origin:

WHERE ARE YOU COMING FROM ?
- ☐ Your home   ☐ Another shopping centre
- ☐ School   Which one ? : _____
- ☐ Your place of work   ☐ Other : _____
- ☐ Refusal

- The transportation mean:

WHAT MODE OF TRANSPORTATION DID YOU TAKE TO THE MALL ?
- ☐ Automobile   ☐ Bike
- ☐ Taxi   ☐ Walk
- ☐ Bus   ☐ Other : _____
- ☐ Motorcycle/scooter   ☐ Refusal

- The household income:

WHICH RANGE BEST DESCRIBES YOUR HOUSEHOLD'S ANNUAL INCOME?
- ☐ Less than $20 000   ☐ $60 000 – $70 000
- ☐ $20 000 – $30 000   ☐ $70 000 – $100 000
- ☐ $30 000 – $40 000   ☐ More than $100 000
- ☐ $40 000 – $50 000   ☐ Refusal
- ☐ $50 000 – $60 000

A.1.3 Section 2: Shopping objectives and goals

This section aims to gather data about the shopper's objectives or his/her shopping purposes. It contains an oral interview, which is composed of two parts. The first part is filled before the shopping trip and is related to the planned objectives, while the second part is filled after the shopping, and aims to gather the shopper's unplanned objectives, which are accomplished during the shopping trip. The two sections contain two types of objectives: general objectives and specific objectives. The general objectives are related to the general activities that can be done in the mall, such as exploring, browsing, etc. The specific objectives are related to visiting specific stores, kiosks or places in the mall in order to purchase specific product or service.

This part of the questionnaire begins with some instructions clauses, which are the following:

Instructions
- I will read the questions and I will write down your answers
- If the question is not clear, don't hesitate to tell me.
- You can refuse to answer by telling me "I refuse to answer".

- Sub-section pre-shopping trip:
  - General objectives (planned):

I WILL FIRST ASK YOU A FEW QUESTIONS ABOUT YOUR OBJECTIVES. AFTER EACH STATEMENT, ANSWER WITH YES OR NO.
As a general goal:

Did you come to:	Estimated duration
☐ Accompany a person (if yes) tell us who (code):	
☐ Meet a person (if yes) tell us who (code):	
☐ People watch	
☐ Do some window shopping	
☐ Walk in the shopping centre for some exercise	
☐ Be a spectator for an event (if yes) which event: _____ _____ _____	_____ _____ _____
☐ Other: _____	

Codes
1. Self
2. Spouse
3. Children
4. Friends
5. Colleagues
6. Other

  - Specific objectives (planned and expected):

WILL ASK YOU SOME QUESTIONS ABOUT SOME MORE SPECIFIC OBJECTIVES. DID YOU PLAN TO VISIT SOME STORES, TO PURCHASE SOME PRODUCTS OR SERVICES, OR TO DO SOME SPECIFIC ACTIVITIES THAT ARE NOT ALREADY MENTIONED?

	Section I (Pre-Shopping)						Section II (Post-Shopping)			
								If accomplished		If not accomplished
Planned priority	Place (store or other)	Product (code)	Service (code)	Specific activity	Estimated duration	For who? (code)	Accomplished objective	Real priority	Real duration	Reason (code)
1.							☐			
2.							☐			

3.						☐			
4.						☐			
5.						☐			
6.						☐			
7.						☐			
8.						☐			
9.						☐			
10.						☐			

For who (code) (Codes)
1. Self
2. Spouse
3. Children
4. Friends
5. Colleagues
6. Other

Product or service code
1.Women's Clothing
2.Men's Clothing
3.Unisex Clothing
4.Children's Clothing
5.Shoe Store
6.Jewelry Store
7.Eyeglass/Sunglass Store
8.Houshold shops
9.Travel Agency
10.Sports Stores
11.Leisure Activity Store
12.Music, Electronics, Photo developing Store
13.Book/Stationary Store
14.Gift shop
15.Speciality Food/Candy or Tabacco Store
16.Restaurant
17.Hair/Salon Products
18.Financial Services
19.Complementary Services
20.Other Services
21.Department Store

- Sub-section pre-shopping trip:
  - General objectives (unexpected):

IF YOU PLAN TO RETURN TO THE MALL, WHAT ELSE WILL YOU DO?	
What would you do?	Estimated duration
☐ Accompany a person (if yes) tell us who (code):	
☐ Meet a person (if yes) tell us who (code):	
☐ People watch	
☐ Do some window shopping	
☐ Walk in the shopping centre for some exercise	
☐ Be a spectator for an event (if yes) which event: _____ _____ _____	___ ___ ___
☐ Other: _____	

Codes
1. Self
2. Spouse
3. Children
4. Friends
5. Colleagues
6. Other

o Specific objectives (for department and big stores):

DEPARTMENT STORES

Department Store	Did you visit this store?	Did you make a purchase?
The Bay	☐	☐
Zellers	☐	☐
Sears	☐	☐
Walmart	☐	☐

DID YOU SHOP AT PEROPHERAL STORES OR VISIT NEARBY SERVICES?

Store	Did you visit this store?	Did you make a purchase?
Famous Players Coliseum	☐	☐
Canyon Creek	☐	☐
Sport Check	☐	☐
Jack Astor's	☐	☐
Alice Fazooli's	☐	☐
Chapters	☐	☐
Playdium	☐	☐
Living Arts Centre	☐	☐
Mississauga Central Library	☐	☐

A.1.4 Section 3: Questions about the spatial knowledge

This section aims at gathering data about the spatial use of the two floors of Square One mall.

(PARKING) ON EACH OF THE DIAGRAMS ON THE NEXT PAGE, CIRCLE THE P SIGN CLOSEST TO YOUR USUAL PARKING SPACE (FACING THE DOOR YOU USUALLY ENTER FROM)

(ENTRANCES) ON EACH OF THE DIAGRAMS ON THE NEXT PAGE, CIRCLE THE DOOR THAT YOU USE MOST

FREQUENTLY TO ENTER THE SHOPPING CENTRE.

(**ZONES**) ON EACH OF THE DIAGRAMS ON THE NEXT PAGE, IDENTIFY THE ZONES OF THE SHOPPING CENTRE THAT YOU VISIT MOST FREQUENTLY. DEFINE THE TYPE OF ACTIVITY THAT YOU USUALLY DO IN EACH OF THE SPECIFIED ZONES USING ONE OR MORE OF THE LETTERS LISTED IN THE FOLLOWING TABLE.

S	Shop in a particular store
W	Window shop
P	Purchase product/ Eat food
R	Relax
Z	Socialize or meet people
O	Other (specific)

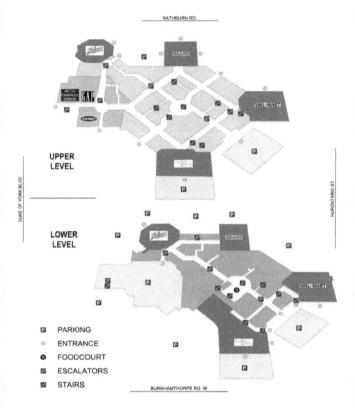

(**ITINERARY**) THINK FOR A MOMENT OF ONE OR MORE TYPICAL PATHS (MAX 3) THAT YOU FOLLOW WHEN YOU COME TO SQUARE ONE.

TRACE OUT THESE PATHS ON THE FOLLOWING DIAGRAM.
Please indicate your point of entrance along with your points of interest that you generally visit.

286

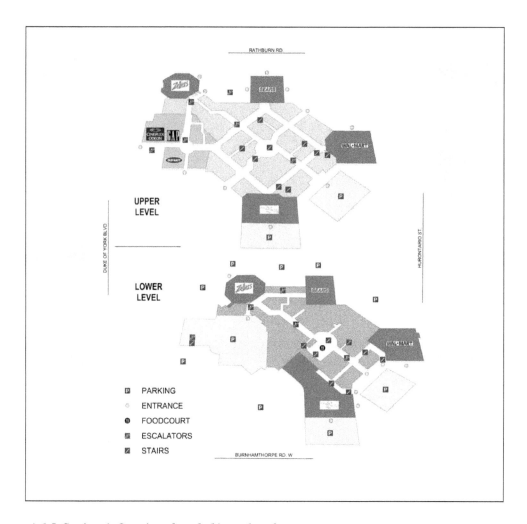

A.1.5. Section 4: Question about habits and preferences

In this section, we gather data concerning the habits, preferences, and interests of the respondents.

- Parking preferences:

WHAT TYPE OF PARKING DO YOU PREFER?	
☐ Interior	☐ No particular preference
☐ Exterior	☐ Refusal

- The usual used parking:

WHEN YOU USE THE PARKING, YOU...	
☐ Always park in the same spot	☐ Other: _____
☐ Park near your shopping destination ☐ Refusal	

- Preferred shopping period-s :

Instructions: For this question, you may check more than one answer.
DURING WHICH TIMES OF DAY DO YOU PREFER TO SHOP IN THE SHOPPING CENTRE?
☐ Morning   ☐ Evening
☐ Before noon   ☐ It varies
☐ Noon   ☐ I don't know
☐ Afternoon   ☐ Refusal

- Preferred shopping day-days:

Instructions: For this question, you may check more than one answer.
WHICH DAYS OF THE WEEK DO YOU PREFER TO SHOP IN THE SHOPPING CENTRE?
☐ Monday   ☐ Saturday
☐ Tuesday   ☐ Sunday
☐ Wednesday   ☐ It varies
☐ Thursday   ☐ I don't know
☐ Friday   ☐ Refusal

- Preferred shopping floor-s in the mall-s :

ON WHICH FLOOR DO YOU USUALLY SHOP?
First floor   ☐
Second floor   ☐
No particular floor   ☐
Refusal   ☐

- Preferred mall corridors:

WHICH CORRIDORS DO YOU FREQUENT THE MOST WHEN "WINDOW- SHOPPING"?
☐ Major Corridors
☐ Secondary Corridors
☐ Both
☐ No particular window shopping habits
☐ Other: _____
☐ Refusal

- Preference of density and crowding:

WHEN YOU SEE AN AREA WHERE THERE ARE LOTS OF PEOPLE,
DO YOU TEND TO GRAVITATE TOWARDS IT?
☐ Yes
☐ No
☐ Other: _____
☐ Refusal

- The emotional states in crowding:

WHEN YOU ARE IN AN AREA WITH LOTS OF PEOPLE, HOW DO YOU FEEL?
☐ Angry   ☐ Happy
☐ Worried   ☐ Other: _____
☐ Uncomfortable   ☐ Refusal
☐ Indifferent
☐ Comfortable

- Sense of orientation and wayfinding :

WOULD YOU SAY THAT YOUR SENSE OF DIRECTION IS...
☐ Very developed   ☐ Developed enough   ☐ Slightly developed   ☐ Not developed
☐ Refusal

- Odor preferences:

GENERALLY, DOES A PLEASANT SMELL CAPTURE YOUR ATTENTION?				
☐ Always	☐ Often	☐ Sometimes	☐ Rarely	☐ Refusal
Comments: _____				

- Lighting preferences:

WHAT TYPE OF LIGHTING MAKES YOU FEEL MOST COMFORTABLE?	
☐ Natural lighting	☐ Coloured lighting
☐ Fluorescent lighting	☐ Other: _____
☐ Muted lighting	☐ Refusal

- Colors preferences (display colors)

WHAT ARE YOUR THREE FAVOURITE COLOURS IN AN AD, INCLUDING BLACK AND WHITE?		
1. : _____	2. : _____	3. : _____
☐ Refusal		

- Colors preferences (decoration colors)

WHAT ARE YOUR THREE FAVOURITE COLOURS IN THE DÉCOR OF A STORE OR ANY OTHER LOCATION IN THE SHOPPING CENTRE INCLUDING BLACK AND WHITE?

1. : _____	2. : _____	3. : _____
☐ Refusal		

- Advertisment preferences:

WHAT ATTRACTS YOU IN THE CONTENT OF A POSTER ADVERTISEMENT?

Contents	Degree			
	Definitely	A lot	A little	Not at all
Ads for sales and special offers	☐	☐	☐	☐
Prices for products/services	☐	☐	☐	☐
Description of products/services in a store (or another location)	☐	☐	☐	☐
Information on the warranty for a product/service	☐	☐	☐	☐
Other: _____	☐	☐	☐	☐
Refusal				

- General interests:

INDICATE YOUR INTERESTS IN THE FOLLOWING TABLE.
- Choose the degree which corresponds the most to your interest.
- The sub-categories of interests (small boxes) are optional.

Interests/Preferences	Degree			
	Definitely	A lot	A little	Not at all
Cultural Activities	☐	☐	☐	☐
Theatre/Shows	☐	☐	☐	☐
Music	☐	☐	☐	☐
Cinema/Television	☐	☐	☐	☐
Reading	☐	☐	☐	☐
Other: _____	☐	☐	☐	☐
Motorsports	☐	☐	☐	☐
Automobiles	☐	☐	☐	☐
Motorcycles	☐	☐	☐	☐

New Technologies	☐	☐	☐	☐
Computers/Internet	☐	☐	☐	☐
Telecommunication	☐	☐	☐	☐
Other: _____	☐	☐	☐	☐
Home and Decor	☐	☐	☐	☐
Interior design	☐	☐	☐	☐
Crafts	☐	☐	☐	☐
Gardening	☐	☐	☐	☐
Other: _____	☐	☐	☐	☐
Sports	☐	☐	☐	☐
Outdoor sports	☐	☐	☐	☐
Indoor sports	☐	☐	☐	☐
Other: _____	☐	☐	☐	☐
Clothing, Fashion and Accessories	☐	☐	☐	☐
Beauty	☐	☐	☐	☐
Beauty products	☐	☐	☐	☐
Beauty services (hair salons, tanning salons, etc.)	☐	☐	☐	☐
Other: _____	☐	☐	☐	☐
Jewelry	☐	☐	☐	☐
Cooking	☐	☐	☐	☐
Other: _____	☐	☐	☐	☐
Refusal	☐	☐	☐	☐

- Musical preferences:

WHAT TYPE OF MUSIC ATTRACTS YOU TO A PRODUCT, A STORE OR ANOTHER LOCATION?				
Types of Music	Degree			
	Definitely	A lot	A little	Not at all
Classical	☐	☐	☐	☐
Rock/Alternative	☐	☐	☐	☐
Country	☐	☐	☐	☐
Dance	☐	☐	☐	☐
Jazz & Blues	☐	☐	☐	☐
Pop	☐	☐	☐	☐
Rap & Hip-Hop	☐	☐	☐	☐

A.1.6. Section 5: Questions about shopping situations

In this last section of the individual questionnaire, we put the respondent in specific shopping situation and we ask him/her about his/her emotional states or actions when he/she is in this situation. In the following points we present these situations.

- Satisfaction or dissatisfaction:

SCENARIO
YOU'RE IN THE MALL AND YOU HAVE JUST BOUGHT A PRODUCT OR RECEIVED A SERVICE. YOU REALIZE THAT IS PRODUCT/SERVICE DOES NOT LIVE UP TO YOUR EXPECTATIONS. HOW DO YOU FEEL?
☐ Disappointed   ☐ Indifferent
☐ Worried   ☐ I don't know
☐ Anger   ☐ Other: _____

□ Discomfort
Comments: _____

SCENARIO
YOU'RE IN THE MALL AND YOU HAVE JUST BOUGHT A PRODUCT OR RECEIVED A SERVICE. YOU REALIZE THAT IS
PRODUCT/SERVICE MEETS YOUR EXPECTATIONS. HOW DO YOU FEEL?
□ Happy   □ I don't know
□ Content   □ Other: _____ -
□ Comfortable   □ Refusal
□ Indifferent
Comments: _____

- Don't have enough time:

SCENARIO
YOU NOTICE THE TIME AND YOU REALIZE THAT YOU
HAVE VERY LITTLE TIME TO FINISH YOUR SHOPPING.
HOW DO YOU REACT?
□ You spend less time in the stores (or in other places)
□ You move more quickly
□ You quit your shopping
□ You visit less stores (or other places)
□ You postpone your shopping
□ Other: _____
□ Refusal

- Reactions in specific emotional state:
  o Happy or joyous:

Instructions: For this question your may check off more than one answer.
HOW DO YOU BEHAVE WHEN YOU FEEL HAPPY OR JOYOUS?
□ You spend more time in stores (or other places)
□ You spend less time in stores (or other places)
□ You move more quickly
□ You move less quickly
□ You spend more (you purchase more products/ services)
□ You spend less (you purchase less products/services)
□ You visit more stores (or other places)
□ Your visit less stores (or other places)
□ Other: _____
□ Refusal

  o Sad or Worried:

Instructions: For this question your may check off more than one answer.
HOW DO YOU BEHAVE WHEN YOU FEEL SAD OR WORRIED?
□ You spend more time in stores (or other places)
□ You spend less time in stores (or other places)
□ You move more quickly
□ You move less quickly
□ You spend more (you purchase more products/ services)
□ You spend less (you purchase less products/services)
□ You visit more stores (or other places)
□ Your visit less stores (or other places)
□ Other: _____
□ Refusal

  o Disappointed:

Instructions: For this question, you may check off more than one answer.
HOW DO YOU BEHAVE WHEN YOU FEEL DISAPPOINTED?
□ You spend more time in stores (or other places)
□ You spend less time in stores (or other places)

291

> ☐ You move more quickly
> ☐ You move less quickly
> ☐ You spend more (you purchase more products/services)
> ☐ You spend less (you purchase less products / services)
> ☐ You visit more stores (or other places)

   o   Angry:

> Instructions: For this question your may check off more than one answer.
> HOW DO YOU BEHAVE WHEN YOU'RE ANGRY?
> ☐ You spend more time in stores (or other places)   ☐ Other: _____
> ☐ You spend less time in stores (or other places)   ☐ Refusal
> ☐ You move more quickly
> ☐ You move less quickly
> ☐ You spend more (you purchase more products/ services)
> ☐ You spend less (you purchase less products/services)
> ☐ You visit more stores (or other places)
> ☐ Your visit less stores (or other places)

   o   Satisfied pr comfortable:

> Instructions: For this question you may check off more than one answer.
> HOW DO YOU BEHAVE WHEN YOU FEEL SATISFIED OR COMFORTABLE?
> ☐ You spend more time in stores (or other places)
> ☐ You spend less time in stores (or other places)
> ☐ You move more quickly
> ☐ You move less quickly
> ☐ You spend more (you purchase more products/ services)
> ☐ You spend less (you purchase less products/services)
> ☐ You visit more stores (or other places)
> ☐ Your visit less stores (or other places)
> ☐ Other: _____
> ☐ Refusal

   o   Unsatisfied or uncomfortable:

> Instructions: For this question, you many check off more than one answer.
> HOW DO YOU BEHAVE WHEN YOU FEEL UNSATISFIED OR UNCOMFORTABLE?
> ☐ You spend more time in stores (or other places)
> ☐ You spend less time in stores (or other places)
> ☐ You move more quickly
> ☐ You move less quickly
> ☐ You spend more (you purchase more products/ services)
> ☐ You spend less (you purchase less products/services)
> ☐ You visit more stores (or other places)
> ☐ Your visit less stores (or other places)
> ☐ Other: _____
> ☐ Refusal

A.2. Group questionnaire

The second part of the questionnaire is addressed to gather data about a group of shoppers. This group can be formed by members' family, friends, colleagues, etc. who come to the mall in order to do shopping together. Before filling the group questionnaire, we need to fill the individual questionnaires for each member of the group who is over than 13 years. When the members finish filling the questionnaire, we choose one member from this group, and we ask him/her to fill the group questionnaire. The selected member must be able to fill the questionnaire, such as the leader of the group. The group questionnaire is composed of the following sections:

A.2.1 Section 0: Identification and instruction

Like the individual questionnaire, the first section aims to identify the questionnaire and to give some instructions for the respondents. It contains a head and a part for the instructions. The head is the following:

```
KIOSK No _____
ADMINISTRATOR No_____
GROUP No_____
DATE-HOUR_____
```

The instructions are the following:

This questionnaire is addressed to the entire group. Members of the group who are able to respond to this questionnaire are invited to read the question attentively and to respond to the best of their ability.

- Certain questions are preceded by instructions: these instructions apply only to this question.
Unless the instructions indicate otherwise, select only one answer among the proposed answers by ticking in the corresponding box (☐).
- When you select an answer, which is followed by a line (e.g. ☐ other: _____) you may write your answer on that line.
- If you do not want to answer a question, you can tick the refusal box (з Refusal).
- Have a good questionnaire

A.2.2. Section 1: The group identification

This section aims to identify the group concerned with this questionnaire. We have the following questions:

- The type of the group:

Instruction: For this question you may tick more than one answer.

ARE YOU A MEMBER OF ONE OF THE FOLLOWING TYPES OF GROUPS…
☐ Family
☐ Work colleagues
☐ Friends
☐ Couple
☐ Other:_____
☐ Refusal

- The composition of the group:

INDICATE THE NUMBER OF PEOPLE IN YOUR GROUP WHO BELONG TO ONE OF THE FOLLOWING AGE RANGES
☐ 0-4 years_____   ☐ 36 – 50 years_____
☐ 5-12 years_____   ☐ 51 - 65 years _____
☐ 13-17 years _____   ☐ 66 years and older _____
☐ 18-25 years _____
☐ 26-35 years_____

- If there is a planned separation:

DURING THIS SHOPPING TRIP ARE YOU PLANNING FOR YOUR GROUP TO SPLIT UP.
☐ Yes
☐ No
☐ Refusal

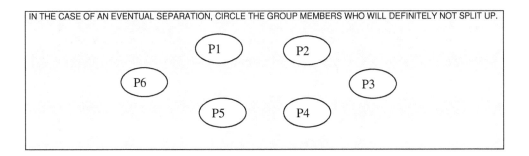

IN THE CASE OF AN EVENTUAL SEPARATION, CIRCLE THE GROUP MEMBERS WHO WILL DEFINITELY NOT SPLIT UP.

P1   P2

P6   P3

P5   P4

A.2.3. Section 2: The group's movement

In this section, we gather some data about the potential separation of the group members and about the movement of the group members inside the mall.

- If the group is separated:

WAS YOUR GROUP SEPARATED DURING THIS SHOPPING TRIP
☐ Yes
☐ No
☐ Refusal

Instruction: for this question you may tick more than one response
IF YOUR GROUP SPLIT UP, GIVE A REASON.
☐ We did not have enough time to do everything we had planned.
☐ We wanted to save time.
☐ We couldn't agree on what we wanted to do.
☐ Other:_____
☐ Refusal

IF YOU GROUP WAS SEPARATED DRAW THE MAKE UP OF THE SUB-GROUPS AFTER SEPARATION.

P1   P2

P6   P3

P5   P4

DRAW ON THE PLAN, ON THE FOLLOWING PAGE, THE ITINERARY, WHICH YOUR GROUP OR THE SUB GROUPS FOLLOWED.

a- In the case of a separation of the group, indicate the point of separation of the group with an "S"
b- In the case of the rejoining of the sub groups (after a separation), indicate the point of re-grouping with an "R"

RATHBURN RD.

UPPER
LEVEL

DUKE OF YORK BLVD.

HURONTARIO ST.

LOWER
LEVEL

P	PARKING
o	ENTRANCE
●	FOODCOURT
▨	ESCALATORS
▨	STAIRS

BURNHAMTHORPE RD. W.

Annexe B: Descriptions of the multi-agent based models of shopping behavior in a mall

This annex aims to present the details of structures and behaviors of the agents composing the geosimulation models of the shopping behavior in a mall.

B.1. The agents of the physical environment (the mall):

Agent name and description	Agent attributes and methods

Door_Agent: This agent represents any door in the simulated environment (the mall).	This agent inherits from Stationary_Agent. It inherits all the properties of this agent.
	 Attributes:
	 -**Door_Agent_Type: Integer**: This attribute represents the type of the door agent. It can have the following values:
	     1: Shopping mall door
	     2: Store door
	     3: Kiosk door
	     4: Toilets door
	 -**Door_Agent_State: Integer**: This property indicates the state of the door agent. It can have the following values:
	     1: Enter only
	     2: Exit only
	     3: Enter_Exit
	 -**Door_Agent_Open: Boolean**: This attribute indicates if the door is open or not.
	 -**Door_Agent_Electric: Boolean**: This attribute Indicates if the door is electric or not.
	 -**Door_Agent_Emergency: Boolean**: This attribute Indicates if the door is an emergency exit or not.
	 -**Door_Agent_Id_Related_Agent: Integer**: This attribute contains the identification of the related agent. The agent which is related to the door agent can be a store, a floor, or anything in the environment which can have a door.

Electric_Door_Agent: This agent represents any electric door in the simulation environment (the mall).	This agent inherits from Stationary_Agent, Door agent, and Active agent. It inherits all the properties and methods of these agents. *Methods*: +**Open ()**: This method is used by the agent to open. +**Close ()**: This method is used by the agent to close.
Retail_Agent: This agent represents all types of retail in the simulated environment. These 'retails' can be stores, kiosks, etc.	This agent inherits from Stationary_Agent. It inherits all the properties of this agent. *Attributes*: -**Retail_Name: String**: This attributes contains the name of the retail. -**Retail_Opening_Hour: String**: This attributes contains The opening hour of the retail. -**Retail_Closing_Hour: String**: This attributes contains the closing hour of the retail. -**Retail_Phone_Number: Integer**: This attributes contains the phone number of the retail. -**Retail_Owner: String**: This attributes contains the name of the owner of the retail. -**Retail_Type_1: Integer**: This attributes contains the main type of the retail. A type of a store represents its category: Clothes, food, electronics, etc. -**Retail_Type_2: Integer**: This attributes contains the second type of the retail. -**Retail_Type_2: Integer**: This attributes contains the third type of the retail.
Store_Agent: This agent represents all stores in the simulated environment (the mall)	This agent inherits from Retail. It inherits all the properties of this agent.
Kiosk_Agent: This agent represents all kiosks in the simulated environment (the mall).	This agent inherits from Retail. It inherits all the properties of this agent.
Room_Agent: This agent represents panoply of rooms in the simulated environment (the mall). It can represent a washroom, a security room, a mechanical room, a maintenance room, a first aid room, etc.	This agent inherits from Stationary_Agent. It inherits all the properties of this agent.
Wash_Room_Agent: This agent represents all washrooms in the simulated environment (the mall).	This agent inherits from Room. It inherits all the properties of this agent. *Attributes*: -**Wash_Room_Agent_Type: Integer**: This attribute indicates the type of washroom. It can have the following values: 1: Washroom for women

	2: Washroom for men 3: Washroom for handicapped persons
Cloak_Room_Agent: This agent represents all cloak rooms in the simulated environment (the mall).	This agent inherits from Stationary_Agent. It inherits all the properties of this agent.

Desk_Agent: This agent represents any desk in the simulated environment (the mall). For example, it can represent an information desk, a service desk, etc.	This agent inherits from Stationary_Agent. It inherits all the properties of this agent.
	Attributes:
	- **Desk_Type: Integer**: This attribute indicates the type of the agent. It can have the following values:
	    1: Information_Desk:
	    2: Service_Desk:

Window_Agent: This agent represents all windows of stores, kiosks, etc.	This agent inherits from Stationary_Agent. It inherits all the properties of this agent.
Product_Agent: This agent represents all products that exist in the simulated environment (the mall).	This agent inherits from Stationary_Agent. It inherits all the properties of this agent. *Attributes*: -**Product_Price: Float**: This attribute contains the price of the product.
Stairs_Agent: The agent represents all stairs in the simulated environment (the mall).	This agent inherits from Stationary_Agent. It inherits all the properties and the methods of this agent. *Attributes*: -**Shopping_Mall_Floor_One_Id: Integer**: This attribute contains the identification of the origin floor. -**Shopping_Mall_Floor_One_Id: Integer**: This attribute contains the identification of the destination floor.
Seat_Agent: This agent represents all seats that can exist in the simulated environment (the mall).	This agent inherits from Stationary_Agent. It inherits all the properties of this agent. *Attributes*: -**Seat_Agent_Capacity: Integer**: This attribute contains the number of places of the seat.

Notice_Agent: This agent represents all notices that can exist in the simulated environment. These notices can be information, advertisement, or signage notices.	This agent inherits from Stationary_Agent. It inherits all the properties of this agent.
	Attributes:
	-**Notice_Agent_Type: Integer**: This attribute contains the type of the notice. This attribute can have the following values:
	    1: Information notice
	    2: Ad notice
	    3: Sign and orientation notice

Electronic_Notice_Agent: This agent represents all electric notices that can exist in the simulated environment (the mall).	This agent inherits from Notice_Agent. It inherits all the properties of this agent.

Escalator_Agent: This agent represents all escalators that can exist in the simulated environment (the mall).	This agent inherits from Stationary_Agent and Active_Agent. It inherits all the properties and methods of these agents.
	Attributes:
	-**Shopping_Mall_Floor_One_Id: Integer**: This attribute contains the origin floor of the escalator.
	-**Shopping_Mall_Floor_One_Id: Integer**: This attribute contains the destination floor of the escalator.
	-**Escalator_Agent_Direction: Integer**: This attribute contains the direction of the escalator. This attribute can have the following values:
	    1: Up
	    2: Down
	Methods:
	+ **Go_Up ()**: This method controls the escalator in the up direction.
	+ **Go_Down ()**: This method controls the escalator in the up direction.

Elevator_Agent: This agent represents all elevators in the simulated environment (the mall).	This agent inherits from Stationary_Agent and Active_Agent. It inherits all the properties of these agents.
	Attributes:
	-**Shopping_Mall_Floor_Id (0-3): Integer**: This attributes contains the identification of the floors which are related by the elevator.
	-**Elevator_Agent_Status: Integer**: This attribute contains the status of the elevator.
	    1: Descending
	    2: Ascending
	    3: Stopped
	-**Elevator_Agent_Current_Floor: Integer**: This attribute contains the current floor where the elevator is.
	Methods:
	+**Go_Up ()**: This method controls the elevator to go up.
	+**Go_Down ()**: This method controls the elevator to go down.
	+**Stop ()**: This method controls the elevator to stop.

Phone_Agent: This agent represents any phone in the simulated environment (the mall).	This agent inherits from Stationary_Agent. It inherits all the properties of this agent.
	Attributes:
	-**Phone_Agent_Type: Integer**: This attribute indicates the type of phone. It contains the following values:
	    1: Public phone
	    2: Deaf phone
	    3: Taxi phone
	    4: Security phone
	-**Phone_Agent_Occupied: Boolean**: This attribute indicates if the phone is occupied or not.
	-**Phone_Agent_On: Boolean**: Indicates if the phone is functional or not.

Fountain_Agent: This agent represents any fountain belonging to the simulated environment (the mall).	This agent inherits from Stationary_Agent. It inherits all the properties of this agent.
	Attributes:
	-**Fountain_Agent_Type: Integer**: This attribute indicates the type of fountain. It can have the following values:
	    1: Drinking fountain
	    2: Decoration fountain

Area_Agent: This agent represents the open areas in the simulated environment (the mall). These areas can be for: food, for socialization, for smoking, etc.	This agent inherits from Stationary_Agent. It inherits all the properties of this agent.
	Attributes:
	-**Area_Agent_Type: Integer**: This attribute contains the type of the area in the mall. It can have the following values:
	    1: Food_Area
	    2: Smoking_Area
	    3: Presentation_Area
	    4: Relaxing_Area
	    5: Playing_Entertainment_Area:
	    6: Shopping_Area

Slot_Machine_Agent: This agent can represent any slot machine existing in the simulated environment (the mall).	This agent inherits from Stationary_Agent. It inherits all the properties of this agent.

Table B.1. The structure and behavior of the agents within the physical environment (the mall).

B.2. The agents of the athmospheric environment (the mall):

Agent name	Agent attributes and methods
Zone_Agent: This agent represents any zone, representing an atmospheric element of the simulated environment (the mall).	This agent inherits from Mobile_Agent and Stationary_Agent. It inherits the attributes and methods of these agents.
Odor_Zone_Agent: This agent represents an odor zone in the simulated environment (the mall).	This agent inherits from Mobile_Agent and Stationary_Agent. It inherits the attributes and methods of these agents. *Attributes*: - **Odor_Zone_Agent_Source_Agent_Id: Integer**: This attribute contains the identification of the source agent that spreads the odor. - **Odor_Zone_Agent_Odor_Type: Integer**: This attribute contains the type of the spreaded odor.
Lighting_Zone_Agent: This agent represents a lighting zone in the simulated environment (the mall).	This agent inherits from Mobile_Agent and Stationary_Agent. It inherits the attributes and methods of these agents. *Attributes*: -**Lighting_Zone_Agent_Source_Agent_Id: Integer**: This attribute contains the identification of the agent that spread the lighting. -**Lighting_Zone_Agent_Lighting_Type: Integer**: This attribute contains the type of the spreaded light.
Sound_Zone_Agent: This agent represents a sound zone in the simulated environment (the mall). This sound can be: music, a sound information message, an advertisement sound message, etc.	This agent inherits from Mobile_Agent and Stationary_Agent. It inherits the attributes and methods of these agents. *Attributes*: -**Sound_Zone_Agent_Source_Agent_Id: Integer**: This attribute contains the identification of the agent which broadcast the sound. -**Sound_Zone_Agent_Sound_Level: Integer**: This attribute contains the level of the broadcasted sound.

Music_Sound_Zone_Agent: This agent represents a music zone in the simulation environment (the mall).	This agent inherits from Sound_Zone_Agent. It inherits the attributes of this agent.
Message_Sound_Zone_Agent: this agent represents a sound message in the simulated environment (the mall).	This agent inherits from Sound_Zone_Agent. It inherits the attributes of this agent. *Attributes*: -**Message_Sound_Zone_Agent_Message_Sound_Content: String**: This attribute contains the content of the sound message. -**Message_Sound_Zone_Agent_Message_Sound_Type: Integer**: This attribute contains the type of the sound message. 1: Information 2: Advertisement

Table B.2. The structure and behavior of the agents belonging to the atmospheric environment (the mall).

B.3. The Shopper agent:

Agent name and description	Agent attributes and methods
Shopper_Agent: This agent represents the shopper which is the most important agent in our simulation.	This agent inherits from the Mobile_Agent. It inherits the attributes and the methods of this agent. *Properties*: -**Shopper_Agent_Shopping_List_Id (0-19): Integer**: This attribute contains the identification of the stores or places to be visited by the shopper agent (the shopping list). -**Shopper_Agent_Shopping_List_Type (0-19): Integer**: This attribute contains the types of the stores or places to be visited by the shopper agent (the shopping list). -**Shopper_Agent_Gender: Integer**: This attribute contains the gender of the shopper agent. -**Shopper_Agent_Age_Group: Integer**: This attribute contains the age group of the shopper agent. -**Shopper_Agent_Occupations (0-5): Integer**: This attribute contains the list of the occupations of the shopper agent. -**Shopper_Agent_Sector_Of_Employment (0-8): Integer**: This attribute contains the list of the sectors of employment of the shopper agent. -**Shopper_Agent_Location_Of_Study: String**: This attribute contains the location of study of the shopper agent. -**Shopper_Agent_Location_Of_Work: string**: This attribute contains the location of work of the shopper agent. -**Shopper_Agent_Marital_Status (0-7): Integer**: This attribute contains the marital statuses of the shopper agent. -**Shopper_Agent_Life_Mode (0-8): Integer**: This attribute contains the life modes of the shopper agent. -**Shopper_Agent_Postal_Code: string**: This attribute contains the postal code of the shopper agent. -**Shopper_Agent_Frequency_Of_Visit_SqO: Integer**: This attribute contains the frequency of visit of the Square One mall by the shopper agent. -**Shopper_Agent_Origin: Integer**: This attribute contains the origin of the shopper agent (where does this agent come from). -**Shopper_Agent_Mode_Of_Transportation: Integer**: This attribute contains the mode of transportation used by the shopper agent when it comes to the Square One mall. -**Shopper_Agent_Preference_Type_Of_Parking: Integer**: This attribute contains the preferred type of parking. -**Shopper_Agent_Preference_Usual_Parking: Integer**: This attribute contains the preferred usual parking. -**Shopper_Agent_Preference_Shopping_Period (0-7): Integer**: This attribute contains the preferred shopping periods. -**Shopper_Agent_Preference_Shopping_Day (0-9): Integer**: This attribute contains the preferred shopping days. -**Shopper_Agent_Preference_Shopping_Mall_Floor_SqO (0-1): Integer**: This attribute contains the preferred shopping floor in Square One mall. -**Shopper_Agent_Preference_Corridor (0-7): Integer**: This attribute contains the preferred shopping corridor. -**Shopper_Agent_Preference_Crowded_Space: Integer**: This attribute contains the preference of crowded spaces. -**Shopper_Agent_Preference_Treeless_Space: Integer**: This attribute contains the preference of treeless spaces. -**Shopper_Agent_Preference_Pleasant_Smell: Integer**: This attribute contains the preference of pleasant smell. -**Shopper_Agent_Preference_Display_Color (0-2): Integer**: This attribute contains the preference of the display colors. -**Shopper_Agent_Preference_Decoration_Color (0-2): Integer**: This attribute contains the

prefernec of the decoration colors.

-**Shopper_Agent_Preference_Type_Of_Lighting (0-6): Integer**: This attribute contains the preference of lighting.

-**Shopper_Agent_Interest (0-29): Integer**: This attribute contains the degree of the interests of the shopper agent. This attribute can have the following values:

        0: The percentage for the interest: Cultural activities
        1: The percentage for the interest: Theatre shows
        2: The percentage for the interest: Music
        3: The percentage for the interest: Cinema_Television
        4: The percentage for the interest: Reading
        5: The percentage for the interest: Motorsports
        6: The percentage for the interest: Automobiles
        7: The percentage for the interest: Motorcycles
        8: The percentage for the interest: Marin_Vheicles
        9 The percentage for the interest: Land_Vheicles
        10: The percentage for the interest: Tourism_Travels
        11: The percentage for the interest: Games
        12: The percentage for the interest: Video_Games
        13: The percentage for the interest:Society_Games
        14: The percentage for the interest: New_Technologies
        15: The percentage for the interest: Computer_Inernet
        16: The percentage for the interest: TeleCommunication
        17: The percentage for the interest: Home_Decor
        18: The percentage for the interest: Interior_Design
        19: The percentage for the interest: Crafts
        20: The percentage for the interest: Gardening
        21: The percentage for the interest: Sports
        22: The percentage for the interest: Outdoor_Sports
        23: The percentage for the interest: Indoor_Sports
        24: The percentage for the interest: Clothing_Fashions_Accessories
        25: The percentage for the interest: Beauty
        26: The percentage for the interest: Beauty_Porducts
        27: The percentage for the interest: Beauty_Services
        28: The percentage for the interest: Jewelry
        29: The percentage for the interest: Cooking

-**Shopper_Agent_Musical_Interest (0-8): Integer**: This attribute contains the degree of preference of music. It can have the following values.

        0: The percentage for the music interest: Classical
        1: The percentage for the music interest: Rock and alternative
        2: The percentage for the music interest: Country
        3: The percentage for the music interest: Dance
        4: The percentage for the music interest: Pop
        5: The percentage for the music interest: Rap and HipHop
        6: The percentage for the music interest: R and B and Soul

-**Shopper_Agent_Entrance_Door: Integer**: This attribute contains the entrance door used by the shopper agent to enter to the mall.

-**Shopper_Agent_Exit_Door: Integer**: This attribute contains the exit door used by the shopper agent when it leaves the mall.

-**Shopper_Agent_Need_To_Eat: Integer**: This attribute contains the value that indicates if the shopper agent needs to eat.

-**Shopper_Agent_Need_To_Drink: Integer**: This attribute contains the value that indicates if the shopper agent needs to drink.

-**Shopper_Agent_Need_To_Visit_A_Restroom: Integer**: This attribute contains the value that indicates if the shopper agent needs to go to the rest room.

-**Shopper_Agent_Need_To_Visit_A_Restroom: Integer**: This attribute contains the value that indicates if the shopper agent needs to go to the rest room.

-**Shopper_Agent_Need_To_Play_Entertain: Integer**: This attribute contains the value that indicates if the shopper agent needs to entertain and play.

-**Shopper_Agent_Need_To_Rest_Relax: Integer**: This attribute contains the value that indicates if the shopper agent needs to relax.

-**Shopper_Agent_Need_To_Leave: Integer**: This attribute contains the value that indicates if the shopper agent needs to leave the mall.

-**Shopper_Agent_Usual_Path (0-19): Node_Agent**: This list contains the path that can be followed by the shopper agent when it explores the mall.

-**Shopper_Agent_Group_Id: Integer**: This attribute contains the identification of the group of the shopper agent.

-**Shopper_Agent_Group_Type: Integer**: This attribute contains the type of the group of the shopper agent.

-**Shopper_Agent_Role_In_Group: Integer**: This attribute contains the role played by the shopper agent in the group.

Methods:

+**Make_Decision** (): This is the most important behavior. This behavior depends upon what the agent perceives, the values of its attributes (static attributes, or dynamic attributes (needs)), what it memorizes, etc.

+**Post_Decision** ():

	+**Observe** (): Using this behavior, the shopper agent notes everything that it does in the mall.

Table B.3. The structure and behavior of the shopper agent (main actor)

B.4. The Group of Shoppers agent:

Agent name and description	Agent attributes and methods
Group_Shoppers_Agent: This agent represents a group of shoppers.	This agent inherits from the Group_Agent. *Attributes*: -**Group_Shopper_Agent_Members_Id (0-29): Basic_Agent**: This list contains the agents that belong to the group. *Methods*: +**Make_Decision** (): This method implements the decision-making process of the agent group.

Table B.4. The structure and behavior of the group of shopper agents.

B.5. The Crowd of Shoppers agent:

Agent name and description	Agent attributes and methods
Crowd_Agent: This agent represents a crowd of shoppers.	This agent inherits from the Group_Agent. *Attributes*: - **Crowd_Shopper_Agent_Members_Id (0-199): Group_Shoppers_Agent**: This attribute contains the list of the individual shopper or groups of shoppers belonging to the crowd agent.

Table B.5. The model of a crowd of shoppers in the simulation.

Annexe C: The specification of behaviors in the MAGS platform

This annex aims to present the specification of some behavior patterns of shopping behavior in a mall.

C.1. The goal Go_To_A_Shop x:

This goal specifies the shopping behavior pattern (go to a shop, store, or kiosk). It is activated if the next destination is shop x. The specification details of this goal are presented in Fig C.1.

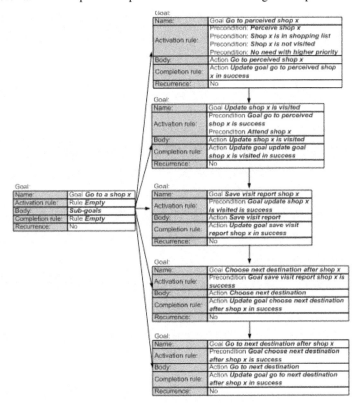

Fig. C.1. The specification of the objective Go_To_A_Shop x.

This goal is composed of the following sub-goals:

- Sub-Goal **Goal Go_To_Perceived_Shop** *x*: This sub-goal allows the shopper agent to move to shop x.

- *Recurrence*: This sub-goal is not recurrent.

- *Activation rule* **Precondition Perceive_Shop_x and Precondition_Shop_x_Is_Non_Visited and Precondition Without_Big_Need**: In order to move to the shop x, the shopper agent must perceive this shop (perception capability); and it must not have previously visited this shop; and it must not have another objective with a higher priority, such as one related to a need to satisfy (as for example go to a restroom).
- *Body* **Action Go_To_Perceived_Shop_ x**: This action allows the shopper agent to move to the perceived shop x.
- *Completion rule* **Action Update_Goal_Go_To_Perceived_Shop_x_Success**: This rule contains an action that updates the sub-goal's life–cycle as finished with success.

the next sub-goal is:

- Sub-Goal *Goal Update_Shop_x_Is_Visited*: Using this goal, the shopper agent updates the shop x as visited in the shopping list.

- *Recurrence*: This sub-goal is not recurrent.
- *Activation rule* **Precondition Goal_Go_To_Perceived_Shop_x_Is_Success and Precondition Attend_Shop_x**: The previous sub-goal must be successfully completed.
- *Body* **Action Update_Shop_x_Is_Visited**: This action allows the shopper agent to update its shopping list, and make the shop x as visited in this list.
- *Completion rule* **Action Update_Goal_Update_Shop_x_Is_Visited_Success**: This rule contains an action that updates the sub-goal's life-cycle as finished with success.

the next sub-goal is:

- Sub-Goal *Goal Save_Visit_Report_Shop_x*: This sub-goal allows the shopper agent to save the trace of the shop x's visit.

- *Recurrence*: This sub-goal is not recurrent.
- *Activation rule* **Precondition Goal_Update_Shop_x_Is_Visited_Is_Success**: The previous sub-goal must be successfully completed.
- *Body* **Action Save_Visit_Report**: This action allows the shopper agent to save the trace of its visit to the shop x.
- *Completion rule* **Action Update_Goal_Save_Visit_Report_Shop_x_Success**: This rule contains an action that updates the sub-goal's life-cycle as finished with success.

the next sub-goal is:

- Sub-Goal *Goal Choose_Next_Destination_After_Shop_x*: This sub-goal allows the shopper agents to choose its next destination.

- *Recurrence*: This sub-goal is not recurrent.
- *Activation rule* **Precondition**
  Goal_Save_Visit_Report_Shop_x_Is_Success: The previous sub-goal must be successfully completed.
- *Body* **Action Choose_Next_Destination**: This action allows the shopper agent to choose its next destination after visiting shop x. This destination may be another shop, or another place in the virtual mall.
- *Completion rule* **Action**
  Update_Choose_Next_Destination_After_Shop_x_Success: This rule contains an action that updates the sub-goal's life-cycle as finished with success.

the next sub-goal is:

- Sub-Goal *Goal Go_To_Next_Destination_After_Shop_x*: This sub-goal allows the shopper agents to move to the next chosen destination within the previous sub-goal.

- Recurrence: This sub-goal is not recurrent.
- Activation rule **Precondition**
  Goal_Choose_Next_Destination_After_Shop_x_Is_Success: The previous sub-goal must be successfully completed.
- Body **Action Go_To_Next_Destination_After_Shop x**: This action allows the shopper agent to move to the destination chosen during the previous sub-goal.
- Completion rule **Action**
  Update_Goal_Go_To_Next_Destination_After_Shop x: This rule contains an action that updates the sub-goal's life-cycle as finished with success.

C.2. The goal Go To A_Restroom:

This goal allows the shopper agent to move to the restroom in order to satisfy a physiological need, when it feels the need to go to this place. The details of this goal specification are presented in Fig C.2.

Fig. C.2. The specification of the objective Go_To_A_Restroom.

This goal is composed of the following sub-goals:

- Sub-Goal *Goal Update_Navigation_State_Big_Need_ON*: This sub-goal updates the shopper agent's navigation state related to the need big-need of the shopper agent. Therefore, the main target of the shopper agent becomes the search for the restroom in order to satisfy its need.

- *Recurrence*: This sub-goal is not recurrent.

- *Activation rule* **Precondition Need_To_Satisfy_Big_Need**: This sub-goal is activated when the agent needs to go to restroom is activated. This rule is triggered when the current value of the dynamic state related to this need is less than its threshold.

- *Body* **Action Update_Navigation_State_Big_Need_ON**: This action allows to update the shopper agent's navigation state to 1.

- *Completion rule* **Action Update_Goal_Update_Navigation_State_Big_Need_ON_Success**: This rule contains an action that updates the sub-goal's life-cycle as finished with success.

the next sub-goal is:

- Sub-Goal *Goal Choose_Next_Destination_Big_Need*: This sub-goal represents the shopper agent's decision-making process when it feels the need to go to restroom.

  - *Recurrence*: This sub-goal is not recurrent.
  - *Activation rule* **Precondition Goal_Update_Navigation_State_Big_Need_ON_Is_Success**: The previous sub-goal must be successfully completed.
  - *Body* **Action Choose_Next_Destination**: This action allows the shopper agent to make decisions about its next destination.
  - *Completion rule* **Action Update_Goal_Choose_Next_Destination_Big_Need_Success**: This rule contains an action that updates the sub-goal's life-cycle as finished with success.

the next sub-goal is:

- Sub-Goal *Goal Go_To_Next_Destination_Big_Need*: This sub-goal allows the shopper agent to move to the next destination chosen during the previous sub-goal.

  - *Recurrence*: This sub-goal is not recurrent.
  - *Activation rule* **Precondition Goal_Choose_Next_Destination_Big_Need_Is_Success**: The previous sub-goal must be successfully completed.
  - *Body* **Action Go_To_Next_Destination_Big_Need**: This action allows the shopper agent to move to the next destination chosen during the previous sub-goal.
  - *Completion rule* **Action Update_Goal_Go_To_Next_Destination_Big_Need_Success**: This rule contains an action that updates the sub-goal's life-cycle as finished with success.

the next sub-goal is:

- Sub-Goal *Goal Go_To_Perceived_Restroom*: This sub-goal allows the shopper agent to move to the restroom.

- *Recurrence*: This sub-goal is not recurrent.
- *Activation rule* **Precondition Perceive_Restroom and Precondition_Need_To_Satisfy_Big_Need**: This sub-goal is activated when the shopper agent is already feeling the need to use the restroom; and when it perceives it.
- *Body* **Action Go_To_Perceived_Restroom**: This action allows the agent to move to the perceived toilets.
- *Completion rule* **Action Update_Go_To_Perceived_Restroom_Success**: This rule contains an action that updates the sub-goal's life-cycle as finished with success.

the next sub-goal is:

- Sub-Goal *Goal Save_Visit_Report_Restroom*: This sub-goal allows the shopper agent to record the information about its visit of the restroom.

- *Recurrence*: This sub-goal is not recurrent.
- *Activation rule* **Precondition Goal_Go_To_Perceived_Restroom_Is_Success and Precondition Attend_Restroom**: The previous sub-goal must be successfully completed; and the shopper agent attends the restroom in order to satisfy its need.
- *Body* **Action Save_Visit_Report**: This action allows the agent to record the information about the restroom visit.
- *Completion rule* **Action Update_Goal_Save_Visit_Report_Restroom_Success**: This rule contains an action that updates the sub-goal's life-cycle as finished with success.

the next sub-goal is:

- Sub-Goal *Goal Update_Navigation_State_Big_Need_OFF*: This sub-goal aims to update the shopper agent's navigation state related to the need to use the restroom.

- *Recurrence*: This sub-goal is not recurrent.
- *Activation rule* **Precondition Goal_Save_Report_Restroom_Is_Success**: The previous sub-goal must be successfully completed.
- *Body* **Action Update_Navigation_State_Big_Need_OFF**: This action aims to update the shopper agent's navigation state related to the need to use the restroom.
- *Completion rule* **Action Update_Goal_Update_Navigation_State_Big_Need_OFF**: This rule

contains an action that updates the sub-goal's life-cycle as finished with success.

the next sub-goal is:

- Sub-Goal *Goal Initlialize_Dynamic_State_Big_Need*: This sub-goal aims to update the shopper agent's dynamic state related to the need to use the restroom. This update sets the current value of the dynamic state to 0.

- *Recurrence*: This sub-goal is not recurrent.

- *Activation rule* **Precondition Goal_Update_Navigation_State_Big_Need_OFF_Is_Success**: The previous sub-goal must be successfully completed.

- *Body* **Action Initialize_Dynamic_State_Big_Need**: This action aims to update the shopper agent's dynamic state related to the need to use the restroom.

- *Completion rule* **Action Update_Goal_Initialize_Dynamic_State_Big_Need_Success**: This rule contains an action that updates the sub-goal's life-cycle as finished with success.

the next sub-goal is:

- Sub-Goal *Goal Choose_Next_Destination_After_Restroom*: This sub-goal specifies the decision-making process about the next destination after using the restroom.

- *Recurrence*: This sub-goal is not recurrent.

- *Activation rule* **Precondition Goal_Update_Navigation_Big_Need_OFF_Is_Success**: The previous sub-goal must be successfully completed.

- *Body* **Action Choose_Next_Destination**: This action allows the shopper agent to make decisions about the next destination after using the restroom. The agent can take again the destination fixed before feeling the need to go to the toilets.

- *Completion rule* **Action Update_Choose_Next_Destination_After_Restroom_Success**: This rule contains an action that updates the sub-goal's life cycle as finished with success.

the next sub-goal is:

- Sub-Goal *Goal Go_To_Next_Destination_After_Restroom*: This sub-goal allows the shopper agent to visit the destination determined in the previous sub-goal.

  ▪ *Recurrence*: This sub-goal is not recurrent.

  ▪ *Activation rule* **Precondition Goal_Choose_Next_Destination_After_Restroom_Is_Success**: The previous sub-goal must be successfully completed.

  ▪ *Body* **Action Go_To_Next_Destination**: This action allows the shopper agent to visit the destination determined in the previous sub-goal.

  ▪ *Completion rule* **Action Update_Goal_Go_To_Next_Destination_After_Restroom_Success**: This rule contains an action that updates the sub-goal's life cycle as finished with success.

C.3. The goal Leave_The_Mall:

This goal specifies the behavior pattern *Leave the mall*. We suppose that the shopper agent leaves the mall for two reasons: (1) it can leave the mall normally, when it reaches its time limit planned for shopping, or (2) it can leave the mall in a panic situation (when a problem occurs). Here, we only present the first mode for leaving the mall in a normal situation. If the shopper agent reaches the fixed time limit for its shopping, it decides to leave the mall. The shopping time is recorded in its static state called *Shopper_Shopping_Duration*. The doors used by the agent to leave the mall can be the entrance door (used to enter the mall), the first perceived door, or the closest door to the agent when it decides to leave the mall. This goal is specified in Fig C.3.

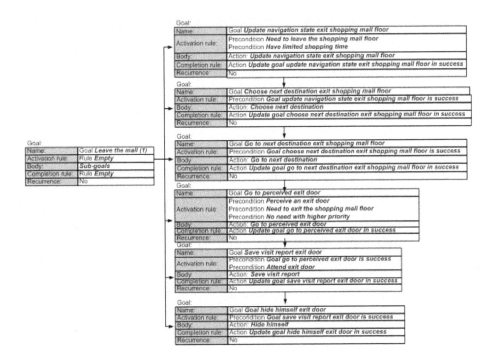

Fig. C.3. The specification details of the objective Leave_The_Mall.

The sub-goals that compose this goal are the following:

- Sub-Goal *Goal Update_Navigation_State_Exit_Shopping_Mall_Floor*: This sub-goal aims to update the navigation state related to the desire to leave the mall. Then, the agent's main target becomes the search of an exit door. This door may be the one the agent used to enter the mall, the first one perceived by the agent, or the closest one when the shopper agent decides to leave the mall.

- *Recurrence*: This sub-goal is not recurrent.

- *Activation rule* **Precondition Need_To_Exit_Shopping_Mall_Floor and Precondition Have_Limited_Shopping_Time**: This sub-goal is activated when the shopper agent reaches the time limit of the shopping trip; and when it has already designated a time limit for this shopping trip.

- *Body* **Action Update_Navigation_State_Exit_Shopping_Mall_Floor**: This action aims to update the shopper agent's navigation state concerning leaving the mall.

- *Completion rule* **Action Update_Goal_Update_Navigation_State_Exit_Shopping_Mall_Floor_Suc**

cess: This rule contains an action that updates the sub-goal's life-cycle as finished with success.

the next sub-goal is:

- Sub-Goal *Goal Choose_Next_Destination_To_Exit_Shopping_Mall_Floor*: This sub-goal allows the shopper agent to choose the door by which it wishes to leave.

- *Recurrence*: This sub-goal is not recurrent.
- *Activation rule* **Precondition Goal_Update_Navigation_State_Exit_Shopping_Mall_Floor_Is_Success**: The previous sub-goal must be successfully completed.
- *Body* **Action Choose_Next_Destination**: This action allows the agent to choose the next door by which it wishes to leave.
- *Completion rule* **Update Goal_Choose_Next_Destination_To_Exit_Shopping_Mall_Floor** This rule contains an action which updates the sub-goal's life-cycle as finished with success.

the next sub-goal is:

- Sub-Goal *Goal Go_To_Next_Destination_To_Exit_Shopping_Mall_Floor*: This sub-goal allows the agent to move to the exit door determined in the previous sub-goal.

- *Recurrence*: This sub-goal is not recurrent.
- *Activation rule* **Precondition Goal_Choose_Next_Destination_To_Exit_Shopping_Mall_Floor_Is_Succ ess**: The previous sub-goal must be successfully completed.
- *Body* **Action Go_To_Next_Destination**: This action allows the shopper agent to move to the exit door determined in the previous sub-goal.
- *Completion rule* **Action Update_Goal_Go_To_Next_Destination_To_Exit_Shopping_Mall_Floor_S uccess**: This rule contains an action that updates the sub-goal's life-cycle as finished with success.

the next sub-goal is:

- Sub-Goal *Goal Go_To_Perceived_Exit_Door*: This sub-goal allows the shopper agent to move to the perceived door, if this door is the one determined door in the decision-making process.

- *Recurrence*: This sub-goal is not recurrent.

- *Activation rule* **Precondition No_Objective_With_Higher_Priority and Precondition Is_In_Exit_Navigation_State and Precondition Perceive_An_Exit_Door**: The previous sub-goal must be successfully completed; there is no objective having a higher priority; and when the shopper agent perceives an exit door.
- *Body* **Action Go_To_Perceived_Exit_Door**: This action allows the agent to move to the perceived door it is the one decided upon in the decision-making process.
- *Completion rule* **Action Update_Go_To_Perceived_Exit_Door**: This rule contains an action that updates the sub-goal's life-cycle as finished with success.

the next sub-goal is:

- Sub-Goal *Goal Save_Visit_Report_Exit_Door*: This sub-goal aims to record the door that is used in the previous sub-goal in order to leave the mall.

- *Recurrence*: This sub-goal is not recurrent.
- *Activation rule*: **Precondition Goal_Go_To_Perceived_Exit_Door_Is_Success and Precondition Attend_Exit_Door**: The previous sub-goal must be successfully completed.
- *Body* **Action Save_Visit_Report**: This action aims to record the door which is used to leave the mall.
- *Completion rule*: **Action Update_Goal_Save_Visit_Report_Exit_Door**: This rule contains an action that updates the sub-goal's life-cycle as finished with success.

the next sub-goal is:

- Sub-Goal *Goal Hide_Himself*: This sub-goal allows the agent to hide itself when it leave the mall. Hence, the agent is invisible for the user of the simulation.

- *Recurrence*: This sub-goal is not recurrent.
- Activation rule: **Precondition Goal_Save_Visit_Report_Exit_Door_Is_Success**: The previous sub-goal must be successfully completed.
- *Body* **Action Be_Invisible**: This action allows the agent to hide itself when it leaves the virtual mall.

- *Completion rule*: **Action Update_Goal_Hide_Himself_Success or Nothing**: This rule contains an action that updates the sub-goal's life-cycle as finished with success.

C.4. The goal Explore:

This goal specifies the exploration behavior of the shopper agents in the virtual mall. A shopper agent can explore the mall for two purposes:

- *Exploring for exploration*: The agent explores the mall without the intention to visit a shop or specific place for two reasons: (1) the agent does not have any store or place to visit, or (2) it finished visiting all the planned stores or places to visit, but still has enough time to continue shopping. When the agent is in this exploration mode, its behavior is easily influenced by its preferences, and it takes its time during the shopping trip, etc. In this mode of exploration, we suppose that the agent follows its preferred path when exploring the mall. This preferred path is recorded in a sequence of static states containing the identification of the agent nodes composing the path. Details of this goal are not presented in this dissertation.

- *Exploring for search*: If the agent wants to visit a store or place, but it does not know it, then it starts by exploring the mall in order to search for this specific store or place. When the agent perceives this store or place, it moves to it. When the agent is in this exploration mode, it begins by navigating in all the nodes of the various paths in order to find the store or place it wishes to visit. Details of this goal are not presented in this dissertation.

www.ingramcontent.com/pod-product-compliance
Lightning Source LLC
LaVergne TN
LVHW062307060326
832902LV00013B/2080